A cook's tour:

Baking Blind goes global

Penny Melville-Brown

Penny

Happy cooking

ISBN: 978-1-7397990-0-7

Editor: Kimberley Miller at www.morethan-words.com

Interior design and publication: Clint MacDonald at www.mac-nificent.co.uk

Cover design: Alice Kennedy at www.glow-designs.co.uk

Dedication.

For Mummy, Christine Melville, who constantly supported, challenged and inspired me when I lost my sight. She wasn't very interested in cooking, and thought that anything that took more than 10 minutes wasn't worth the bother. But she was an intrepid traveller into her 80s, usually "gallivanting", as she described it, for at least three months every year on solo explorations of Australia, New Zealand, the Pacific Islands and many countries en route. Having survived two cancers, she was already planning her next adventure to Peru and South America only a few weeks before the next big C finally got her in 2015. She would have been wildly envious of my trip and absolutely determined to come too.

And for my great co-cook Karen, who has saved me from many mishaps at home, plus all those brave chefs and cooks worldwide who feature here.

Last, but not least, Toby, without whom none of this would have been possible. His patience, humour and determination were invaluable throughout the trip and even more so when my recovery made the editing more difficult. His cover design and illustrations here are just the tip of his enormous talent (www.tobymelvillebrown.com).

Acknowledgements.

My thanks to Kimberley Miller and her team of Alice and Clint who turned my very rough text into this superbly finished article.

Table of contents

Notes ix

1. The way to win a small fortune 11
2. Hello, San Francisco 17
3. Sticky mess 26
4. Michelin star 33
5. Food for the soul 42
6. Sourdough masterclass 53
7. Fine dining in the jungle 62
8. Escaping hurricane Nate 80
9. Celebrating 100 years of women in the Navy 86
10. Loaves and fishes 99
11. Families and friends 115
12. The largest city in the world 131

13. Out and about in Chongqing .150
14. The sounds of Chongqing .175
15. Hello, Kiama 195
16. High drama .205
17. Enabled cooking .212
18. Iranian barbecue 223
19. Melbourne Cup 236
20. Three gastronomettes .246
21. The warm heart of Africa 267
22. Cooking under the African sun 278
23. Ghosts and spirits 282
24. By the skin of my teeth (literally) .289
25. Hampshire home cooking 302
26. On my travels again .316
27. Lessons learned .331
Index 338

Notes.

Recipes.

Each chapter concludes with recipes. There is an index at the end of the book and over 50 have links to cookery demonstrations. Ingredients (and their preparation) are listed in the order they are needed to make it easier to organise the work surface. Where possible, metric measurements have been used with oven temperatures in Celsius, Gas and Fahrenheit. Throughout, I have worked on the principle that an American or Australian cup is about 240ml or 120g. A few recipes are more interpretative as it wasn't always possible to pin down quantities etc.

Videos.

There are links to nearly 90 individually named videos. They are on my Baking Blind YouTube channel https://www.youtube.com/channel/UCWTJYx7jGA3xaR4830wJSRg but please forgive any adverts.

Website: www.pennymelvillebrown.com

Chapter 1.

The way to win a small fortune.

How did I get here? Unable to move or see, breathing with a ventilator, a fibre-glass brace encasing me from neck to armpits. In a French Intensive Care ward without the words to express my utter fury at being tied to the bed rails.

I put it all down to that fateful email that floated in 12 months earlier. Could anyone resist the lure: "Up to $25,000 for blind folks with awesome ideas!". One seemingly innocent missive and the plans for the next few years went up in smoke.

It all seemed too good and the timing too perfect. I was in the midst of a long battle with the laughably named Department for Work and Pensions. My 18-year-old business had been terminally blighted. A new challenge was just what I needed: motivation, inspiration and creativity. Somehow, San Francisco's LightHouse Organisation for the Blind (www.lighthouse-sf.org had found and invited me to their inaugural prize, celebrating someone called James Holman (www.jasonroberts.net). But who was he? The answer completely convinced me that this wasn't a hoax but a spooky coincidence.

As I learned more about him, those similarities kept slotting into place. Just like me, he'd lost his sight while serving in the Royal Navy – but 200 years apart. We almost certainly had the same inflammatory eye condition (uveitis). Neither of us had been willing to sit back quietly on our military pensions: he'd explored the world and become the renowned travel writer of the 19th century, while I'd been helping other disabled people get back to work.

In his day, James would have had to rely on strangers as he travelled by coach and sailing ships. With the common belief that syphilis was the cause of blindness, he may not have had welcome receptions. My own forays abroad for work and play had been easier by plane. But people haven't changed much: while strangers are often invaluable, they still want to know all about the medical causes of blindness.

Checking out that dangling bait, I realised it wouldn't be just free money but was to fund a project. It was a chance too good to miss, and I'd already started working on a new idea – but would it be "awesome" enough? The naval similarities might have given me an edge, but only if my idea could grab the judges' attention. I'd created some distinctly amateur videos, but their goal of disrupting stereotypes of disability could have legs. Toss in an international perspective, attract mainstream audiences, and it could even run.

"Baking Blind" had been a short and simple diversion. In November 2016, I was cooking 50 mini-Christmas cakes for friends' seasonal hampers. Someone thought that this was a rather odd and ambitious activity, especially for a blind person. For me, it was just what I've always done, but the comment showed how disabled people can be underestimated.

Posting a video online seemed to be the perfect antidote, and my brother, Martin, had some time to spare.

Video: Christmas cakes for presents

The video was embarrassingly amateur, and far too long, but there was no stopping us. Gradually, the subsequent YouTube videos got shorter and showed my growing confidence, especially when I started cooking alongside other people.

The prize opportunity seemed the ideal next step, but trying to honour James's courage and travels meant I couldn't stay safe and sound at home in my own kitchen. I needed to match his spirit of adventure and cook around the world. And so the global Baking Blind idea was born.

Why not do something sexier than cooking? After all, disabled people get lots of public attention and have changed thinking through the Paralympics and other sports. But super-athletes are very distant from the rest of us. Instead, food is more achievable for us mortals. Everyone needs it and anyone can make it. All the television cooking programmes show that food has mass appeal. And, after a lifetime of cooking, I could probably manage to appear vaguely competent.

And so the work began, and the 90-second video pitch would attempt to bring all my ideas together.

Video: Baking Blind: a taste of the world

Next I needed a project plan and a network of international supporters. Luckily, I'm never happier than when pounding on a keyboard and writing hundreds of emails, press releases, lists of every description, even the odd erudite paper and more. To a military mind like mine, little compares to the delights of a detailed itinerary (preferably with numerous serials, annotations and annexes).

With my computer well set up to use screen reading software, I am probably quicker than most sighted people. I taught myself to touch-type decades ago and it has been immeasurably useful. As I press each key, the software speaks the letters, the words and the punctuation. Reading is just as easy but even faster. The frantic garble of spoken words is too much for many people to bear but, after years of practice, I could listen to hundreds of pages, absorb the detail and remember it.

Not even all the experts fully understand screen readers. I vividly remember turning up for three months work with the Olympic Delivery Authority before the London 2012 Games. We were on the 21st floor of the posh Canary Wharf Building, and they were immensely proud to have installed the screen reader software within 24 hours. But it took them another week or so to get the speakers I needed (that they'd forgotten). Meanwhile, I had to type on the desk with my head part under it to hear the tinny sound from the PC tower.

My laptop is a constant companion and would be top priority in a fire. It holds my life and allows me to work, rest and play. But don't be beguiled into thinking that modern IT is the answer to everything: the websites, social media and online shopping used every day by anyone else remain Dark Matter.

But back to the benefits of being able to send all those emails. Within months a network of supporters across the world were cajoling professional chefs and home cooks to welcome this stranger into their kitchens and even perform on camera. These were the true heroes who played the key roles in the Baking Blind tour: Noam from Costa Rica was a contact-of-a-contact who simply rang me up to find out more; Jo in Virginia Beach remembered me from Navy days nearly 40 years earlier; Andrew was a friend-of-a-friend who could call on Rotary Club support in China; Rosemary in Kiama, Australia, had guided me years earlier to European Blind Union conferences; Colin in Melbourne was a former naval commander and colleague of brother Martin; Suzie had worked with niece Jessica in Malawi. And so the visit locations fell into place completely randomly.

The competition was no walkover – 200 video entries from 27 countries – but that uncanny naval link was probably the tipping point. I'd been especially fortunate to gain the support of two experts in their fields: Mike "Fin" Finlayson who filmed the original and authentic "Railway Man" and international chef/patron/restaurateur Larry of Lauro's Brasserie. My ideas would ultimately be tested by the judging panel, including a cross-section of some of the most successful blind people in the world, each a leader in their separate fields. This was a nail-biting time: yet another trans-Atlantic interview was scheduled and I could scarcely believe they wanted even more information.

But, within seconds, the whole tone had changed: I was listening to the LightHouse Chief Executive, Bryan, congratulate me on being one of the three winners. The rest of the conversation is a fog. I only remember a huge sense of relief. But there was a sting in the tail: the news had to be kept secret until the official announcement. After whipping up so much interest at home and abroad, it felt very sneaky fending off questions and pretending ignorance for another three long weeks.

Video: UK's Baking Blind is a worldwide winner

There were two other prize-winners: Apiarist Ojok in Uganda aiming to train other blind people to work with bees, gather honey and sell their produce to become more financially independent; Ahmet who lived in San Francisco but, in celebration of his Turkish heritage, planned to kayak across the Bosphorus having developed navigational equipment for blind people. My cooking ambition seemed very humble in comparison.

And let me introduce my nephew Toby, a professional freelance illustrator specialising in architectural drawings. He had been producing our cooking videos for the Baking Blind YouTube channel for months, and now volunteered to donate his time to capture the world tour. His superb artistic eye helped enormously, and he was an ever-patient and caring travel companion.

Finally, all the tickets were booked, inoculations jabbed and bags packed. Different coat hangers each held sets of clothes, all interchangeably coordinating with each other. "Dinner medals" are part of the inescapable spills and thrills of life when you can't see the plate, the cutlery or the food. Using a knife and fork together doesn't give enough feeling to judge the size of a mouthful, the unctuousness of a sauce or the dimensions of a lettuce leaf. I knew that regular changes of non-clashing camera-friendly clothes would be vital.

Safely tucked away was my essential cooking equipment: talking scales, favourite knife and trademark striped apron. We were ready, and a whole world of new tastes, experiences and people beckoned.

Video: Baking Blind going global

Chapter 2.

Hello, San Francisco.

Nine months after that fateful email, I was flying to San Francisco for the induction week with the prize organising team from LightHouse – the opening salvo.

Video: Baking Blind goes west

Their headquarters on Market Street, at the heart of the city, offered everything that a blind person wants: training and equipment, motivation and independence, understanding and care.

But the overwhelming memory of their accommodation was that it took me straight back to naval New Entry training in the 1970s. Back in those days I'd been sharing bunk beds in a cabin with another trainee. Nearly 40 years later, the other single bed was luckily empty, but the communal ablutions were still over-familiar. Imagine that midnight loo dash: shoe in the door to stop it locking automatically, navigating strange corridors by touch and memory, hoping to find the room again as there was no help around. An en-suite is my top priority nowadays with a much more mature bladder.

Getting to the loo is a perennial issue. There's a certain delicacy about asking strangers, and unfamiliar surroundings add further complications when every element of the facilities must be located and explained. At one stage I was regularly flying to Leeds for day meetings with a government department – up at the crack of dawn, flight, meeting, flight, home at dusk. Colleagues tended to forget to ask if I needed the loo during the day, and I was too embarrassed to ask. I developed cast-iron plumbing to cope with those long days.

At those prestigious offices at Canary Wharf, I'd explained that I needed a way to navigate through the huge open plan space to the loo. Solution: a tactile plastic strip would be laid on the carpet so I could find the way with my stick. Drawback: it would take two weeks. They seemed to think it funny when I asked if I had to cross my legs for the duration.

The first test of my cooking ambitions came early during that hectic week in San Francisco: I had to prove I could do more than just walk, talk and wave a pan. Local entrepreneur and major LightHouse supporter, Michael, had opened his "One Market" restaurant (www.onemarket.com) for a cooking session. It had been decades since my teenage Saturday job in my first and last professional kitchen. Relying on just my ears, the noise of his restaurant in full lunch service was overwhelming: every voice and utensil ricocheted off the tiled walls. The relative cool and peace of the pastry section was a welcome haven. Too cowed to dress up in the proffered cook's whites, I hid behind that familiar, homely stripey apron made by my mother – my comfort blanket.

That morning with specialist pastry chef, Mack, was to set the pattern for so many cooking sessions to come. Under the unforgiving eye of the LightHouse video team's camera, we were both nervous. He was fearful that this unknown quantity might not be up to the job and, worse, be distinctly dangerous. But gathering ingredients, swapping recipes and comparing methods was soothing, and quickly got us on an even keel. I knew that with a work surface in front of me, familiar equipment, and a clear route to the sink and oven, I could probably cook anywhere. Soon we had become just two food enthusiasts sharing the common language of our shared passion with a job to do.

A biscuit seems an odd measure of success. Mack had started me on a distinctly simple basic peach galette and his "pie dough" alone made the whole morning worthwhile. My galette crimping was far from perfect but I'd managed to produce something respectable. I knew that I'd graduated – and proved myself – when he let me loose with tuile biscuits.

Named after traditional French roof tiles, these oval-shaped biscuits are taken hot from the oven and wrapped around a wide rolling pin to harden into the classic curved shape. Making the biscuit mix was simple. Much trickier was getting the right amount of mix into an even circle on the baking sheet – and still leaving room for spreading. It's a recurrent problem with biscuits, choux pastry and meringues for me.

The final element of Mack's dessert was a blackberry coulis to make a rustic dish full of flavour and texture.

Hours later I emerged fragrant with baking and triumphant to share my creations with Michael and others from LightHouse for a celebratory lunch. I felt far more confident about making a success of the future tour.

Mack's recipes.

Peach galettes.

450g butter, grated from frozen and then refrozen.
60ml apple juice.
120ml ice-cold water.
1 teaspoon orange zest.
100g granulated sugar.
570g plain (all-purpose) flour and extra for dusting.
A large pinch of salt.
15 peaches halved and stones removed and cut into 1cm cubes.
1 teaspoon lemon juice.
4 tablespoons soft brown sugar.

Method.

Day/hours before weigh and freeze the butter then grate from frozen and refreeze.

Mix the apple juice, water and orange zest.

In a separate bowl mix the sugar, flour and salt before adding the frozen grated butter.

Rub and grab/squeeze the butter into the dry ingredients to reduce the pieces to the consistency of rough sand – chunkier than for a shortcrust pastry.

Mix in the liquid and bring the dough together into a rough ball, adding a little more water if needed.

Push the dough into a neat oblong and place in a plastic bag before chilling for 30 minutes.

Roll the peach cubes in the lemon juice and sugar to macerate.

Dust a board and rolling pin with flour. Roll out the pastry to about 5mm thickness and re-chill.

Cut out rounds of pastry about 6 inches in diameter.

Place a mound of the fruit in the centre of the disc and fold up two edges of pastry – you are aiming to make about 5 "corners" around the top rim of the galette that are pinched together and then all folded neatly in the same direction. Re-chill.

Cook for 8 minutes at 180C, Gas 4, 350F to set the pastry, and then for a further 8 minutes at 160C, Gas 3, 325F.

This quantity makes 15-20 small individual galettes.

My tips.

Mix the sugar, flour and salt the day before in a plastic bag in the mixing bowl.

Store in the fridge overnight so that everything is well chilled.

Add extra orange zest. Mack's commercial version was very concentrated.

When the block of pastry is removed from the fridge, it may need to be slightly warmed with the palms of your hands in order to roll out.

If preferred, use clingfilm to wrap the chilling pastry in place of food-quality plastic bags.

Blackberry coulis.

Rinse the berries and place in a pan with a little sugar. Any water remaining in the fruit will help to create a rough textured sauce when gently simmered.

Tuile biscuits.

100g white granulated sugar.
115g almonds, skinned and slithered.
4 tablespoons egg whites.
30g butter, melted.

Method.

Mix sugar and egg whites.

Fold in nuts and melted butter.

Chill in the fridge for at least 30 minutes.

Line baking tray with silicone mat and lightly spray with oil.

Place rounds of biscuit mix on the tray and spread out evenly – especially the almonds. Chill in the fridge for 10 minutes.

Cook at 135C, Gas 1, 275F for 6 minutes, then rotate the tray back to front and cook for a further 6 minutes.

Place on a rolling pin to cool and become curved.

My tips.

Use a lightly oiled round pastry cutter or ring. Place the mix in the ring, spread the mix with a spoon or finger and then remove the ring before chilling.

French galettes.

Since that first experience I've discovered other authentic French versions. The galette des rois is usually served on the first Sunday of January in celebration of the Three Kings of the Christmas story.

Traditionally, these galettes contain a bean or "fève" hidden in one of the slices that are eaten amongst family, friends or workmates. In some families, the youngest child sits under the table directing the allocation of slices so that there's no cheating! The eventual lucky person finding the bean is crowned either King or Queen with the golden paper crown sold with the cake and is expected to choose someone else as their partner King or Queen. Galettes are still available throughout January, as each bean-winner may be expected to buy the next one (or a bottle of wine), and so the chain of sharing continues.

This galette des rois is the frangipane (almond) version typical of northern France, although sometimes the almond has chocolate pieces added or is replaced with apple purée. The southern version is more like an enriched brioche dough containing cherries and dried fruit shaped into a crown-like circle. Another Anjou version combines the two, and the brioche-type dough is studded with chocolate commemorating Good King René. The fève is still used in the southern galettes but has often been replaced with other collectable favours elsewhere. The one I found was made of glass and in the shape of a small cow – watch out for your teeth! There are probably historic links to the tradition of a silver sixpence in the British Christmas pudding.

Finally, there is another galette available all year round, a sort of buckwheat pancake similar to a crêpe but crisp. It can be filled with savoury combinations of egg, ham, cheese, potato and more.

Galette des rois à la frangipane.

2 sheets puff pastry, enough to line the baking tin and cover it.
75g butter.
100g caster sugar.
2 eggs.
140g ground almonds.
1 fève (a large dried red kidney bean would do).
1 egg yolk, beaten to glaze.

Method.

Cream the butter and sugar together.

Beat in the eggs.

Fold in the ground almonds.

Line a loose-bottomed baking tin with one sheet of pastry.

Pour in the filling and press in the fève.

Top with the remaining pastry and glaze with the beaten egg.

Cook in a preheated oven at 200C, Gas 6, 390F for 20-30 minutes, checking regularly.

My tips.

Add a drop of almond extract to the filling to enhance the flavour, and scatter flaked almonds on the pastry top before baking to add crunch.

Chapter 3.

Sticky mess.

It was the last day at LightHouse and I urgently needed a break. We'd been on the go from dawn to dusk all week. Often there hadn't even been time to get to the loo, let alone to manage real life, check emails and make a series of phone calls to sort out a freezer happily defrosting at home. It had been a whirlwind program: breakfast and lunch with sponsors; journalists teaching us story-telling and promotion; a walking tour of the city; hours struggling to get to grips with inaccessible social media and much more. Every day was so packed with new people and experiences that we hardly had a chance to sleep. But we were still luckier than the homeless people living on the street outside.

Ojok blew in like a ray of sunshine from Uganda, six foot seven of fun and self-confidence. Visa problems and a long layover en route had stopped him getting to us until mid-week. It was good to finally have the three of us together.

Thursday was blissful. We escaped from the vacuum-packed, air-conditioned building and walked on Ocean Beach, breathing fresh air, smelling the sea, hearing the waves and the birds wheeling and cawing above us. It was a powerful sensation on the edge of the Pacific Ocean to know that each puff of wind had come thousands of miles. I felt very small and inconsequential alongside that enormous expanse of ocean that had pulsed with life and energy for millions of years.

Walking on the beach was another strange sensation. My stick crunched through the wind- and sun-baked crust of sand to feel yielding softness below before reaching firm ground. It was like feeling my way over soft, bloated bodies.

We drove on to meet local bee-keeper, Meredith, at a community garden. Land around San Francisco is at such a premium that, in some places, homes are too tightly packed for private gardens. Instead, people wait years to get one of the big wooden boxes (about four foot high and 12 foot square) set out in the community space to grow anything they can fit inside.

Meredith had brought protective bee suits and whisked Ojok, Ahmet and others away to inspect her hives. I simply sat basking in the sun, snoozing in the blissful peace of the garden. They brought back a honeycomb frame for me to feel, and the tiniest pressure from a fingertip cracked each fragile hexagonal wax cell to ooze honey. It was still very new and thin – not yet mature enough to match the smokily complex and exotic honey Ojok had brought from Africa.

That final Friday Ahmet, the "Blind Captain", was in his element sailing in the bay with Ojok. Rather than risk being seasick, I volunteered to help cook our last team lunch with LightHouse instructor Sydney. Her own limited vision is a distinct advantage when she is teaching other visually impaired people how to cook, and her training kitchen is designed and equipped with blindness in mind: straightforward layout with plentiful tactile knobs and buttons, voice-activated timers, a library of audible recipes and more. It was a delight to explore.

Sydney is the consummate cook: organised, inventive and enthusiastic. Her chicken had marinaded overnight ready for oven-baking, and while saffron rice cooked she whipped together a salad with sliced apple and pecans, dressed with a blueberry vinaigrette.

Meanwhile, inspired by Ojok, I was creating a honey cake that I'd made only once before under the supervision of professional MasterChef champion Stephen Edwards (www.steven-edwards.co.uk). It probably wasn't a brilliant idea to try something so ambitious on my first solo Holman effort, especially when feeding the people to whom I'd flaunted my cooking credentials! At least I had the sense not to risk Ojok's special honey, but resorted to something local and less precious.

It all seemed simple until I got to the egg whites. Perhaps American chickens are fed differently, but those eggshells collapsed rather than cracked. Holding a disintegrating egg in one hand, I attempted to pour it into a little basket-like separator hanging very precariously on the side of the bowl, trying not to drop the broken shell too – you try it, with your eyes closed! – but I gave up and simply strained the eggs through my fingers. By then there was egg white everywhere, so a bit more didn't make much difference.

Weighing the whites was no problem with the talking scales, and whipping up the rest of the cake was straightforward. But the end result seemed far too wet and runny, and I couldn't imagine how it would ever cook. With disaster looming, Sydney and I held high-level consultation over the sloppy mix and resorted to another tablespoon each of flour and ground almonds – sorry, Steve. And I didn't have the right shape baking tin either, but we substituted a ring mould with the advantage of heat reaching the centre of the cake.

Our improvisations seemed in vain as the cake refused to cook through, and I began dreaming up alternative desserts. Surely there was something possible with a loaf of bread and the remaining honey? I could see my cooking reputation crashing and burning. And, of course, I'd had the temerity to tinker with the MasterChef recipe too, adding orange and candied walnuts – sometimes one needs the sense to just leave a good idea alone.

The walnut concept had seemed so simple: dry roast in a pan, drop into boiling honey for a few minutes, and cool to a crisp finish on a plate. It remains a mystery to me as to how I could have made everything so sticky! The whole work surface and everything on it, every handle and knob, bowl and pan, each utensil and plate, the taps and sink. Me too, up both arms, my apron and, somehow, right through my T-shirt, back and front! Every stitch had to go into the washing machine.

But, thanks to Steve's great recipe, and double cooking time rather than my bumbling efforts, the cake was a triumph! It was light and full of flavour but, surprisingly, not too sweet. The walnuts added crunch and it disappeared in minutes. I don't think anyone realised the kitchen drama I'd survived more by luck than skill.

Sydney's chicken Marbella.

2 chickens (2 and half pounds each) quartered – or 8 chicken quarter portions.
Half a bulb of garlic, peeled and finely puréed.
1 tablespoon dried oregano.
Coarse salt and freshly ground black pepper to taste.
60ml red wine vinegar.
60ml olive oil.
100g pitted prunes.
50g pitted Spanish green olives.
50g capers with a little of liquid from the jar.
3 bay leaves.
100g brown sugar.
120ml white wine.
2 tablespoons Italian parsley or cilantro (coriander), finely chopped.

Method.

Mix all the ingredients except sugar, wine and parsley in a bowl, cover and marinade overnight in the fridge.

Preheat oven to 180C, Gas 4, 350F.

Arrange chicken in a single layer in one or two large, shallow roasting tins.

Spoon marinade over the chicken evenly.

Sprinkle chicken pieces with brown sugar and pour white wine around them. Bake for 50 minutes to 1 hour, basting frequently with pan juices.

With a slotted spoon transfer chicken, prunes, olives and capers to a serving platter and pour over some of the pan juices and sprinkle with parsley. Serve the remaining juices in a sauce boat.

My tips.

This seems a long time cooking. The chicken will be done when the thickest part reaches around 70-75C on a cooking temperature probe.

Steven Edwards' honey cake.

80g butter, melted and browned in a pan then cooled.
160g icing sugar.
60g ground almonds.
60g plain flour.
10g baking powder.
200g egg whites.
15g honey.
More honey for topping.

Method.

Mix the dry ingredients with an electric mixer.

Add the egg whites and whisk to combine.

Whisk in the cool browned butter followed by the honey.

Lightly spray a square high-sided baking tin with a little oil and then pour in the cake batter.

Rest in fridge before baking.

Cook at 160 C, Gas 3, 320F for 22 minutes.

Remove and cool on a cooling rack.

Spike all over with a knife and drizzle more honey.

My tips.

When butter heated in a pan stops making a bubbling/boiling sound, most of the water has evaporated and you can smell that the butter is becoming cooked/darker/nuttier.

Different types of honey contain different amounts of water so be prepared to add a little more flour and/or cook longer.

Don't be afraid to change the 2013 professional MasterChef champion's winning recipe. For example, add orange zest to the mix and the bottom of the tin, plus the orange juice to the honey glaze syrup. Top with candied walnuts.

Chapter 4.

Michelin star.

There's still that difference in language between English and American; the old potato and tomato "let's call the whole thing off" debate. Being called "badass" was rather staggering. I'd misheard and misunderstood – it might be big, but it isn't bad! At the time, it was reassuring – only just – to hear that this farewell valediction from the Holman team was their way of saying tough, competent and relentless! Years later I discovered they had really said "ass" when I'd spent all that time believing they'd been referring to my posterior.

All of that came to the fore when I moved into a hotel for my second week in California. There was no room at LightHouse and Toby was due to fly in late the next day. A brilliant chance to catch up on a week's lost sleep, I thought. But the best laid plans... I never did pursue the travel company about their interpretation of a "disability accessible" room, and it was certainly an alien concept for the hotel staff too. But they were kind in running out to get me food. There was no catering in the hotel, but a nearby pizza place was OK if, like me, being cheese-intolerant you could survive on the BBQ chicken version for lunch, supper and lunch again! Welcome to the culinary delights of America.

It was the bathroom that finally did it. Not enough space to swing a bathmat, not a grab rail in sight, and a slippery step over the bath side with just the swinging open door to hold on to. Probably tight but manageable if you can see, but downright treacherous if you can't. With two months of travel ahead, the consequences of falling over were far too risky.

Thank goodness for Ben and Blanche. I'd met them at the final LightHouse function as blind sailor Ben had been part of Ahmet and Ojok's sailing trip. As soon as they heard about my imminent move to the hotel, they spontaneously offered beds in their Oakland home on the other side of the bay. I'd been shy of accepting the generosity of virtual strangers: too much imposition on too short an acquaintance. But my stiff upper lip and English reserve wobbled when I faced that hotel room the next day. I was in touch with Blanche within the hour, and she didn't hesitate to take on two unknown guests. With the escape route planned, I just had to wait the 36 hours for Toby's arrival.

He was a Trojan, unphased by a change of plans and happy to make the move after a good night's sleep. We'd never had a warm cuddly aunt/ nephew relationship, but real friendship flowered while battling with the challenges of the coming months.

Our bags were already packed as we set off the following morning to cook in San Francisco's famous Chinatown. Luis, the Michelin-experienced executive pastry chef at "China Live" (www.chinalivesf.com) introduced us to his sleekly modern fine dining area of this emporium of Chinese cuisine: a ground floor café, and shops for authentic ingredients and implements, banqueting and more.

After a week of many meals across the city's eating outlets, that morning with Luis was a welcome return to the simplicity of good food. Too often I'd found that, in a land of plenty, cooks couldn't resist the temptation to throw far too many ingredients onto the plate. Dishes just became a muddle of flavours and textures.

His explanation was: "Several recessions shrunk the catering and hospitality sector, with many of the most able chefs moving out of the industry. There were still many other cooks with little experience but a drive to make money. At the same time, they were being persuaded by the phenomena of the "Hot Rock" celebrity chef boom in America that anyone could become a cooking superstar. The result was lots of pop-up restaurants and chefs creating their reputations with just a couple of dishes or gimmicks. Some of these people only had two- or three-years' experience, without actually learning the basics, so that combinations and techniques weren't well executed. But because they did something crazy or created two great plates, they captured an audience and now they have a restaurant that is successful, but they don't really offer anything more than the cooking on which they built themselves."

Both a top professional and college lecturer, Luis shared his philosophy: "The hardest thing is to make the students focus on the flavours they want to express to the customer." He taught me to decide first on the tastes and textures of a dish and, only then, how I could make this work on a plate rather than being beguiled by complexity of process and confusion of ingredients.

A fan of fusion cooking, Luis said, "I think that a lot of Asian cuisines are perceived as cheap and easy, fast and using very simple ingredients. Here we are more about the technique and history; the passing of knowledge that just isn't reflected in the 10-minute fire order that you might find on a street stall. In China, a lot of ingredients have been combined and techniques passed down the generations."

He'd chosen a perfect example: seagrass cake with passionfruit mousse and seagrass cracker, explaining, "A favourite ingredient at China Live is imported seagrass. It's a little bit different from traditional seaweed or nori. It grows in the marshland, predominantly on the east side of the country."

The dried grass felt disturbingly like long hanks of coarse hair before Luis ground it into a rough textured brown flour flecked with bright green. It combines high protein levels, starch and gelling properties, similar to the Irish carrageen, to help stabilise the sponge mix. We mortals without access to such exotic ingredients can use ordinary wheat flour instead, but will find the sponge a bit tougher. If you can find the authentic seagrass, why not use it like Luis to top sea urchin toast and in petit fours to add that extra layer of saltiness and sea savour? But perhaps a pinch of salt is as close as most of us can get.

This dessert matches his philosophy by making subtle variations of two or three flavours through texture, temperature and fine tuning the sweetness and sourness. His sponge and cracker have different concentrations and textures of the seagrass: the sharpness of the fresh passionfruit element is mellowed in the mousse and everything changes again when tasted in different combinations. Every sense is stimulated.

An electric hand whisk is nearly essential for this type of sponge. Egg yolks and sugar are whisked over a pan of hot water to start cooking the egg before pouring all into a fresh, cold bowl and whisking fast until the mix has cooled. Then yet more whisking for 3 to 5 minutes, although at a slower speed, to break down the air bubbles and create a marshmallow texture before the ground seagrass can be carefully folded in. Then even more whisking of the egg whites and sugar to a soft peak meringue into which the seagrass mix is folded. The finished sponge goes into a hot oven and the temperature is immediately reduced. All eminently achievable.

On the other hand, the crackers separate the cooks from the chefs: seagrass combined with under-cooked rice! It doesn't sound great and, worse, there's so much heat-generating starch in the mix that you risk burning out the blender. The paste is dried for two days in a dehydrator, another 24 hours in the kitchen, and the cracker is fried before using tweezers to impale the mousse with shards. For those few without a dehydrator, Luis recommended: "Dry in an oven with just the pilot flame for 2 or 3 days and then dry for another day at room temperature." Anyone can do it and then boast about transforming fishy porridge into fishy wallpaper paste to create this perfect finishing touch to wow friends and family.

But the dish wasn't quite finished yet. Inspired by a beach scene after a bonfire, Luis brought all the elements together: "We have the seagrass cake. You'll have a little bit of the cream, prepared overnight, which gets the best texture. With that, we'll be placing our crackers, creating a seascape base, some pickled seaweeds and adding freeze-dried passionfruit pieces that look like little rocks. Coated with cocoa butter, they are waterproofed and have a matt Corian stone look to them. We have little marigold flowers from Japan and have stripped some of the petals off them. The final piece is smoked bubbles: sugar, egg whites, xanthium gum, and edible smoke powder. The thickened liquid is aerated by an aquarium pump and the bubbles are dolloped very lightly on to the dessert. The wave break of an ocean – that residue of sea foam." Aquarium pumps will be flying off the shelves.

A year later, Luis and I met up again in San Francisco to swap news. He'd moved on from the restaurant to be even more wildly creative: featuring in a television series on the edible properties of newly legalised marijuana. He had been using the plant's relaxation properties in another outstanding dessert.

Luis's recipes.

Seagrass cake.

Video: Passionfruit cream and seagrass cake

50g egg yolks.
148g whole eggs.
30g roasted tea oil.
148g sugar.
40g seagrass powder.
90g egg whites.
16g sugar.

Method.

Preheat oven to 220C, Gas 7, 425F.

Mix yolks, whole eggs, tea oil and sugar over water bath heated on hob until hot.

Whisk on high speed to ribbon stage.

Whisk on medium speed for 3-5 minutes to stabilise.

While mixing, slowly add in seagrass powder (in 3 additions). Remove from heat.

Meanwhile, whip egg whites to frothy and soft peak.

Slowly add in sugar while whisking to stiff peak.

Fold a third of the seagrass mix into the egg whites, repeat with another third and then the final third.

Spoon mix into one or two baking trays.

Place tray in oven and reduce heat to 190C, Gas 5, 375F.

Bake for 8 minutes, rotate and continue for another 4 minutes.

Once cooled, remove from the tray and cut into portions.

My tips.

Tea oil might be replaced with a nut oil and the seagrass powder with plain flour (although it will make the sponge a little tougher).

I'd probably line the baking tray with parchment.

Passionfruit cream.

230g passionfruit purée (pulp with seeds removed).
3 leaves gelatine.
225g sugar.
10g passionfruit powder.
65g egg yolks.
450g whipping cream.

Method.

Heat passionfruit puree in a pan to a boil.

Soak gelatine in ice water.

Sift sugar and passionfruit powder into a bowl, add egg yolks and mix well. Gradually add warm passionfruit puree to the egg mix, whisking.

Return to the hob and return mix to a boil, whisking continuously.

Remove from heat, add gelatine and mix before straining into a clean bowl.

Allow to cool to below 26C, 80F.

While cooling, whip cream to soft peak, reserve until ready.

Fold whipped cream into cooled passionfruit mixture. Chill until needed.

Seagrass crackers.

Video: Seagrass crackers and finishing touches

120g small grain rice.
420ml water.
Three quarters teaspoon salt.
3 tablespoons seagrass powder.
360ml water.

Method.

Place rice, water salt and seagrass in pan, bring to the boil then reduce heat and cook for 10-15 minutes.

Place in a blender with the second amount of water and blend until smooth.

Spread onto parchment paper and dehydrate overnight at 61C, 142F.

Next day, lay out the crackers on their parchment and leave at room temperature for one day.

When serving on the third day, fry the crackers at 175C, 350F.

Chapter 5.

Food for the soul.

Cooking with Luis had been daunting in its exactitude and refinement, but at least the spacious kitchen had been quiet and empty. But the videos show me at rather a low spot, tired and despondent after two days caged up in the miserable hotel from which I was desperate to escape. Within an hour of completing the session at China Live, Toby and I were in the taxi to Ben and Blanche in Oakland. After all the accommodation issues during the previous days, it felt like coming home.

By the next day, with a good night's sleep and supper of real rather than processed food cooked by gastronome Ben, we were all set for the renowned West Oakland "Brown Sugar Kitchen". It was my first experience of traditional southern food created by chef-owner Tanya Holland. This was a completely different restaurant experience: not much space, positively vibrating with cheerful noise, and nearly too many cooks rushing to feed the constant stream of customers who could watch everything we did. And another different style of food that developed in the 1950s with close links to soul music, as Tanya explained: "Wherever there's a population of African Americans, whether in the west like Oakland, the northwest like Seattle, or the northeast like New York, you are going to find soul food. The origin is the south. Soul food is the cooking that developed from what the Africans brought to this country, what ingredients they found in the south, what they brought with them and the fusion of cultures that, over time, has produced dishes, whether it is fried chicken, gumbo, corn bread or mac and cheese, that are associated with an African American cuisine."

Her authentic Creole spice mix was at the heart of many dishes, reflecting the very essence of her heritage. The glorious fried and spiced shrimp, oozing with extra beery barbecue sauce amidst a slurry of grits, was a prime example.

Grits are a porridge-like concoction made from hominy – the dried and reconstituted scrapings from corn cobs once the golden nuggets of sweetcorn have been removed. The result is an alternative to more familiar potatoes, pasta or rice, with enough carbohydrate punch to sustain a day's physical hard labour. They are a stark reminder of the poor food upon which slave labour survived. Modern taste demands less frugal fare, with the enrichment of butter and cheese. But, regardless of great seasoning, the cheese made grits a dish too far for me.

In the past Oakland had been the terminal for the railway and, with many African Americans working on the trains, they had naturally gravitated to make their homes around the last stop on the track. They brought their own taste in food and now, hearing the diversity of Tanya's customers, it hit the spot for many more. She was rightly proud of the Oakland heritage and used local artists to capture the history and culture in the restaurant's artworks.

Sustaining 50 covers in a restaurant far from usual transport links and in a complicated socio-economic area was daring, but Tanya's success proved that people will travel to find good food. Like any community, people and their tastes constantly change. The original vibrant middle-class community was mutating with better road access, urban development and gentrification, pricing out many of the original residents. Tanya had moved with the changes, creating menus to reflect increasing demand for local, organic and seasonal food. There was entertainment too. The pace of the seeming multitude of cooks in the narrow galley kitchen was fast and furious. The customers could watch each flashing blade and flipping pan. The whole lunchtime atmosphere was boisterous with good cheer and friendliness.

Not surprisingly, Southern fried chicken and waffles was the most popular dish on the menu. I could understand rubbing spices into the meat, and even the overnight marinade in buttermilk before frying, but serving with sweet waffles was a strange combination for those less familiar with typical food from the American south.

It was a cuisine laden with treats such as the homemade marshmallows bobbing in a mug of hot chocolate with a comforting slice of red velvet cake. I was intrigued by the prospect of the peanut butter cake, but it had all been snaffled by her customers. The whole sense of the food, the cooking and atmosphere was generosity; hospitality seasoned with a wicked touch of self-indulgence.

But Covid ended Tania's Oakland restaurant. Undaunted, she has an even bigger audience on television with Oprah (www.oprah.com/app/tanyas-kitchen-table.html).

Tanya's recipes.

Creole spice mix.

3 tablespoons (kosher) salt.
3 tablespoons herbes de Provence.
3 tablespoons ground cumin.
45g cayenne pepper.
30g freshly ground black pepper.
30g sweet paprika.

Method.

Stir all the ingredients together and store in an airtight container for up to 6 months.

Makes about 200g of spice mix.

Creole sauce.

1 tablespoon unsalted butter.
2 spring (green) onions (white parts only), chopped.
1 teaspoon garlic, peeled and minced.
360ml wheat beer.
180ml Worcestershire sauce.

Method.

Melt the butter over low heat in a medium pan.

Add the onions and garlic, cook until softened (about 5 minutes).

Add the beer and Worcestershire sauce and increase the heat to bring the pan contents to boiling.

Reduce to simmering point and cook for 15-20 minutes until the sauce is thick and syrupy.

The sauce should be reduced to about 240ml. Remove from heat and cool.

To make ahead, refrigerate sauce in an airtight container and store in the fridge for up to 1 week.

White cheddar grits.

Video: Creole shrimp and cheddar grits

660ml water.
95g quick-cooking grits.
2 tablespoons double (heavy) cream.
2 tablespoons unsalted butter.
115g sharp white cheddar cheese, grated.
1 and a half teaspoons (kosher) salt.
Pinch of white pepper.

Method.

Boil the water in a medium pan and whisk in the grits.

Reduce the pan to a simmer and cook for about 4 minutes, stirring constantly, until the grits are fully cooked and thick.

Stir in the remaining ingredients to serve 4.

Creole shrimp.

2 tablespoons vegetable oil.
50g diced green (bell) pepper.
50g diced red (bell) pepper.
3 spring (green) onions, all thinly sliced.
2 garlic cloves, peeled and minced.
2 teaspoons **Creole spice mix** (see recipe above).
680g medium prawns (shrimp), peeled and deveined.
180ml **Creole sauce** (see recipe above).
60ml double (heavy) cream.
2 tablespoons unsalted butter.
140g baby spinach leaves, washed.
2 teaspoons fresh lemon juice.

Method.

In a large sauté pan, heat the oil over medium heat until simmering.

Add the green and red peppers, spring onions, garlic and **Creole spice mix**. Cook until the vegetables are softened, about 5 minutes.

Add the prawns and sear for about 2 minutes until opaque and starting to feel firm, turning once.

Stir in the **Creole sauce**, cream and butter. Bring to a simmer.

Add the spinach, a handful at a time, stirring to wilt and coat with sauce.

Once all the spinach has been added, remove from the heat and stir in the lemon juice.

Makes 4 servings with the cheddar grits.

Buttermilk fried chicken.

Marinade.

2 tablespoons fresh parsley, minced.
1 tablespoon dried tarragon.
1 teaspoon dried oregano.
1 teaspoon dried thyme.
1 tablespoon sweet paprika.
1 teaspoon cayenne pepper.
2 teaspoons garlic powder.
1 tablespoon onion powder.
2 teaspoons (kosher) salt.
1 teaspoon freshly ground black pepper.
1.6kg chicken, cut into 8 pieces.
240ml buttermilk.

Coating.

1 tablespoon salt.
1 tablespoon ground black pepper.
185g plain (all-purpose) flour.
Vegetable (canola or rice bran) oil for deep-frying.

Method.

Mix all the marinade herbs and spices in a large bowl before adding the chicken pieces. Stir to coat and then pour the buttermilk over.

Cover the bowl and chill for at least 8 hours or overnight.

Preheat the oven to 180C, Gas 4, 350F.

Line a rimmed baking sheet with paper towels and set a wire rack on top.

In a large wide bowl, combine the coating flour, salt and pepper.

One piece at a time, and letting any excess buttermilk drip back into the bowl, transfer the chicken to the flour mixture.

Dredge the chicken with the flour mixture, shaking off the excess.

In a large cast-iron frying pan, add oil to a depth of 2cm and heat the oil to 180C, 350F over medium heat until hot but not smoking.

Fry the chicken, a few pieces at a time, taking care not to crowd the pan and turning occasionally, until crisp and browned, 5-7 minutes.

Transfer the chicken to the rack over the baking sheet to continue cooking in the oven for about 20 minutes until the temperature reaches 75C, 165F. Remove from the oven.

Allow to rest for 5-10 minutes. Repeat with the remaining chicken.

Serve immediately with cornmeal waffles and cider syrup for 6 to 8 servings.

Cornmeal waffles.

Video: Cornmeal waffles

2 teaspoons active dry yeast.
180ml warm water.
3 eggs.
720ml whole milk.
140g cornmeal.
255g plain (all-purpose) flour.
1 and a half teaspoons (kosher) salt.
1 and a half teaspoons granulated sugar.
170g unsalted butter, melted.
Vegetable oil for the waffle iron.
Half a teaspoon baking soda.

Method.

In a small bowl, combine the yeast with the warm water and allow to stand for about 10 minutes until foaming.

In a large bowl, whisk the eggs and milk together.

Place the cornmeal, flour, salt and granulated sugar in a sieve and sift together into another large bowl.

Add the yeast mixture to the eggs and milk, then whisk in the flour mixture until thoroughly combined.

Whisk in the melted butter until just combined.

Cover the bowl with clingfilm and refrigerate for at least 4 hours or overnight. The batter will thicken as the yeast continues to ferment and the butter solidifies.

Preheat the oven to 120C, Gas 1/2, 250F.

Set a wire rack over a baking sheet.

Preheat the electric waffle iron and brush lightly with oil.

Remove the waffle batter from the refrigerator and stir in the baking soda.

Ladle some of the batter into the waffle iron.

Close the lid, and cook the waffles until golden and cooked through, about 3 minutes or according to the manufacturer's instructions.

Transfer the waffles to the rack to keep warm in the oven. Repeat with the remaining batter, placing the 8 to 10 waffles in a single layer on the rack.

Serve the waffles warm with warm apple cider syrup.

My tips.

The batter should not be beaten for too long to avoid the flour's gluten making the dough too elastic.

It is important that the final batter isn't too thick, or the waffles won't be light and crisp.

Tania's commercial waffle iron cooked the waffles at about 200C, 400F for about 3 minutes.

Apple cider syrup.

300g brown sugar.
1 and a half teaspoon apple cider vinegar.
960ml apple cider.
2 cinnamon sticks.
115g unsalted butter.

Method.

In a large pot, mix the ingredients and heat to boiling point before reducing to simmering for about 45 minutes.

The mix should reduce by about two-thirds to about 360ml.

Remove the cinnamon and either keep the syrup warm over a low heat or store in an airtight container in a fridge for up to one month.

Chapter 6.

Sourdough masterclass.

Our final day in California was at the Cheeseboard Collective (www.cheeseboardcollective.coop), not far from the renowned Berkeley University across the bay from San Francisco, and an inspiration to anyone who wants to make, smell and greedily devour absolutely fantastic sourdough bread. Famous bakers have beaten a path to their door, including The Great British Bake Off's Paul Hollywood, who filmed there too.

Operating for over 50 years, this successful emporium of bread delights is a true collective, with each member of staff having a stake in the business, inspiring them to excellence. Their ethos creates real workplace equality and shared responsibility based on the essentials of home cooking: wholesome ingredients, handcrafted with care and love. It is no wonder that generations of customers have championed the collective concept and the quality of what they produce.

Cathy had been elected to take charge of my visit, but passed me around to Tina on dough, then Matt and Erin on shaping and finishing. Talking to the crew, it was obvious how much they enjoyed their work, were proud of their products, and were a strong team. It's difficult to imagine a better basis for a successful business – and it clearly was with their delicious food flying off the shelves. They were all generous with their time, patient with my efforts, and professional enough to tell me when I got things wrong. And Erin turned out to be a close friend of Ben and Blanche – the world of people enthusiastic about cooking can be surprisingly small.

The Collective's famous "pizza of the day" demonstrated their success, so popular that customers queued up in the street. Being cheese-intolerant, I was completely the wrong person to explore their extensive selection of those cultured and fermented milk products that I find so revolting. However, I did pay closer attention to the racks upon racks of different sourdough breads – not the industrial woolly sliced stuff reliant upon yeast enhancers, but wholesome grains bursting with flavour and texture from the natural yeasts that surround us.

One of my tasks was to "feed" their sourdough starter, up to my elbows in a large plastic tub, hand-mixing extra flour into the cold, slippery, pungent goo that had been fermenting for years.

A few hours later, the starter was ready for use in their giant-size basic sourdough mix. It took a massive cement mixer-size bowl to handle over 245 pounds or 110 kilos of dough. But, with a hoist and chains, it was a one-woman job for Tina! Perhaps not your idea of an easy morning in the kitchen, but I learned some key principles to apply to my own bread making. By translating the huge weights of the Cheeseboard ingredients into their respective proportions, I've scaled down their mix to something more achievable at home.

Starch heats up with the friction of mixing. Luis at China Live had been careful not to overheat the blender full of rice and seagrass. With bread, warmth helps activate the yeast. The temperatures of the room, the flour and water plus the mixing/kneading friction should, ideally, bring the dough to nearly 24C/75F. Then it is in peak condition for proving.

Tina was constantly alert to the dough temperature in the mixer, which seemed to be the key for deciding when to slow or speed up the machine and, most importantly, when to stop it.

A long slow cool prove can produce more flavour and a better texture. At Cheeseboard they allow the dough to rise overnight in a dedicated proving room. Back at home, I've found that sourdough left in a cool porch doubles in size while I sleep and dream.

Once the sourdough had completed its first proving, it was ready for shaping and finishing by Matt and Erin cutting into different sizes and adding flavours and finishes before further proving. It wasn't easy to keep up with their professional speed, so I only managed to make a few of their range: focaccia, bialys and zampanos. The last were named after Anthony Quinn's character in the film ***La Strada*** when they marked the death of director Fellini. These rolls are indented with a fingerprint pattern, topped with sea salt, chilli flakes and parmesan. Once you have the sourdough base, the variations are only limited by your imagination.

I managed to capture some of their other professional tricks, but recommend the Cheeseboard Collective cookbook for the real sourdough enthusiasts:

- Shape small dough rounds tightly to create surface tension.
- Line baking trays with cornmeal to prevent sticking and add extra crunch.
- Allow breads to rest and part-rise under a floured tea towel for about an hour before further shaping and adding flavourings.
- Allow at least 2 hours further rising time.
- Bake in moderate ovens (375F, Gas 5, 190C) to avoid too much crust. (At home I check the temperature inside the bread has reached about 95C to be confident it has cooked through.)
- Rotate the trays back to front and between lower and higher shelves in the oven during the baking time.

- Finish with any more flavouring while the bread is still warm.

After a hard morning's work, Erin and I sat at a sunny table outside, sampling some of the products while she reviewed my performance. Her verdict: fun to work with, a quick learner, and lack of sight hadn't been a problem. That was good enough for me as I departed, laden with breads to share with Ben and Blanche.

I'd survived the first week of the tour without major mishap. Despite unfamiliar professional kitchens and new ingredients, cuisines and equipment, I'd been in the safe hands of those competent and professional chefs. I felt far more confident about the next stage. But I hadn't fully realised the tests we were about to encounter – the language differences, the jungle kitchen, and risky, unconventional and interpretative cooking.

Video: Hello from San Francisco

Next day Toby and I were excitedly on our way to Costa Rica. I still haven't forgotten the encounter at San Francisco airport, probably the first time I'd been confronted by blindness since arriving in America. The check-in clerk clearly thought that it was a contagious condition and absolutely couldn't talk to me directly. Perhaps some people don't realise that, like anyone else, I am completely aware when they are directing their talk, face and eyes elsewhere. I reminded him that I was the paying passenger with whom he was dealing, with a total sense of humour failure, somewhat firm language, keeping my temper through gritted teeth.

Thankfully, the passenger assistance staff were better trained and understood how to help without being condescending. Toby was a hero, managing our carry-on luggage and guiding me too.

Talking about guiding, don't imagine that most guides are in charge of more than navigation. Over many years and many knocks, bumps and scrapes, I've learned that the guidee needs to take charge of the guidor. There's no way that I'm going to allow a complete stranger to hold my safety in their hand. I know that most people who generously offer to be a guide are complete amateurs at it: they won't tell me if a slope or steps go up or down; they forget to say left or right; they miss the hazards at head height. Instead, I'm the one taking a firm grip on their arm so I can feel our progress through their body, the momentary pause that heralds an obstacle, the head movements of uncertainty, the body surge of confidence. Me holding their arm means no escape until I'm done. Many a time the haplessly inexperienced guide has been resolutely steered from one location to another as I complete my mission, transit or shopping. Outside the professional assistants at airports and railway stations, there are few guides who appreciate that they have become the means to my end.

But being upfront and personal is one of the joys of being guided. While others have to be satisfied with a handshake or hug, I get continuing physical contact that makes conversation and the sharing of personal stories almost inevitable. As I've been guided on my travels, I've heard about family triumphs and break-ups, about health and money worries and, most startling, the intimacy of tattoos. Being guided adds an entirely unexpected and magical dimension to life.

Toby and I had practiced our guiding techniques back in the UK so we could cope with the odd hitch, like the adventure of changing planes in Los Angeles as we circumnavigated the huge airport a couple of times on the shuttle bus after being misdirected.

Finally, we found the correct terminal and embarked on the overnight flight to San Jose, capital of Costa Rica in South America. Not even the long flight could stop me talking about food and cooking with anyone who'd listen. Kate, one of the Delta flight attendants, volunteered her fruity salad dressing recipe before sleep silenced me.

Cheeseboard Collective recipes.

Sourdough.

Video: Sourdough

You are probably unlikely to use the quantities of these commercial bakers but I've included them to give a sense of the size of their operation, which needed a catering cement mixer, hoist and chains. Instead, I've translated the quantities into comparable proportions. Hence, if you are using 750g flour, you would need 510g water, 263g sourdough starter and 7.5g salt. You just need to scale the ingredients to the amount of flour you are using.

100% strong white bread flour (120 pounds).
68% water (about 82 pounds).
35% sourdough starter (about 42 pounds).
1% non-iodised salt (about 19 ounces). Americans call this kosher salt.

Your goal is to create smooth and shiny dough with a temperature of about 24C, 75F. All the following will impact the temperature:

- **The ambient room temperature.** In California the temperature was over 26C, 80F. This will affect the temperature of the flour, starter and the mixer (whether a machine or hand-draulic).
- **The water temperature.** In California, their normal coolest water for the dough was about 7C, 45F.
- **The mixing time and speed.** The friction of the mixture with the bowl and dough hook creates heat. With the enormous mixer at the cheeseboard collective, they alternated between slow and high speeds.

Start by mixing the flour, water and starter together slowly and then increase the speed for a few minutes.

Add the salt and mix again, first slowly and then fast.

Check the temperature is around 24C, 75F with your trusty cooking thermometer.

When the dough is smooth and shiny, oil one or more containers that have enough space to allow the dough to double in size.

Place the dough into each container and roll to cover with a thin layer of oil.

Cover with a floured tea towel and place in your proving room, which has a constant temperature of about 15C, 60F to rise overnight and develop the best sourdough flavour. If you don't run to such a room, the rise can take place in the kitchen or other warm place for about 4 hours, but will be quicker and less flavourful. You could also leave the covered dough in a colder place or the fridge overnight, but allow it to return to ambient room temperature and rise for a couple of hours before the next step.

Then you can move on to shaping the breads for baking and various toppings.

Sourdough variations.

Video: Sourdough variations

Focaccia.

These breads are usually rather flat, perhaps having risen an inch or two but not much higher. The proven dough can be pressed out to line the bottom of a large tin or cut into smaller individual rounds.

Once the breads have rested and risen for a while, there are endless variations in adding different flavours before the second rise: simply pushing stoned black olives into the dough; pressing finger prints into the dough before brushing with garlic-infused oil; spiking with rosemary and adding a salt crunch; spreading with a sun-dried tomato paste; combining some of these and more.

Bake individual small breads for 25 minutes at 375F, Gas 5, 190C and place larger breads direct on to a preheated stone or tray in the oven to crisp the bottom.

Zampanos.

The proved dough for each individual bread is rolled as tightly as possible and flattened before resting and rising for an hour.

Brush with garlic-infused olive oil and dimple the bread with fingertips before sprinkling with sea salt.

Cover with a floured tea towel and allow to rise for at least two hours.

Bake for 20-25 minutes at 375F, Gas 5, 190C so that they are cooked but don't form a crust.

Once removed from the oven, brush again with the garlic-infused olive oil and top with flakes of dried red chilli and shavings of parmesan cheese.

Bialys.

Divide the proved sourdough into small rounds of flattened dough and place on a tray.

Combine finely sliced onion, poppy seeds, sea salt and olive oil in a bowl.

When the dough rounds have rested and risen for an hour, make a small well in the centre for a tablespoon of the onion mix.

Allow to rise again for at least 2 hours.

Bake for 25-30 minutes at 375F, Gas 5, 190C so that they barely have any crust and just a light golden colour.

My tips.

These were variations used with sourdough, but could also transform bread dough made with yeast.

Kate's salad dressing.

Avocado, tomatoes, green chilli and mango, all whizzed together and seasoned to taste.

Chapter 7.

Fine dining in the jungle.

Video: Baking Blind coming to Costa Rica

Our arrival in Costa Rica was somewhat befuddled and disorientated after the long overnight flight. But there was no time for leisurely breakfast or acclimatisation. Our first task was to tackle the capital's traffic and somewhat haphazard approach to location finding. It seemed there weren't formal street names or addresses in San Jose. Total lack of any useable Spanish was an additional hurdle. Our heartfelt thanks went to the excellent Tourist Information agent, helpfully located outside the airport's Arrivals hall. We were put into a taxi with his handwritten directions for the National Association of Blind People and were duly delivered. I never discovered where we were.

Members of the Association ushered us into a classroom where we could wait, rest and relax for the several hours before my afternoon presentation. Our generously hospitable hosts quickly arranged delivery of an extremely welcome typical Costa Rican breakfast of rice and beans with fried chicken and plantains. A hot meal, time to catch our breath, and even a short snooze was enough to recharge our batteries.

Most important, it was my first face-to-face meeting with the extraordinary Noam, our host for the week. I'd simply had a phone call out of the blue many months earlier making the invitation. I'd been innocently sitting in Hampshire and, suddenly, was talking to someone in South America, explaining my cooking tour ambition. Noam hadn't hesitated for a moment in inviting me to cook in the Tamarindo jungle fine dining restaurant on the Pacific Coast. I hadn't hesitated either, and that part of the travel plan was fixed.

Noam said, "I knew that we had at least one thing in common: she's completely bonkers, she's completely mad, and she's willing to push limits, and that's the kind of person I like to work with because it fits my personality." Others had received the same warm invitation to cook: one Michelin-starred chef, two specialist vegan chefs, and, now, this home cook too.

Noam described hirself as one of the many "capitalist hippies" from Europe and elsewhere who had decamped to Costa Rica to relish alternative, off-grid lifestyles. A cosmopolitan background**:** "My grandparents were Polish Jews who left Poland during the war. I was born in Belgium. I left when I was 18 to study civil engineering in the UK and, since then, I've been travelling the world coaching entrepreneurs, business owners and artists to create masterpieces and experience life as magical."

Video: Not for the faint-hearted: blind cook in South American jungle

After more of the staple Costa Rican rice and beans for lunch, there was increasing chatter as members of the Blind Association gathered to hear me perform. The entertainment opened with stirring renditions of popular Costa Rican songs, plus vociferous choruses from the audience. Several lengthy speeches of welcome followed, with a local priest providing nearly simultaneous translation.

They were an exuberantly enthusiastic bunch, and listened patiently to a rather disjointed account of the tour and my own experiences. When both speaker and audience are invisible to each other, building rapport is even trickier when pausing after each sentence for translation, but their determined attention made it work. Asked about myself, I explained that, "Blindness is no longer important. I have an incredibly good life; I am very happy." We debated technological solutions for sight loss. For me, it would take a great deal of persuasion to accept that some form of bionic eye would change life. There was more general support for my credo: "We want to show the whole world that blind people can do anything. We have lots of ambition. We have learned to solve lots of problems. We've learned to live our lives in a different way and those are huge skills for us to take to our communities, to our families and to the workplace. Give us a chance!"

Video: Blind people everywhere want their chance of success

Many of those people were highly motivated to get back to work or start their own businesses. Like so many disabled people, everyone wanted to make more of their lives, with more involvement and more independence rather than being seen as needy blind people.

I was immensely heartened and my confidence was boosted by their positive response. Some immediately offered accommodation, and another volunteered me to take the Holman tour to El Salvador. The cooking theme clearly touched a chord: many were asking for their own course, while others had skills and recipes to share. Within minutes we'd organised our next gathering for a week later when I returned from Tamarindo: I'd lead a demonstration at the capital's top cookery school.

By the end of the afternoon our common aspirations and experiences had overcome the language difficulties. I was reluctant to leave them when there seemed so much we could do together. But the road to Tamarindo beckoned.

Noam had arranged a big four-by-four car and Victor had abandoned his medical studies to drive us for the week. As the light faded, we set out on the long journey to the resort town of Tamarindo on the Pacific Coast. In Costa Rica, the new cross-country single carriageway had substantially improved transport and communications. Nevertheless, it was a six-hour drive in the growing dark to the thrum of windscreen wipers battling heavy rain and the bounce of wheels on the road, treacherously awash with water, riddled with potholes and "sleeping policeman". It felt somewhat unnerving being driven into the unknown by two strangers. On the other hand, in those weather conditions, I was thankful to have rejected the quicker but riskier alternative: flying in a single-engine aircraft to land in a field once cleared of grazing horses and cattle. As our headlights lit each cluster of small houses, Noam explained that the villages were all centred around a football pitch, post office, school and church – the staples of Costa Rican communities.

It was after 10 o'clock that night when we eventually arrived in Tamarindo. Neither Toby nor I had slept much on the overnight flight from San Francisco. We had been on the go for nearly 36 hours. With both body and brain aching, it was a relief to find a good simple hotel bedroom, ample bathroom and a large bed for instant sleep.

Tamarindo.

Another day. Noam and Victor collected us for breakfast at the local Venezuelan café: Arepa, a sort of cornmeal roll filled with an omelette. Toby had already been exploring the sandy Pacific Coast beach, which is increasingly attracting tourists, but he hadn't thought to watch out for the crocodiles. The locals know all about them so assume that visitors will too!

Noam guided us on a stroll through a cook's dream of a Saturday farmers' market, where the stallholders generously cut up samples of their strange and exotic fruits for me to taste amidst the hustle and bustle of their customers. There was a bewildering selection of mangostan (small black fruit with the flower sepals still attached), Chinese mamanchino, Lemon mandarino (the small malaquina orange), and dragon fruit.

Although most of the growers were local people, many other stallholders were those "capitalist hippies" with international roots. Many had moved to Tamarindo for the lifestyle, culture and relaxation, often wanting to avoid the structures and bureaucracies of modern Western life. Some were keen to maintain their anonymity and Toby was warned to ask permission before taking pictures.

These stallholders were selling an intriguing cross section of their artisan handcrafted food: French croissants and eclairs; bagels; fermented kimchi, ice creams and much more. One seller shared his tips on cooking bagels: poach for 1 minute before 16 minutes in the oven, rotating front to back, top to bottom halfway through. I was allowed to sample the 95% cocoa solids chocolate on offer, a revelation of subtle, complex and sometimes bitter flavours that lasted on the tongue. I moved on to learn some new ice cream flavour combinations – coconut milk and lime spiked with lime zest and a little white sugar; cinnamon with nuggets of chocolate brownie – and was disappointed that the peanut butter version had already sold out. Another stallholder gave me a taste of pineapple kombucha and explained her cane sugar and tea escobi: "What escobi does is eat the sugar and the product of the black and green teas, creating probiotic enzymes and a variety of different vitamins. It gets the good bacteria into our system which helps our digestive system, our kidneys, our liver and our overall general good health – and it's a great hangover cure."

With the blare of the market music and the loud chatter of the people in the background, I was swapping charcuterie recipes with the producer of German sausages and other preserved, smoked meats. I hadn't imagined such a cosmopolitan mix of people and cuisines.

Noam and fellow immigrants were welcome when they tried to learn the language and integrate into the community, but they had increased prices through demand for land and houses. On the other hand, this influx of foreigners had brought employment and improvements, such as the new cross-country highway, the increase in hotels and food outlets, the cinema and much more in Tamarindo. There was a delicate balance between maintaining the desirability of the original town character and the economics of progress.

A classic example of these international nomads, Noam had a strong sense of adventure: "Since I was about 13 or 14, I've been fantasising of living in the jungle and living in nature as a sort of hermit/Indiana Jones figure. I hate clothes. I don't wear shoes. And so this felt like a childhood dream." Noam cut a striking figure in the small resort town, long hair swept into a topknot and dressed only in shorts. It had taken three months' foot-hardening to achieve that shoeless ambition. Noam guided me around the market and, later, the fine dining creation amidst the damp, dripping trees and muddy puddles. That bare arm and torso in the hot, sticky, wet rainy season was almost too intimate.

Blind people are lucky and don't judge others by their appearance. We can't! Colour, hair, clothes – none of them matter. When I still had a little sight, I went up to two young people for help. They turned out to be the local punks with fully-spiked hair, piercings and the rest of the paraphernalia. They couldn't have been kinder or more helpful, but clearly no one else talked to them because of their looks. I can guess someone's height by hearing their mouth position, while depth of sound usually indicates their size. Don't forget that I can hear whether someone is talking to me or the person beside me. That very subtle change of sound as the head and eyes turn, even a fraction, is a complete giveaway.

HIR[1] fine dining.

Market purchases made, and Victor at the wheel again, we were soon off road along bumpy jungle tracks to Noam's HIR culinary adventure fine dining restaurant (www.elmundodenoam.com). First we visited the beginnings of the new premises – the construction by two extremely friendly and garrulous local builders had been delayed by the torrential rain. Noam's ambitious vision included tree houses for guests, a spacious kitchen, outside dining area, entrepreneurial coaching programmes during the day and culinary discovery at night.

Stepping along the precarious jungle track under the dripping trees, we made our way back to the original restaurant where we would be creating two nights' dinner services. This was a small simple structure comprising a domestic-size kitchen, storage room and toilet, with living accommodation in the roof above. The large outside decked area proved to be a useful additional food preparation space and, beyond, was the dining area of tables and chairs on the jungle floor, for about 12 guests, all under corrugated tin roofing that thrummed in the rain. The guests would be sitting in the open air, amidst all the trees, plants and wildlife. The whole area was teeming with ants and insects, birds and Noam's own pet cat and dog, plus others that popped in for a visit. And everything, including me, having stepped into a deep muddy puddle, was damp and soggy in the rain.

That puddle was the last straw. Thoroughly overtired, with muddy feet, legs hurting and swollen after nearly 48 hours sitting, I was a rather weepy mess and couldn't imagine how I would be able to invent new recipes for the next day. But a glass or two of wine and some supper restored self-confidence and determination.

1 HIR refers to unspecified or non-binary gender.

After a good night's sleep, and with Toby, Noam and Victor clucking over me like mother hens, I was ready to start cooking. Noam described the approach: "One of my big, big passions is integrating opposites. That's my personal research. I create seven-course discovery menus. People don't know what they are going to eat."

We spent the day concocting some strange flavour combinations. My first attempts were distinctly uninspiring – the tomato and avocado savoury crumble was just plain boring – but we were making progress by discarding the failures. I was learning to work in the unfamiliar kitchen, locating the key equipment and workspaces, finding the sink and tap. It was delightful sitting at the table on the decking, preparing ingredients, listening to the rain falling on the metal roof above and the jungle living and breathing around me.

Perfect 360-degree perception is a massive benefit of relying on hearing. It's not that ears are any more acute, but concentration on and interpretation of every sound is honed to bat-like accuracy. Simultaneously chopping vegetables in one place, monitoring a bubbling pan elsewhere, a machine whisking or even the level of wine in a glass is child's play. In contrast, loud muzak, chatter or machine noises create the sensory deprivation of having my head in a bucket that's being beaten. I lose all sense of the space around me, what is happening and who is about. My bonus was sitting in that jungle creating an entire three-dimensional soundscape of everything around me.

Back in the hotel, a little fruit was sufficient supper for Toby and me after a day of tastings. Somewhat optimistically I attempted some clothes washing, but the prospect of it drying on the shower rail was slim when the air was thick with damp.

Another Venezuelan breakfast heralded the new day, to end with our first dinner service for paying guests. And the seven-course menu still wasn't fully finalised or tested.

Creating completely new dishes in Noam's tiny premises was not easy with strange ingredients, unfamiliar equipment, the pressure, the heat and deluges of rain. As in most Costa Rican kitchens, there was only a cold water supply, and even this failed for over six hours during the last stages of preparation. Toby, Noam and Victor resorted to collecting rainwater pouring off the roof to top up the toilet cistern and give us some basic washing up facilities. Luckily I wasn't distracted from the cooking by the vision of three fit bare-chested people due to the sticky heat and torrents of rain.

Our menu aimed to give an English twist to the local ingredients – hence versions of fish and chips, a curried Coronation salad and more. Having helped Noam with the design and testing, my responsibility rested with the two desserts. I took the easy course with variations on classics: lemon meringue pies and Victoria sponges. I roped Victor in to squeeze all the lemon mandarinos for a citrus curd filling for the shortcrust tartlets. My silicone trays brought from home were ideal, although the pastry made with damp and lumpy flour was less so. My repeated attempts at meringue failed every time. I could whisk the egg whites perfectly but they collapsed immediately any damp sugar was added.

Individual coriander and chilli flavoured Victoria sponges were easier. Victor had plunged into the deluge to gather tiny wild chilli peppers. Together we prepared the sponges for their final drenching of pineapple, tamarind and chilli sauce – oddly successful alongside roast pineapple brushed with chilli oil and banana ice cream.

The guests that first night were a party of nine Americans celebrating a birthday, beautifully dressed, although stiletto heels must have been tricky on the wet jungle floor. The clearing was filled by their music and laughter while the tin roof above their heads rang with the torrents of rain.

Noam and I juggled our way through the complicated elements of each course without any (hopefully) obvious problems or delays. Each course was proudly announced to the increasingly appreciative and festive diners – I suspect that the food, two unusual cooks, and the jungle dining all contributed to the experience they'd wanted.

It was another exhausting day. Toby and I had been on the go from early morning and did not get back to the hotel until late, without lunch or supper. Next morning, thankfully we could sleep for a little longer and, starving hungry, ate huge breakfasts of homemade burgers, bacon and chips in one of the local cafés – true gastronomes! Forewarned, Toby was resolute that we would buy enough provisions to feed ourselves throughout the coming day.

With much of the dinner preparation already completed, there was less work, which gave me another opportunity to attempt the ill-fated meringues. No success. Rather than being crisp and puffy, they were sweet egg white pancakes. In desperation I made a quick lemon mandarino sorbet to top the citrus tartlets which, with the mangostan sauce and segments, just about passed muster. The trick I learned from Noam was to be confident and convincing that this had been the plan all along!

There was a little time to review other many food plants growing wild in the jungle:

- Okinawa spinach – green on one side and purple on the other and used as you'd expect.
- Mayan tree spinach, which definitely needs cooking to remove its toxicity.
- Turmeric plants with large leaves – just dig out some roots.
- Ginger plants with thin strap leaves for fragrance and light flavour, while the bulbous growths emerging from the ground could be cut for a real hot spicy punch.

And every home needs cleaner ants. They don't eat our food but will get rid of other insects, including cockroaches and even something as large as a scorpion. They might not eat human food, but weren't averse to giving us a sharp nip. You need to know which ant is which and keep the good ones.

One of the guests that second night was a neighbour whose garden bananas had become our ice cream. Another couple had travelled for hours and made a dramatic arrival: they were hours late, and had taken a wrong turn in the jungle. Eventually they rang to explain they were lost amongst the trees with their car wedged in a hole. It isn't often that the chef-patron drops kitchen utensils for a pickaxe to dig the customers out, but it was totally in keeping with Noam's "culinary adventure" philosophy in which the fine dining was the least of the experiences.

Since then Noam has written a book on fine dining, opened pop-up restaurants in America, explored gender identity and made hir own transition. As they say in Costa Rica: "Pura vida" – the answer to everything.

Noam's HIR jungle culinary adventure menu.

Rather than a recipe, this gives a sense of the food that Noam and I served on the two evenings at the jungle restaurant. Some of the dishes were inspired by English classics, and then turned on their heads!

Fish soup.

A sliced onion and chopped carrot were sautéed before adding a selection of mixed fish, seafood and crab (shells and all). Simmered in water, this produced a fragrant soup that was flavoured with wasabi and fish sauce before being sieved and poured over shredded kale and courgette.

Seared scallops.

Before searing in the pan, the scallops were seasoned with peppery ground papaya seeds and salt and then were served on a bed of Okinawa spinach (the leaves have purple undersides). On the first night, this was accompanied by a Chinese lychee granita that included rum and orange juice, topped with whole papaya seeds. On the second night, we replaced the granita with more leaves on warm rice noodles in homemade teriyaki sauce.

Coronation seafood.

This was an adaptation of the cold curried chicken dish served at the Queen's coronation but with prawns and mango or papaya. We made a curry base with sautéed onions and Indian spices that was strong enough to flavour the homemade mayonnaise, and added citrus juice to lighten and part-cooked papaya or mango. The chilled curry was served on discs of under-ripe plantain that had been fried at a low temperature, removed from the pan and smashed flat with a saucepan before frying again at a high temperature to become crisp like poppadums. Each serving was topped with diced fresh fruit and coriander.

Ceviche of sea bass.

The fish was cured in lime juice for 24 hours for serving on shredded beetroot leaves and diced beetroot stalks to give crunch. The fish was accompanied by a wasabi sauce, including finely diced mango and topped with colourful red dried avocado seeds.

Fish in batter with tartar sauce.

The mai mai fish was cooked in a crisp beer batter. The sauce was a mixture of mayonnaise, capers and slithers of watermelon skin pickled in beer and vinegar. The fish was served with kale leaves (stalks removed) that had been scrunched in a little oil and then dressed with nutritional yeast powder before being cooked in the oven so that it became crisp.

Lemon mandarino tartlets.

These were served with mangostan sauce and segments, plus a soft meringue topped with a citrus sorbet (mainly lemon mandarin juice, a little orange juice, rum and sugar).

Chilli pineapple and Victoria sponges.

The sponges were topped with pineapple and tamarind sauce and accompanied a slice of pineapple seared in butter and brushed with chilli oil. The pan cooking liquor was flambéed with rum and poured over the pineapple, before adding a scoop of banana and pineapple ice cream.

My tips.

First find the jungle of your choice in a country that offers wonderful fish, fruit and vegetables. Let your imagination and palate run riot as you combine familiar cooking methods and ingredients with unexpected tastes, textures, temperatures and smells. Make sure it all looks beautiful and colourful.

Noam's teriyaki sauce.

Water.
Soy sauce.
Rice wine vinegar or Nicaraguan rum.
Whole cloves of garlic, peeled.
Sugar.
Fresh root ginger.

Method.

Use about the same quantities of water and rum.

Heat all the ingredients and reduce.

Keep for about a week.

Lemon mandarino tartlets.

Video: Lemon mandarino tartlets

Pastry.

225g plain flour.
110g butter, cold and cubed.
About 40ml water.

Curd.

75g caster sugar.
2 lemon mandarinos (or 1 large lemon), rind and juice.
2 large eggs.
50g unsalted butter, cubed.

Method.

Rub the butter into the flour until it resembles breadcrumbs.

Add the water a tablespoon at a time and, using a palette knife, mix into the flour and butter before starting to bring together with your hands.

Form the pastry into a ball and place in a plastic bag before chilling for at least 30 minutes.

Meanwhile, make the curd by placing the sugar and lemon zest in a heatproof bowl.

Whisk the lemon juice and eggs together before pouring over the sugar and zest.

Add the butter cubes to the mixture and place over a pan of simmering water, taking care that the water doesn't touch the bowl.

Stir until the mixture has thickened as the eggs cook (about 20 minutes).

Place the bowl in the fridge to cool.

Remove the pastry from the bag and roll out on a lightly floured board.

Cut out rounds and place into tartlet tray, pricking the bottoms with a fork.

Chill again for 20 minutes while the oven heats to 220C, Gas 7, 425F.

Take squares of kitchen foil and scrumple into balls.

Place a ball in each tartlet and cook for about 10 minutes until the pastry is starting to firm.

Remove the foil balls and cook for a further 3-5 minutes until the pastry is cooked.

When the pastry cases are cool, fill with the curd and serve.

My tips.

Lemons may be easier to find than lemon mandarinos.

If using a food processor to make the pastry, take care not to process for more than a few seconds after adding the water to avoid the pastry becoming tough.

You can enrich the pastry by adding a tablespoon of caster sugar and replacing some of the water with an egg yolk.

If serving later, store the tartlets unfilled.

Chilli and coriander Victoria sponge.

Video: Chilli and coriander sponges

3 eggs, weighed.
Same weight butter.
Same weight sugar.
Same weight self-raising flour (or plain flour plus a teaspoon of baking powder).
1 red chilli, de-seeded and finely chopped.
Stalks of coriander finely chopped.

Topping.

3 slices of fresh pineapple.

2 teaspoons tamarind paste.

Method.

Weigh the eggs and then measure out the same weight in butter, sugar and flour.

Cream the butter and sugar together using a whisk or food processor.

Beat in the eggs one at a time, adding a little flour if there is any risk of curdling.

Fold in the flour.

Fold in the finely chopped chilli and coriander to taste.

Place the mixture into individual bun or muffin tins.

Cook for about 20 minutes at 180C, Gas 4, 350F.

Put the pineapple and tamarind paste into a food processor and whizz until smooth.

Once the cakes are out of the oven, prick the tops with a wooden toothpick and spoon a little of the pineapple mix on to each.

Chapter 8.

Escaping hurricane Nate.

Following those hot, wet, steamy, exhausting days of jungle cooking, we were set for our return drive across country back to San Jose for the final events and flight back to America. Knowing the road difficulties, we started early with breakfast in hand, but without fully appreciating that we would be hit by tropical storm Nate. Rivers were flooding onto the road, trees uprooted by blasting winds, vehicles abandoned, visibility limited, and all accompanied by the continuous noise of the rain, wind and windscreen wipers. It was a tense and gruelling journey for driver Victor, and probably foolhardy to have done it. After nearly six hours he was shattered by the conditions and the responsibility. He pulled in for a break and late lunch at a roadside café amidst others marooned by the storm. It was only our second experience of authentic Costa Rican food: chifrijo (a plate of pork, rice, pinto beans, tomatoes, avocado and cream) and empanadas (similar to a deep-fried cornmeal tortilla folded to enclose different fillings such as chicken and rice). The relative quiet of the café was blissful, the hot food delicious, and the affectionate service by our very aged waitress restored a sense of humanity to a day riven by the noise and ferocity of the storm that had been re-categorised as a full hurricane.

After several hours more driving, we finally arrived at the hotel in the capital to dump our luggage. We were imminently due for supper cooked by local chef Mario and had no time to lose. But it was also our farewell to Victor, who had been such a stalwart and caring support throughout the week.

Getting to our new destination in the city was fraught. The usual rush hour was a slow and grinding affair lasting from mid-afternoon well into the evening. Once again, while the taxi driver knew our approximate destination, we had no specific address. It was a matter of ringing ahead and trying to spot Mario as he came to find us on the roadside. And all of this in the dark shuttered streets, amidst driving rain and wind, uprooted trees on the ground, flying debris and other vehicles trying to escape the storm.

After the long and hot working days in Tamarindo, the chaotically difficult journeys and the overwhelming racket of Nate, we arrived to the calm of Mario and Ariana's home, a peaceful haven of conviviality. Their kitchen quickly filled with the gentler sounds and smells of home cooking. It was exquisite to relax with a glass of wine and excellent, simple food cooked by someone else.

Mario had cooked professionally in restaurants in both Costa Rica and America following catering college, and explained how he was taking his skills further: "I'm at university now studying food engineering – the physical and chemical changes during cooking – to work in the food industry." His partner, Ariana, was studying environmental law and her excellent English helped me understand his recipes.

Frazzled by the day, I did little more than stand alongside him as he created comforting classic Costa Rican dishes: simple, warming and delicious. His Caribbean chicken with curry flavours, tomatoes and peppers reflected the African influence of the coastal slave heritage, accompanied by the traditional national dish of pollo con patatas. For dessert he made bunuelos

– a fried dough of yucca flour and smoked cheese drenched with a wicked syrup of raw cane muscovado-type sugar heated with water. Topped off with a couple of glasses of wine, I was finished for the day.

But back in the hotel, there was still work to be done: tomorrow afternoon was the cooking session with the blind group at the country's top cooking school. I had to finalise the recipes and a shopping list of ingredients, after which I could slide into bed and sleep.

And the sliding wasn't that easy either. Space is good to avoid bumps and scrapes but can go too far. That "accessible" room in San Jose was enormous and, other than a chest of drawers on one wall, was completely empty other than a narrow single bed in the middle of the opposite wall. Probably perfect for someone manoeuvring a wheelchair but, without any reference points to feel, I just had to launch myself into the yawning space in the hope that I'd connect with the bed.

It was all change the next morning: Noam rang to say that a government weather warning had advised everyone in the capital to stay indoors due to the hurricane. San Jose had been virtually closed down. It was impossible for anyone to travel and the cooking school was almost certainly closed. All that enthusiasm, preparation and expectation dashed.

Video: Cooking in Costa Rica

Meanwhile, hunkered down in the hotel, Toby was sharing news from the UK: flights to San Jose cancelled; the airport likely to remain closed; dramatic coverage of the storm's destruction and escalation into a hurricane. We began to realise how lucky we were not to be stranded in Tamarindo. Noam told us that the road we had battled along the previous day had been closed. If we'd delayed our departure by just an hour, we would not have got to San Jose for another week.

Being stuck in Costa Rica also seemed highly possible. There was every chance that the hurricane's destructive force would disrupt local services. There was a sense of disconnect and unreality cocooned within the modern hotel, but conscious that it might not take much more to disrupt the power and water. We didn't panic, but Toby did scavenge the hotel's breakfast bar for emergency rations of bottled water and sandwiches – just in case. Otherwise, there was little we could do but settle down in our rooms to edit our materials, back up videos, write up recipes, clear emails and generally be super-productive during our forced incarceration. It was a long day of confinement, checking on the airport status every few hours and hoping that we would be able to get away the next morning. Insulated by the double glazing, we were hardly aware of the powerful storm lashing the building, but there was a pervading sense of dread. We went to bed wondering what the next day would bring and whether we would reach Virginia Beach.

There's no doubt, if you want Western comfort mixed with life on the wild side, Costa Rica is perfect – but perhaps better outside the rainy season!

Mario's classic Costa Rican dishes.

Video: Mario's recipes.

I was too exhausted to capture the detail or quantities of these recipes but, like any well-loved traditional dishes, they will vary from home to home as each cook adds their own twist, interpretation or whatever happens to be at hand.

Rice and beans.

This combination of carbohydrate and protein is a staple of the Costa Rican cuisine. It was served for breakfast on our first day in the country.

Dried pinto beans are soaked then boiled until softened.

Sauté the beans in a little oil – coconut oil if available.

Add uncooked short grain rice to the pan and a little more oil if needed.

Briefly sauté the rice with the beans before adding coconut milk, fresh thyme and ground pepper.

Simmer for 12-15 minutes until the rice is cooked.

Cabbage salad.

When served with the rice and beans, this coleslaw-like salad adds a different dimension of freshness and texture to create a well-balanced meal.

Finely shredded cabbage mixed with chopped carrots and sliced tomatoes dressed with chopped coriander, plus lemon juice and salt to taste.

Pollo con patatas.

Mario described this as a modern Costa Rican classic dish that is cooked in every home.

Fry tomatoes and then cover to gently simmer down.

Add finely chopped onions and garlic plus the chicken and potatoes.

Mario used a special local spice which enhances the red colour rather than adding more flavour and gently simmered the pot.

When everything is cooked and unctuously combined, serve with plain rice.

Caribbean chicken.

The sugar was the intriguing part of this dish.

Chicken thighs are rubbed with salt and pepper and then cane sugar before being fried until very crisp and caramelised in coconut oil (which can burn easily).

The chicken is served in a curry-based sauce with rice, both spiked with fresh chillies.

Chapter 9.

Celebrating 100 years of women in the Navy.

We were in luck. The weather in San Jose eventually cleared and we were winging our way north to Norfolk, Virginia. It was nearly 40 years since my last arrival to attend an international NATO naval intelligence conference. Back then I'd been an ambitious young Second Officer WRNS having fun in her first naval job in Naples. That transatlantic flight, all that time ago, had been similarly delayed by storms in Italy. It seemed that Norfolk and I were never destined to have an easy relationship.

We were met by Jo, a diminutive bag of energy and exuberance who I'd last seen those four decades ago when she relieved me in Italy. Back in 1981, after much conspiratorial prevarication to accommodate our respective love lives, she took over from me in the Intelligence Division of the NATO naval headquarters, COMNAVSOUTH, based across the causeway from Naples on the tiny island of Nisida.

Before that, we'd been callow young women at the Britannia Royal Naval College Dartmouth in spring 1978, being turned into officers in the Women's Royal Naval Service. Those three frantic and sleepless months of ridiculous parade drills, practice cocktail parties, shoe polishing, naval history and more hadn't been the time or place for making long friendships. In those days we were commissioned as Probationary Third Officers WRNS, and were let loose on an unsuspecting Navy in our first jobs, bright, shiny, enthusiastic and utterly naive.

I'd completed a month's Divisional Officer training at HMS Excellent, another island close to Portsmouth, allegedly learning how to look after the Wrens in my care. There was a second month of "secretarial" training on the misnamed Long Sec's Course at HMS Pembroke in Chatham. It definitely had nothing to do with shorthand and typing, but tried to equip us and our male counterparts to run the administration of a small ship or naval shore establishment. Going overseas for my first proper work appointment was unusual for a brand-new officer, but I didn't object.

I worked for a United States Navy captain in the small multi-national team. We were still in the grips of the Cold War, so security was tight: layers and layers of combination locks plus grilles on the windows to disrupt any long-range microphones. The administrative stuff quickly became too boring and simple to keep me occupied for more than a couple of hours a day. Instead, I became more involved in the operational briefings, counterintelligence and security inspections, intelligence tasking and reporting.

Our prime role was monitoring the activities of the Soviet Navy, with the highlight being the emergence of their first aircraft carrier, *Kiev*, from the Black Sea. She strutted her stuff across the Mediterranean with a flock of NATO aircraft, ships and others in close surveillance. In those days, women didn't go to sea in the Royal Navy. Men seemed utterly perplexed as to why I wasn't enthusiastic about spending months in a grey metal box being seasick, but I preferred to be ashore where we told them what to do.

Life in Naples wasn't all work and no play. There were endless cocktail parties aboard visiting ships, socialising amongst the international community, and responsibilities as Vice-Commodore of the Naples NATO Yacht Club. The last simply reflected my natural ability to throw good parties. A memorable one combined NATO wives drunk on undiluted cocktails, RAF officers well-lit after a mess dinner, Americans marching through with cornets, UK officers singing rugby songs, a belly dancer and the Wrens trying to sleep on the floor above calling out the Shore Patrol. I travelled too, around Italy and those work junkets to Gibraltar, Athens, Brussels (frequently), RAF St Athan in Wales for a month's driving course plus Norfolk in Virginia, USA. It was a tough life, but someone had to do it.

After three strenuous years, Jo arrived to take over the job while I returned to the UK for the junior officers' staff course at the Royal Naval College in Greenwich. I was the first woman to come top of the course simply by asking visiting speakers the most difficult questions possible. Meanwhile, Jo was having more life-changing experiences. She'd left the WRNS during her time in Italy, swept away to be married to US Navy Commander Nick – the only eligible bachelor out there. Three children and another career under her belt, our lives had gone in completely different directions.

Video: Baking Blind coming to Virginia Beach

Now, many years later, I was back in America and in contact with her. Through the labyrinthine networks of social media, Jo had replied to my Holman request for help. We'd talked on the phone, caught up on news and planned this leg of my adventure in her new home of Virginia Beach – the main residential area for people working at the world's largest naval base at nearby Norfolk.

We hadn't been in contact for years and I learned that Nick had died, two of her children had left home, and she was a Pilates and fitness instructor. With all the organisational skills that had been instilled in us in the Navy, Jo had put together a schedule of home cooking sessions for the coming week, and even included some rest and recuperation times. Not only were Toby and I to have accommodation with her, but she had also given up her own large accessible bedroom and wet room for me. After the dramas of Costa Rica, we anticipated straightforward days of calm, successful cooking.

Our arrival should have warned me of a different scenario. Our feet barely touched the ground after a long day's travel. We dashed in from the airport, dumped our bags and went straight out for dinner with the members of Jo's fitness class. It was my first experience of Mexican food since Naples, all those years ago, and very much better. Toby entertained as the sole man amongst the group of fit females. Wine flowed, proper food I hadn't had to cook sustained us, and the noise level was set to top volume. We bellowed our news, dramatised the adventures of recent weeks and put the world to rights. Shower and bed were a welcome conclusion.

The relaxation continued the following day, with languid strolls to explore parts of Virginia Beach, browse through potential ingredients, refine and polish plans for the week. The sense of orderly control in an environment of familiar languages, experiences and expectations was soothing but, perhaps, misleading.

Throughout the tour I had had to learn every new location, but utterly failed in Jo's house. Navigating by the sound of voices was the only way I managed to get from my room to join the others, and even that failed sometimes. One day I found myself in a room I didn't even recognise, somehow trapped with furniture behind me, my nose against a wall. I dared not move and damage what was around me. The only solution was to shout for help until Toby came to the rescue.

Jo's generosity was further revealed when I discovered that, despite supporting the tour, she had no interest in cooking. Being a fitness freak, it seemed she survived on the salads and vegetables favoured by health fanatics, relying on her daughter, Katie, to rustle up the rare hot meal. After many years, the knobs and dials on her cooker remained a mystery. I began to wonder how we would manage the neighbours' brunch scheduled for later in the week.

That one day of rest disappeared all too fast and I was back to performance mode, helping to cook a celebration lunch for a gaggle of naval women. Like Jo, many former Wrens had met American Navy men while serving in various NATO headquarters, married, emigrated and settled close to Norfolk. Several of their younger counterparts also joined us for the party, now with Royal Navy ranks and uniforms, serving at the nearby American SACLANT NATO base. Our celebration marked 100 years since the formation of the Women's Royal Naval Service, and was hosted by retired Royal Navy Captain Stuart and his wife, Wendy, in their splendid Virginia Beach home. The original plan was that the catering would be led by a US Navy chef, with me doing the donkeywork. But, as always, the exigencies of service come first, and she had to bow out when her admiral scheduled his own official lunch.

Naval wife, arch party organiser and list supremo, Fran, sprang into action and filled the breach by volunteering her husband as head chef. Hence lunch was to be provided by two RN commanders: David, still serving, and me, long retired. I was already in Naples when he joined the RN in 1980 and he was also commissioned at Dartmouth in 1989. I'd been in the "Supply and Secretarial" specialisation and he in the modern "Logistics" version. As the morning progressed, I began to appreciate that his enthusiasm surpassed his kitchen experience. He had been practicing under Fran's close supervision, and they'd been eating the same dishes for the past week.

Life was good for him and Fran, living in Virginia Beach and working in NATO. He explained: "The first thing that strikes you is the temperature. We're here in the middle of October and I'm still in shorts and T-shirt." I decided that, on this occasion, a full inspection of his rig wasn't part of the parade.

His gin enthusiasm was true to Navy form. He told us: "They're now making them with a different mixture of botanics. Grapefruit is probably my favourite at the moment. I would use a Plymouth gin – obviously, being from Plymouth – a nice tonic to go with it and a bit of grapefruit as a garnish. You'd be amazed at the smells and taste coming out, just a little bit differently."

The naval propensity for liquid refreshment was equally apparent amongst our guests.

A crowd of early celebrants were charging their glasses before we had a chance to start cooking, and the noise didn't abate for hours while we put Fran's immaculate party plan into action. It was great in theory, and vital when real life got in the way of our timings.

She had designed two "tray bakes" that feed large numbers for minimum effort. We simply assembled roasting tins of chicken with a herb and lemon dressing, plus salmon layered with goat's cheese and sun-dried tomato, before putting them in the oven.

Our over-confidence collapsed with the profiteroles for dessert: they emerged from the oven like small, sweet pancakes. The good news was I'd discovered that, without the sugar, I could now make blinis for topping with smoked salmon – easier than managing batter in a pan. Fran stepped in behind the scenes and made another batch to save our pride and the lunch finale.

Beyond the kitchen door, our congregation of women was in full voice. There were many stories being shared, friends remembered, glasses lifted and laughter echoing from the far reaches of the resplendent dining hall. I wondered if James Holman could have imagined how his Navy had changed. In his time, nearly 200 years earlier, he'd been patrolling the coast of rebellious America, and any women on board ships had been smuggled there for very unofficial purposes. I doubt he foresaw that, a century later, the first women were in uniforms and, another 100 years later, were fully integrated into the Royal Navy. Nowadays, with a few women commanding ships at sea, equality is making progress, although there's still a long way to go before we achieve our First Sea Lady. I can hear centuries of old sea dogs turning in their graves.

Fran and David's party plan and recipes.

Timetable.

11.00 Preheat oven to 200C, Gas 6, 400F. Make choux pastry.

11.20 Choux pastry to oven.

11.30 Increase oven to 220C, Gas 7, 425F.

11.40 Choux out of oven.

11.45 Prep fish and put in fridge.

12.00 Prep chicken dish.

12.15 Pan fry chicken.

12.30 Chicken to oven.

12.45 Fish to oven.

12.50 Potatoes on.

13.15 Fish out – plate and garnish. Chicken out – serving dish, keep warm. Asparagus in oven.

13.25 Asparagus out – serving dish. Potatoes drained and dressed – serving bowl.

13.30 Lunch is served.

My tips.

If I'm catering for a crowd, I do much the same but also working back from the menu to the shopping lists, food preparation over several days, wine chilling, flowers, table laying etc.

Chicken with lemon, rosemary and garlic.

Video: Chicken tray bake

Dressing.

160ml olive oil.
120ml lemon juice.
100g (1 small jar) capers, drained.
2 large lemons, sliced.
10 garlic cloves, peeled and smashed.
4 tablespoons fresh rosemary leaves stripped from their stalks.
Salt and ground pepper.

Dish.

3 tablespoons olive oil.
12 chicken thighs, bones removed but skin still on.
1kg small new or red potatoes.

Method.

Preheat oven to 230C, Gas 8, 450F and place roasting tray in oven to heat.

Make the dressing by mixing the ingredients in a bowl.

Put the tablespoons of oil in a large frying pan and heat.

Season the chicken with salt and pepper before placing into the pan, skin side down to sear for about 10 minutes until brown.

Transfer the chicken thighs, skin side up, to the hot roasting pan.

Wash and season the potatoes before tucking around the chicken.

Pour the lemon dressing over the pan of chicken and potatoes.

Return the pan to the oven and cook for 45-50 minutes.

My tips.

To make this even faster on the day of your party, prepare the dressing the day before and store in the fridge and do likewise with the potatoes. Use at least two frying pans to sear the chicken.

This seems a long cooking time at a high temperature so check if the chicken has reached 70C, and the potatoes are cooked after 30 minutes, and be ready to reduce the heat if necessary.

Baked salmon with goat's cheese.

Video: Salmon tray bake

1.5kg fillet of salmon.
Half lemon.
300g soft goat's cheese.
4 tablespoons sun-dried tomato paste.
50g fresh white breadcrumbs.
25g parmesan cheese, grated.
2 tablespoons olive oil.

Garnish to serve.

Small red onion, very finely sliced.
Black olives.
Basil leaves, shredded.
Capers.

Method.

Preheat oven to 230C, Gas 8, 450F.

Place the fish in a roasting tray, squeeze lemon over it and season with salt and pepper.

Spread the goat's cheese over the fish.

Spread the tomato paste over the goat's cheese.

Mix the breadcrumbs and parmesan cheese and sprinkle over the fish.

Press down the crumb topping and drizzle with olive oil.

Bake for 20-30 minutes.

Mix the garnish ingredients and scatter over the top of the fish.

My tips.

Get someone with excellent tactile senses to check the fish for any small remaining bones.

Lemon choux buns.

Video: Lemon curd profiteroles

90g strong white bread flour.
2 teaspoons caster sugar.
225ml water.
75g butter.
3 eggs.
Double (heavy) or whipping cream, whipped.
Lemon curd.
2 lemons, juice only.
Icing sugar.
Preheat oven to 200C, Gas 6, 400F.

Method.

Sift flour and sugar onto a folded sheet of silicon paper.

Heat the water and butter in a saucepan on moderate heat and stir with a wooden spoon.

As soon as the butter has melted and the water begins to boil, remove from the heat, and quickly add (shoot) in the flour and sugar in one go. Start beating with the wooden spoon.

Beat vigorously until you have a smooth ball of paste that leaves the side of the saucepan clean.

Gradually add the eggs to the ball of paste. Beat hard to incorporate each addition until you have a smooth glossy paste.

Lightly grease a baking tray, hold it under running water for a second and tap off excess moisture.

Place teaspoons of the mixture 1 inch apart. (Should make about 40-45.)

Bake for 10 minutes and then increase the heat to 220C, Gas 7, 425F for a further 10-15 minutes.

Pierce the side of each bun to let out steam. Cool on a rack.

Mix together half whipped cream and half lemon curd and use to fill buns.

Mix sieved icing sugar with lemon juice to make a glaze for the buns.

My tips.

Instead of buying lemon curd, make your own. See the tamarindo lemon tartlets recipe.

Avoid disasters with choux pastry. In Melbourne I learned tips from Dré.

Warm peaches with honey and rum

6 tablespoons unsalted butter.
4 tablespoons honey.
6 medium ripe peaches, sliced.
8 tablespoons rum.

Method.

Heat the butter and honey in a large non-stick pan on medium heat until the butter melts.

Add the sliced peaches and cook for 5 minutes or until lightly browned and tender.

Place peach slices in serving bowl, reserving juices in the pan.

Add the rum to the juice in the pan and continue to cook on medium heat until the sauce has reduced and thickened (about 3 minutes).

Pour the sauce over peach slices and serve.

Chapter 10.

Loaves and fishes.

Two more days and three more cooking sessions: two loaves, two fishes and more. The piscatorial bounty of the Atlantic coastline of Virginia was about to be set before me.

It started with Kate, one of Jo's friends and neighbours, who'd been emailing with me for months, full of enthusiasm and support for the Baking Blind adventure. Again, I was struck by how sharing a kitchen and cooking together can create such bonds. She told me how love had also brought her to America (but not through the Navy route): "I was a deputy headteacher in the UK and reunited with my college sweetheart. He was working and living in Virginia Beach so I moved too and also created my own business. I'm allergic to every product under the sun and started making my own skincare products. Neighbours liked them, then friends of neighbours and friends of friends – it's just grown hugely."

Alongside us for the morning was reporter Loraine, from the Virginian Pilot newspaper, who also responded to the warmth of that kitchen atmosphere and shared her vision worries, explaining: "I have some tears in the retina of my left eye and some surgery that gave me double vision in my right eye. It's been difficult to be a hard-charging journalist."

But, like so many other people faced with life-changing health conditions during their working lives, she hadn't given up but was determined to keep her career. We talked about how screen magnification and screen reading software could help her keep writing with a computer.

Meanwhile, Kate had chosen a familiar classic English dish to reflect our shared background. "When I decided to do fish pie," she said, "I wanted to choose a locally caught fish. I talked to the lovely chap who is co-owner of the Beach Pub and he suggested puppy drum, which I'd never heard of before. So, he caught and filleted it for us ready for our fish pie today." It was a magnificent specimen, but neither of us realised that it hadn't been skinned until the fish had been cut up. It was far more difficult to remove the skin from those small slippery pieces of fish. But, in my defence, I'm good at finding all those remaining bones.

Fish was on the menu again the next morning with retired US Navy Commanding Officer and Beachmaster Rich, resplendent in an apron bearing a map of his last command. Again we were welcomed into his home and this time cooking gadgets were the great icebreaker. We eagerly compared notes on the best ways of handling garlic, and I drooled over his hunting-style knife sharpener, only to be disappointed later on discovering that the company had stopped trading.

He told me a little of his own military background: "I was a Surface Warfare Officer for about 26 years. Served on five ships. I was in command. It was a wonderful experience. I saw the world. Obviously, I met and worked with literally thousands of people. We have that bond too because you served as well." We were in complete agreement: although the jobs and work were interesting, it had been the people who made life in our different navies special, because so many of us shared the same values and personality traits. I could definitely recognise his clear, no-nonsense approach and utter focus on succeeding at any task – even in the kitchen.

Rich had another fish and another cooking method to show me too: "treasure of the sea" rock fish on his Webber barbecue with applewood smoke. The fish was wonderfully fresh, having only been caught the day before. As he explained: "The boat pulls up to the dock and the fish market is on the dock. This part of Virginia is known for its crab, so they have live crab there and some of the best oysters in the world."

The 1.6 pound whole fish was simply seasoned with salt, pepper and lemon before being enclosed in the barbecue alongside the can of applewood chips. Fourteen minutes later, it was ready, soft and moist, perfumed with the smoke and lemon.

He dished up the fish with vegetables sautéed in excellent Greek olive oil and homemade chicken stock. I could imagine the glorious colour mix of the white celery and onions, golden Yukon potatoes and multi-hued heritage carrots all flecked with green spinach.

Much to the amusement of his non-cooking wife Cathy, we had a heated debate as to whether celery should be peeled (according to the late TV chef, Keith Floyd) or not (according to Rich). He scorned my enthusiasm, but was rather more interested in my idea of roasting a chicken carcass before using it for stock. One all, I thought.

Video: To peel or not to peel

And he produced the first of our loaves for the day: excellent sourdough that brought everything I'd learned from the Cheeseboard Collective in California down to the domestic scale. It isn't easy, as he explained: "I started about seven months ago and it took me three attempts to create a very vigorous sourdough starter."

True to his gadgets, Rich was a fan of glass baking pans which can reduce oven temperatures: "The recipe calls for the bread to be cooked at 425 degrees Fahrenheit (220C, Gas 7) but, because I'm using glass,

I'll lower it to 400F (Gas 6, 200C) for about 28 minutes and it comes out wonderful."

He'd started at an ungodly early hour. "The dough was created this morning at about five thirty," he said. "I let it rise for a couple of hours and then I took it out, flattened it out, and folded it in on itself in five different sections. And I did that process about three times." But the combination of such an active starter, the glass pans, the early start and the warm weather had a critical drawback: the dough had risen so much that, not just overflowing the pans, it was oozing through the handle holes at each end. We could see that those extrusions, once cooked, would lock the bread into the pans. We were right. Extraction required major surgery, but that didn't stop the bread having perfect crust and crumb – wonderful with the rockfish and vegetables for lunch.

Rich had a wealth of cooking knowledge and skill, which gave me more ideas for my own bread by adding dried milk to the mix and baking it until the centre reaches at least 190F /88C. He is a fan of King Arthur flour and recipes, which I discovered online. Their sourdough crackers are an answer to all the flour and water discarded while making the starter.

Back on Jo's terrace after our fish lunch, relaxation turned into a new drama. I could hear lots of movement, thrashing and disturbance in one of Kate's pots of sunflowers. Luckily someone other than me discovered that a large black rat snake had become entangled in the netting. Although they aren't dangerous for humans (but watch out, rats), I'm not sure my nervous system would have managed touching a cool, smooth, writhing body in a restricted space! Instead, a phone call brought a quick response from the Animal Rescue team, and the snake was despatched to pastures new where it could hunt with freedom.

That evening Jo drove Toby and me back to Wendy and Stuart's house where the centenary lunch had been held. This time Wendy had the run of her own massive kitchen, and two recipes from her Irish heritage to teach me. I was wildly impressed that she was ready to knead bread wearing most of her jewellery. But then she was a woman of style and flair who can turn her hand to domesticity but still look ready for her high-powered NATO job. We cooked to the running banter of a small audience, growing increasingly cheerful over a few bottles of wine.

All the links with NATO reminded me of my time in Italy, decades ago, where pretending to know something about intelligence was much more rewarding than paper-pushing. One of the highlights had been flying in a US Navy surveillance aircraft over the Soviet anchorage on the Libyan coast. I was all dolled up in a flight suit with body-length zip, rendered redundant by the men-only onboard facilities: a pipe! Even very junior officers like me were aware of international risk and tension. We felt we were making our small contribution towards peace and stability: minor pawns in a vast game.

Back to my second bread of the day: a wheaten soda bread – a traditional and familiar smell of Ireland. Wendy explained: "Wholewheat flour – it's very much finer ground. A wholemeal flour is more like a porridge, while that's almost like a sand. This is my Auntie Maureen's recipe. She very sadly died just a couple of months ago and we miss her terribly." Wendy was even wearing a much-beloved and elderly Irish linen apron displaying symbols from the Book of Kells – another gift from her aunt and reminder of her own Celtic heritage. We needed to do justice to her aunt's memory.

Wendy added buttermilk to the mix and gave me a tip for making my own: "A normal pint of full cream milk," she explained, "and I add a little dollop of white vinegar and a good squirt (about half a lemon's worth) of lemon juice into the pint of milk. I leave it on the side of the counter for about 10-20 minutes and then it starts to go all sort of curdly and it looks a bit weird. Hey presto, you have buttermilk to make the bread!"

I did manage to get my hands into the mix to pull the ingredients together, fold the dough over a few times and shape it into a ball ready to bake. The final touch was an "Irish blessing" – a crosscut into the top – and the loaf was risen, brown and ready in about half an hour. Wendy warned me to resist the temptation of the delicious smells until the loaf had cooled for 10 minutes, "Because, if, like my husband, you try and eat it straight out of the oven, which he often does, it will just fall to pieces and burn your mouth. If you're going to leave it until the next day, you have to have it as toast."

While the bread was baking, in front of that crowd of increasingly noisy onlookers, we chopped and stirred, sautéed and liquidised to turn the simplest ingredients into another dish. Wendy said, "It's an extremely nice mushroom soup. I've tried this a few times before and my husband, in particular, is a great fan."

She was inspired by the Avoca restaurant in Powerscourt, just outside Dublin, which Wendy and Stuart visit often. "It's a big, old, magnificent house and it's got fabulous grounds, gardens and waterfalls. They pride themselves on their food, which is all homemade, and lots of their ingredients are actually grown in the gardens. It's all very fresh food, all really hearty, very Irish but very glamourous."

It was a simple soup, but Wendy made it her own with a slosh of sherry and a "decorative dollop of whipped cream" (her words!).

Another day closed as our incredibly happy audience downed the soup and bread that was so quick to make that there was still wine left for the hard-working cooks.

Kate's fish pie.

Video: Fish pie

Topping.

1kg Maris Piper potatoes, peeled and halved.
Dash of milk.
Knob of butter.
Handful of grated cheddar cheese (optional).

Filling.

85g butter.
85g plain flour.
4 spring onions finely sliced.
850ml milk.
300-400g puppy drum fish, filleted, skinned and boned, cut into chunks.
1 teaspoon mustard
Small bunch chives, finely chopped.
Handful frozen peas.

Method.

Cover potatoes with salted cold water, bring to the boil and cook until done.

Drain and mash the potatoes with butter, milk, plus salt and pepper to taste.

Heat oven to 200C, Gas 6, 390F.

Heat the remaining butter, flour and spring onions in another pan and cook for 1-2 minutes before whisking in the milk.

Bring to the boil and simmer for a few minutes until thickened, whisking constantly to avoid lumps.

Remove from the heat and add all the remaining ingredients except the topping. Stir gently to start firming the fish, defrosting the peas. Place in ovenproof dish.

Top with mashed potato and cheddar (if using).

Cook in oven for 20-25 minutes.

My tips.

Puppy drum fish may not be available so you can use a mix of salmon, cod and other fish. Smoked haddock is very traditional and luxury versions can include prawns, pieces of monkfish and more.

Peas and sweetcorn add colour and texture.

Rich's recipes.

Video: Sourdough bread

Sourdough starter.

120g wholewheat flour.
120ml water.

(Same quantities required for each subsequent "feed", but use plain flour instead of wholewheat.)

Method.

Day 1: Mix the wholewheat flour and water in your container thoroughly, loosely cover and leave for 24 hours.

Day 2: Stir the starter and discard half. Stir in one feed portion and leave loosely covered for another 24 hours at normal room temperature.

Days 3, 4 and 5: Every 12 hours stir the starter and measure about 120g into a clean container. Add another feed portion.

Day 6: The starter should be doubled in size, bubbly and smelling acidic.

If not, repeat the 12-hour feedings until you see the starter doubling in size within about 4 hours of feeding, each time indicating that there is enough activity to make bread. It can take a few weeks in some conditions.

When the starter is fully active, stir and measure about 120g into a clean container. Add another feed portion and leave for 6-8 hours before using on your first sourdough bread.

When using the starter for that bread, you will always need to leave 120g to be fed again to keep the starter alive.

You can store the starter covered in the fridge and continue the discard-feed routine weekly. When you need starter for your next recipe, remove it from the fridge 12 hours beforehand. Don't forget to reserve 120g and feed it to keep the starter going.

My tips.

You will probably need about 1kg plain flour for the feeding.

If the ambient temperature is cool, use lukewarm water and consider where the starter can be kept during the first few days at a temperature above 20C, 68F.

Discarding starter seems wasteful. There are recipes online for using it to make crackers, or give some to a friend.

Rich took seven months to get his starter perfect, so it might take several attempts. You could end up with a lifetime supply of sourdough starter crackers!

Vegetable sauté.

5 cloves garlic, peeled and chopped.
2 large onions, peeled and sliced.
Bag of Yukon small potatoes.
5 sticks of celery, (peeled) and chopped.
Bag of heirloom carrots.
Bag of spinach, washed.
1 pint chicken stock.

Method.

Sauté all the vegetables except the spinach in a little olive oil.

Add the stock and gently simmer until all are cooked and the stock is reducing.

Add the spinach and adjust the seasoning.

My tips.

Use whatever vegetable proportions suit your taste and what you can find. The aim is to have succulent vegetables in a little light stock.

Apple-smoked barbecued fish.

1 whole rockfish, gutted.
Sea salt and freshly ground black pepper.
Olive oil.
2 lemons, one sliced and the other juiced.

Can of applewood chips.

Method.

Season both the interior cavity and outside of the fish with the salt, pepper, olive oil and lemon juice.

Place slices of lemon in the cavity and on the top of the fish.

Place the fish on the preheated barbecue rack with a can of apple wood chips sitting on the charcoal. Close the lid and cook for 14 minutes.

My tips.

If not using a barbecue, ignore the wood chips.

Other firm white fish such as cod or haddock can be cooked in the same way.

Wendy's recipes.

Wheaten bread.

Video: Wheaten bread

450g whole wheat flour (finer than wholemeal).
1 teaspoon salt.
1 teaspoon baking soda/powder.
590ml buttermilk.

Method.

Heat the oven to 200C, Gas 6, 400F.

Aerate the flour either by sieving or by sifting through fingers.

Add the salt and baking powder/soda.

Gradually stir in the milk to form a firm and sticky dough – it feels like wet sand.

Tip on to a floured surface and lightly knead to form a ball.

Slash the top in the form of a cross – an "Irish blessing" according to Wendy.

Place on a floured baking stone or tray and cook for about 45 minutes.

My tips.

Wendy suggested: "In place of buttermilk, use nearly a pint of full fat milk and add about one teaspoon vinegar and the juice of half a lemon. Mix thoroughly and leave at room temperature for about half an hour before using."

My simple version of soda bread.

1 teaspoon salt.
250g self-raising flour.
170g plain natural yoghurt.
Heat the oven to 200C, Gas 6, 400F.

Method.

Mix all the ingredients in a bowl to make the dough (about 5 minutes).

Place the dough ball on a baking tray lined with baking parchment sprayed with a little oil.

Cut cross on the top and bake for 25 minutes, turn over and cook for final 5 minutes.

My tips.

I test that the bread's internal temperature has reached at least 95C, 200F to know it is cooked.

Slice all the bread and toast any leftovers the next day.

If you make your own yoghurt, the "strainings" work just as well in this recipe.

Video: A taste of the old country

Mushroom soup.

Video: Mushroom soup

25g butter.
2 onions, peeled and finely chopped.
1kg mixed mushrooms, trimmed and chopped.
75g plain flour.
1 litre vegetable stock.
600ml full cream milk.
1 teaspoon fresh thyme leaves.
Glass of sherry.
Whipped cream and chopped parsley to serve.

Method.

Gently sauté the onions in the butter for about 10 minutes.

Increase the heat, add the mushrooms and seasoning and cook for about 3 minutes.

Stir in flour over reduced heat for about 5 minutes.

Add stock and milk and bring to a gentle simmer for 10 minutes.

Place in liquidiser with thyme and sherry to blend, before pouring into serving bowls and topping with garnish of whipped cream and sprinkle of parsley.

Chapter 11.

Families and friends.

Working with other disabled people for over 20 years, I've learned how one person's ill health can impact on the whole family. It's not just the time, energy and pressure of extra care but also, for some, the strain on relationships, the frustration and misery, the difficulty in talking about fears and worries, of not adding more pressure and demands. There are always major dramas in the media but far less visibility of all the small dramas that happen in over one in five homes, day in day out, worldwide. In Virginia Beach, two families allowed me some insight into their experiences.

Kelly and I had met at the fitness class Mexican supper a few days earlier and again at her workplace when she was advising us on ingredients at the busy local supermarket. At the time she was the wine expert, but then moved to online shopping, mastering an even bigger range of products but missing the personal contact with customers.

Like many Mums (and Dads), Kelly was being pulled in all directions, holding down a busy job, managing home life and bringing up children. She was juggling even harder than most to make extra adjustments for her son's disability. Even though she had a stock of those familiar recipes that make meals quick and simple after a day's work, life was more complicated. She explained: "My son has autism and was diagnosed at age three and a half. He definitely has texture issues with a lot of foods. So, when he was little, if he didn't like something, it came out immediately." Some people with autism have specific requirements concerning their food: some will only accept certain colours; others want their food very clearly separated on the plate. For Kelly's son, it was a matter of texture, and the lettuce, water chestnuts and onion in her Asian wraps dish would have been too crunchy and crispy for him.

Kelly was proud of how he was progressing. "He's in high school," she told me, "and they have these programs called community-based involvement. They'll teach him how to behave in social settings, like going to the grocery store or the mall, and how to buy things and money transactions." Her son needs this extra help because, unlike most of us, he doesn't learn such life skills from watching other people. The program is enabling him to communicate better too. Kelly said: "Because of a lot of the therapies and teaching that they give him at school, he's able to tell us things and say 'Oh, I saw this today.' When he does that, it's such a relief to be able to have that conversation. Sometimes he feels bothered because he doesn't want us to ask him questions. But he gets excited when he can explain something to us." The right help was clearly making a huge difference for the whole family.

Kelly was no slouch in the cooking equipment field. The cake she was making was putting her new mixer through its paces with considerable gusto and some alarming noises. I suspected we'd hit the "fast" speed with rather too much enthusiasm. But neither of us had a fool proof solution to getting the right amount of mix into the baking pan. It was still rather a hit and miss approach, with me erring too often on the side of miss.

The banana bread was to be a contribution to the brunch Jo was giving the next day so Toby and I could meet more of her friends. What greater generosity can there be than when a friend cooks for you? And, in Jo's case, it was even more generous for someone who so rarely cooks, but together we rustled up a huge frittata, an extraordinary "overnight egg casserole", which turned out to be like a savoury bread and butter pudding, pumpkin bread (easy when you can buy tins of the cooked pumpkin) and more. As always, cooking together brought us together, and I heard more about her life and, especially, her husband Nick's illness.

But we started with our own Navy connections. Those few months officer training back in 1978. Jo had felt it went on forever and said, "I went back to Dartmouth in 2016 and it seemed to have shrunk. It was much less daunting. It's the bond you get when you go into the trenches together."

We both had very strong memories of the first officer WRNS who had been in charge of us. She'd made it very clear to Jo that, although they had the same last names, "There's no way that we were related." For my part, the highly polished door knob of her office was the lasting impression. We would be summoned to the office for a dressing-down and, when dismissed with sweating hands, it was impossible to get enough grip on the knob to turn it and escape. We all went equipped with a paper tissue to get out of the door. Jo laughed and said, "I've suppressed that memory. But it explains why I always have a tissue stuck up my sleeve!"

There was the time we were doing an exped on Dartmoor, a bevy of very unhappy women trainees all soaking wet and freezing cold being led by an army officer who was determined not to admit that he'd got lost. Jo recalled a joke that, apparently, we might have started: "A rumour that the WRNS were going to go to sea. Enough for Nelson to have turned in his grave." I think she'd found a very old press cutting and suspected that the tale had been fed to another trainee whose father owned a newspaper.

Then there were all the practice cocktail parties, mess dinners and coffee mornings at which we learned the "social niceties": how to talk to the person on one side during the first course, and then the one on the other side during the next one; how to circulate with a cup of coffee, drink it, talk to everyone and eat the chocolate digestive without it melting down the cup. How officers were made!

We lost touch after Dartmouth when I went out to Naples in 1978, until she was due to relieve me there three years later. We manufactured all sorts of courses and training she needed to do because I was seeing someone in Italy and she had someone in the UK. She'd gone to GCHQ at Cheltenham for a course "completely above my pay grade but I did learn how to bluff my way through an intelligence briefing" – as she explained – which brought us to about the same level. We both knew how to give just enough detail to sound really convincing!

Video: Wrens reunited

She'd arrived in Naples in February 1981 when I returned to the UK to pursue my naval career. Within two years, Jo had married US Navy Commander Nick, left the WRNS and started a new life in America. Now, nearly 35 years, a successful marriage, three children and a new career later, she was sharing her thoughts on Nick's long and difficult death.

Her beloved husband had started having problems moving, a few falls, cramps, "foot drop" and more. Jo told their story: "When he turned 65, he went to the doctor and he asked the doc why he was walking like a dork. So they ran all sorts of tests, ruled out any kind of spinal stuff, and eventually he was sent to a neurologist. He had a very painful exam. You stick needles deep into the muscle fibre to see if they're firing. And this woman (I won't even describe what I feel about her) looked at the readouts and said, 'Well, I believe that you have ALS. You have two to five years. You'll become gradually paralysed, unable to move, eat, drink, finally breathe, and you'll die.' There could have been a bit more empathy." All these years later, the doctor's stark words still anger her. But, fortunately, they found more caring attitudes elsewhere.

It had been devastating news. ALS is one of the most serious and terminal diagnoses that anyone can receive. Jo and Nick had the fortitude and courage to get through those remaining years together. Many other people struggle on too. Their own diagnoses may not be terminal, but can have huge consequences on their lives.

In America, Nick's condition is known as amyotrophic lateral sclerosis (ALS) or Lou Gehrig's disease after a famous baseball player with the condition. In the UK, we call it motor neuron disease (MND). As Jo learned too well, "The motor neurons, which control everything in your body except the bowel and bladder or eyesight and hearing, die. They stop sending the signals to the muscles to move so that you gradually become paralysed. There's no known cause, there's no cure, and there's no effective treatment. Once you get it, it's a death sentence." Some people will live for as little as a year, some longer.

Government help was key. Jo explained: "ALS in the States is Service-connected. Because Nick was a Navy veteran, we actually got help from the Veterans Administration. That was huge." But it was probably their own strength and Jo's ability to anticipate what was coming that made the vital difference. "We just got on with it," she said. "Because I knew what was going to happen, I was pretty good at planning ahead. So, when it came to getting equipment for him, if they wanted to give him a particular kind of equipment that I knew wouldn't be effective for that long, I'd say 'Forget that, I'll borrow one.' When we built the addition to the house, because I knew we'd probably end up on a ventilator, I got more electrical outlets so that we could plug in the ventilator and the suction machine. We have a generator because, obviously, if power goes off, the ventilator stops, and you die. I did learn that a couple of times. I had to bag him, which is a bit like doing CPR."

And Nick wasn't a passive patient either. "He was a mute quadriplegic with attitude," Jo said. "His brain was fine. He did all our finances. He did our taxes until the day he died. We had a hospital bed that did percussion vibration to keep his lungs clear because he couldn't cough. We could turn the hospital bed into a chair and, because he was like a rag doll, we would prop him up with pillows, tie his head up in a scarf to the side rail, and then we had a spring attachment where we could put his elbow in a cup. We would tape his finger to the mouse so that he could do lateral movements. He could move the cursor. It just went on. He was fully involved with everything, with the kids. We had a power wheelchair; we had a handicap van. He went to concerts; he went to a couple of ball games."

Nick died in October 2014, six years after his original diagnosis. Jo crowed with pride: "He did outlive what the original doctor told us – just out of spite." Jo also talked about their final moments: "I don't have any regrets about how he died, he was ready to go." She gathered family and friends around him in the hospital, the carers who'd been supporting him, and his sister on the phone. "I held him in my arms, then the nurse turned off the ventilator and took the tube out of his throat. I whispered into his ear, 'You're the best thing that ever happened to me, I love you.' He took about three breaths and he died."

Life without him has been hard. "The first year was a cushion of grief," she told me. "The second year was way worse. Year three and I was coming through it. I focus on how many years and days we had together, and I'm going to have to be 88 before I've lived longer without him than I've lived with him. Accept the grief and move through it."

Video: Handling grief and death

All the family faced a massive struggle with the enormous practical and emotional consequences of Nick's progressive deterioration and inescapable death. The pain and loss is etched on their lives. Jo and her daughter, Katy, continue a daily fight to increase awareness, research and support for those affected by this deadly condition. It had felt intrusive to be unpacking in the bedroom they had shared, that private space still with residual paraphernalia of terminal illness. But Jo was all practicality, explaining the accessibility benefits but, perhaps, it also meant that Nick was part of our visit too. Her advice to anyone in a similar situation was, "Be honest with each other. Reach out for help. Enjoy the time you have."

Four weeks earlier, I'd left home on this Holman adventure thinking it was just about cooking. I'd learned new recipes, new ingredients but, most of all, that people with the same enthusiasms and passion can create bonds of shared experiences, trust and insight. It was all so much more than I'd expected.

Video: Cooking with Wrens and friends in Virginia Beach

And so back to the UK for a week of sleep, washing, repacking and preparation for China, Australia and Africa. Would it match up?

Kelly's recipes.

Oriental turkey lettuce cups.

Video: Oriental turkey lettuce cups

Sauce.

60ml tomato ketchup.
4 teaspoons rice vinegar.
4 teaspoons sesame oil.
1 teaspoon dried red pepper flakes (2 for a spicier flavour).
2 tablespoons brown sugar.

Filling.

2 tablespoons olive oil.
1 medium onion, peeled and diced.
2 garlic cloves, peeled and crushed.
1 (230g) can water chestnuts, drained, rinsed and chopped.
460g finely minced (ground) brown turkey meat.
60ml soy sauce.
1 head iceberg lettuce, separated into individual leaf "cups".
Tablespoon shallot (scallion), finely chopped.
Tablespoon peanuts, chopped.

Method.

Mix the sauce ingredients.

Heat the oil in a frying pan and sauté the onions, garlic and water chestnuts for 3-4 minutes.

Add the turkey and soy sauce, cook for about 5 minutes.

Add the sauce mix to the pan. Cook until the turkey mixture looks like a "thick sloppy joes".

Take the pan off the heat and spoon the mixture into the lettuce "cups" and garnish with the onion and nuts.

Serve with plain basmati rice and the oriental green beans, which can be cooked while the turkey and sauce thicken.

My tips.

The meat is more like sausage meat than mince. Chicken, white turkey meat, pork, beef or other meat could be used, but cooking times will vary.

Oriental green beans.

680g green beans, trimmed.
3 tablespoons soy sauce.
1 tablespoon sesame oil.
1 teaspoon sugar.
6 cloves garlic, peeled and minced.

Method.

Cook the green beans in boiling water for 4-5 minutes.

Meanwhile, combine soy sauce, sesame oil and sugar. Set aside.

Spray a frying pan or wok with spray oil.

Using medium-high heat, cook the garlic for 20-30 seconds until softened, stirring constantly.

Add the drained green beans and cook for 2 minutes, stirring to coat with the garlic.

Add the soy sauce mixture and cook for 1-2 minutes, stirring, until most of the liquid has evaporated.

Video: Classic baking – how a blind cook manages

Banana bread.

Video: Banana bread

170g plain (all-purpose) flour.
1 teaspoon baking powder (soda).
Half teaspoon salt.
2 large eggs (at room temperature).
1 teaspoon vanilla extract.
110g unsalted butter (at room temperature).
110g sugar (use more sugar if you omit the crumb topping).
3 very ripe bananas, peeled and mashed with a fork.

Crumb topping.

55g cold butter.
2 tablespoons pecan nuts, chopped.
2 tablespoons dark brown sugar.
1 tablespoon plain flour.

Method.

Preheat oven to 175C, Gas 3, 350F.

Sift flour, baking soda and salt into a bowl and set aside.

Whisk eggs and vanilla together and set aside.

In a mixing bowl, cream the butter and sugar until light and fluffy, then gradually add the eggs and vanilla mix until all is thoroughly incorporated.

Add the mashed banana and don't worry if the mixture seems a little curdled.

Remove bowl from mixer and fold in the flour mix with a spatula until incorporated.

Spray loaf pan/s with a little spray oil or butter.

Pour the mixture into the pans.

Cut the cold butter into a bowl and rub in the pecans, brown sugar and flour to a crumbly consistency.

Sprinkle the topping over the loaves of uncooked banana bread.

Bake for about 22-25 minutes or until a toothpick comes out clean. If using one large loaf pan bake for about 55 minutes.

My tips.

Kelly said, "I use small individual pans because I think they bake better. But you could use a larger nine-inch by five-inch pan. Just adjust the baking time. These taste the best when still warm!"

Jo's recipes.

Pumpkin bread.

420g plain (all purpose) flour.
2 teaspoons baking powder (soda).
Half teaspoon salt.
1 teaspoon ground cinnamon.
1 teaspoon ground nutmeg.
Half teaspoon ground ginger.
200g softened unsalted butter.
360g granulated sugar.
180ml milk.
425g can of unsweetened pumpkin puree.
2 large eggs.
120g raisins
120g chopped walnuts.

Method.

Heat oven to 175C, Gas 3, 350F.

Grease two loaf tins with butter and then dust with flour.

Whisk together the dry ingredients.

Cream butter and sugar until light and fluffy.

Add milk, eggs and pumpkin puree, beating well after each addition.

Fold in dry ingredients and then raisins and walnuts.

Divide between the two loaf pans.

Cook for 65-70 minutes.

My tips.

Unless you are in America, or somewhere where it is easy to get hold of a tin of pumpkin puree, you might wait until you have a glut of pumpkin that can be gently oven-roasted to produce the puree. Perhaps this is a bread to make for Halloween after carving pumpkins and don't want to throw away all that flesh

Overnight egg casserole.

6 slices "day old" sandwich bread.
12 eggs, beaten.
480ml milk.
240g cheese, grated.
18 sausages.
Spray oil or butter.
Salt and pepper.

Method.

Cook the sausages, drain off any fat and slice.

Meanwhile, prepare an ovenproof dish (approximately 9 by 12 inches) by spraying with a little oil or rubbing with butter.

Spray or very lightly butter the bread on both sides and place a layer across the bottom of the dish, cutting to fit if necessary.

Place a layer of half the cheese on the bread, topped with half the sausage pieces.

Repeat with the remaining cheese and sausage.

Beat the eggs, milk and seasoning together and gently pour over the dish to cover all the other ingredients.

Cover the dish and refrigerate overnight.

Place in a preheated oven at 190C, Gas 5, 375F for 55-60 minutes. By then the eggs should have risen somewhat like a soufflé. Check that the centre is also cooked. Give another 5 minutes if necessary.

The dish will collapse a little after coming out of the oven. Serve warm.

My tips.

The aim is to use bread that won't soak up all the liquid, so lightly toasted bread can be an alternative if yours is too fresh.

There's no end to the alternative or additional ingredients in this savoury bread and butter pudding, but all need to be pre-cooked and the seasoning adjusted. You can use onions, peppers, bacon, mushrooms, peppers, even fish, but avoid adding too much liquid, such as from tomatoes.

Broccoli crunch salad.

1 broccoli head, florets removed and cut into small pieces, stalk peeled and finely chopped.

1 onion, peeled and very thinly sliced.

2 large handfuls seeds/nuts, toasted/roasted (e.g. sunflower, pumpkin, peanuts, cashews, walnuts).

2 large handfuls raisins or sultanas.

2 rashers bacon, cooked, cooled and finely chopped.

Dressing of mayonnaise with a little vinegar (could be rice wine vinegar) and sugar (optional).

Simply combine all the ingredients and season to taste.

My tips.

Cauliflower could replace the broccoli.

Don't bother with the sugar.

Keep the vegetable pieces small to give a good balance of flavours in each mouthful.

Chapter 12.

The largest city in the world.

Refreshed, revitalised and fizzing with excitement after a week at home, I was en route for China. Although there was little sense of Finland during the short stopover in Helsinki, I did get a taste of the country on the second leg of the flight – pine-infused ice cream to celebrate 100 years of Finnish independence – and it was exhilarating to be flying over the top of the world, somewhere near the North Pole. The only glitch was that the handle of one of my suitcases had broken. It was to haunt me during the weeks as we struggled through over 15 airport check-ins!

Many hours and some sleep later, I arrived in the splendidly impressive monumental Chongqing airport. I could tell the sheer size and scale of the building from the sound of so much space. Toby had just flown in from Shanghai and we were met by Andrew and his wife Maggie. Through the roundabout route of friends of friends, he had replied to my original emails begging for help for the Holman adventure. A university professor in Chongqing, Andrew was our primary contact with the local Rotary Club, which was sponsoring that stage of our trip, while former lawyer Maggie kept track of the recipes during the cooking sessions. Andrew and the Rotary Club had done all the hard work, organising accommodation, transport, translation, cooking sessions, entertainment and much more. We needed do no more than surf on the wave of their preparedness, hoping not to crash on the rocks of wholly new cuisine. Their hope was that I could, in turn, promote their own project assisting visually impaired people in Chongqing.

This amazing "mountain city" is virtually unknown outside China. Surrounded by four major mountains, two important rivers, the famous Six Gorges and a huge dam, the dramatic landscape cradles this massive metropolis. With some 37 million inhabitants (more than half the total population of the UK), the city has been a magnet for those who want to work and share the benefits of growth for tens of thousands of years.

Chongqing apparently means "repeated celebrations", and the people have brought a mix of culinary cultures to the city throughout its important history and economic development. Helped by local architects, Julia and Matthew, we learned to appreciate the delicate balance between past millennia of civilisation and the surge of current building. The ancient mudstone rock beneath the city conceals a labyrinth of caves and tunnels above which rise glittering glass and steel towers alongside more traditional homes and businesses. As we heard in Tamarindo, and probably like so many other places, there was tension between the demands of economic development and the preservation of authentic local character. We managed to experience both: singing to the echo of the mudstone caves; walking old, convoluted brick alleys and stairways; the dazzling night-time light displays; the superb modern apartments.

Toby expressed his particular perspective as an architectural illustrator: "As soon as we arrived, I was bowled over by the scale and the energy. I'd never seen so many bright lights and cranes, so many textures. With all the cliffs and waterfalls, it felt like a city built on a mountain. But, amongst all the bombasity, there's another side to Chongqing. One with a more human scale and one you might miss if you're not looking. Places like Charlie's backpacker hostel nestled on the steep banks of the

Yangtze, a wonderfully traditional flower market, the old cable car – once the only means to cross the river before the many bridges. There are smoky teahouses, where locals sit around locked in tense games. All this under the gaze of sparkly new towers."

He captured the dichotomy in a unique illustration and explained: "It represents old China, full of stairways and fortresses and folks going about their daily lives." Using invisible inks, he superimposed a second drawing that is only revealed in ultra-violet light. "Here is modern China," he said, "full of glowing neon towers and cranes."

Video: Toby talking about Chongqing

Video: China Tower by Toby

Our excitement was palpable as the city unfurled before us on the drive to the prestigious Intercontinental Hotel (www.ihg.com/intercontinental/hotels/gb/en/chongqing/chghb/hoteldetail). We were met by welcoming staff, and whizzed aloft in silent lifts to rooms on the 29th floor. Toby was thrilled by the views, while I was especially delighted to be able to open windows and hear the people and activity in the square below. Sound travels very far upwards and gave me a sense of the city's pace, night and day.

More mundanely, the spaciousness, huge walk-in shower and enough flat surfaces to spread out my belongings made my time in the hotel so much easier: a place for everything. What a change from the hotel in San Francisco and the backpacker hostel in Tamarindo. I could get used to this style!

Having space and everything in its place means I have some chance of moving about safely and finding things. At home I try to keep a mental image of every room, every drawer and cupboard, and everything inside them. Trip hazards like furniture and easy-to-knock-off items are placed precisely to the millimetre, helping my memory and reducing the risk of breakages (me or the house contents).

I have my technique for new hotel rooms, developed after work and holidays have taken me to hundreds of places all over the world. One of the hotel staff has to do the full tour from how to lock and unlock the door, along each wall and piece of furniture, around the bathroom, and how to work the shower. Also, where is the rubbish bin? Are the lights on or off, and are the curtains closed? It takes a few minutes as I mentally map the space I'll occupy for, perhaps, just a night. The final check is what happens if the fire alarm goes off. Do I try to escape or stay and pray they've remembered me? Just asking the question reminds them to make a note for the night manager. But it's rather more challenging in different languages.

The next 36 hours were a haze of jet lag. There was some unpacking, a supper to meet Julia and husband Matthew in a room lined with racks of wine bottles, some sleep, time planning cooking sessions with Food and Beverages director, Sam, and a presentation to the welcoming Rotary Club dinner.

The club and their guests were truly international, with some of the city's most influential business people and residents. My task was to sing for my supper, explaining how the ambitions for the Holman Prize linked to their own project. Andrew had warned me that local audiences tended to talk throughout a theatre production or presentation, but they were generously attentive and a gaggle of questioners gathered at the end.

Meeting masses of new people was a challenge without visual clues. It was a matter of recognising the various voices and being able to tie each to a name. Not easy when there were lots of them all talking at once in different languages, and no hiding place for mistakes. Adding to the confusion, most local people I met had adopted English names to overcome our awful Chinese pronunciation. It's generous to relinquish your identity for the convenience of strangers.

And so to sleep...

By ten thirty the next morning I was in the hotel's demonstration kitchen – thankfully separate from the noise and frenzy of the main cooking areas. Julia was on standby to help with the translation, Maggie had her notepad, and the irrepressible Sam kept us all on track. He was a truly memorable character, with boundless energetic enthusiasm and tireless good humour in the face of coping with this strange woman. Add the hotel PR people, head chef Jack keeping an eye on us all, and a few onlookers, and we had the makings of a party! "Knee how" was my best interpretation of how to say "Hello" in Mandarin.

The many videos we made that long day are rather misleading. I look vaguely competent and seem to be knowledgeable about the various dishes. In reality, I had to voiceover later, as the space was too noisy and there were so many people speaking various languages that Julia and Sam struggled to translate, but I was closely supervised by big-hearted, ebullient and boisterous Jack and his team every step of the way.

Confidently relaxed and friendly, chef Dillon was following in the family tradition, with both his father and brother being chefs. His braised pork was fragrant with cinnamon, star anise, garlic and ginger. As he explained, "The typical taste of the Cantonese food is delicate flavours. It is not too strong but light and sweet."

Sichuan-style chicken was just as subtle and fragrant – quite different to local fiery Chongqing cooking. His "magic" sauce was the key. Instead of simmering soy sauce and sugar with a pale vinegar (more often added to cold dishes), Dillon had used a dark Langzhou vinegar. With the ancient name of Langzhong in Sichuan province, this vinegar is made with rice, corn kernels, bran and herbs. My special prize of the morning was being presented with two bottles of his potion, plus one of the vinegar. Rather than risk them on my future travels, they journeyed back to the UK with Maggie and spent months being mistaken for shampoo and shower gel before I realised what her artistically careful package contained.

In contrast, chef Tony's tofu dish was typical of his Chongqing home and very much in line with the move to reduce meat consumption in our diets. He used just a tiny amount of beef, plus chillies, and the fragrant local pepper to bring very uninspiring bean curd to life. We had a little translation problem when "slowly pressing" the curd cubes should have been "stirring gently", but it wasn't a disaster. Raw tofu is chewy and tasteless. It improved a bit after poaching and frying, but would need this type of spicing to achieve the popularity gained by vegan sausage rolls in the UK. It is definitely an ingredient that could play a part in reducing deforestation, methane, chemical input and other negative factors of intensive meat production. Perhaps there will be enough profit in tofu to persuade food producers to save the world?

It was a whirlwind morning, and none of the chefs seemed the least bothered by giving me extra help. Head chef Jack was more concerned that we were all doing a good job rather than having any misgivings about me wielding a knife (although chopsticks floored me). They'd each signed the chef's toque that was ceremoniously presented, before they rustled up yet more dishes for the lunch to welcome our guests, Wan Lin and Lisa.

While I knew there must be blind people in the city, no one had mentioned seeing any in the streets or shops. Hearing the live experiences of these two 20-year-olds gave me better understanding of their situation. Although the recent economic promise of China continued to flourish, they had experienced some of the malnutrition and health problems linked to poverty in their childhoods. Their eye problems and tiny stature were some of the consequences.

In the old days, when families could be very poor, children with visual impairments had to stay at home, with no education or prospects. China's rapid progress had made free places at the blind school available and removed the burden on families.

Following a childhood accident that damaged her vision, Wan Lin had joined the specialist school when she was 11 and, after learning to read and write, graduated to the massage school at 18 with the possibility of future work. She still had some residual sight, so managed without a white cane, but her small size meant she could only treat children. Massage is an important part of Chinese medical treatment, reflecting the principles of acupuncture. Wan Lin showed me how each finger is associated with a specific organ, saying, "There are loads of energy lines in the body."

I thought I might get a quick solution to the chesty cough I'd developed with all the flying. As she held the appropriate finger, she said the massage could, "push it out if you have got phlegm, but this is not going to do the trick because there are so many other things. I'm just showing you a very basic example. If I was doing it properly with babies or children, I would look at their tongues, their eyes, the colour of their face, their skin." We didn't succeed even when I went close to show her my face and tongue because, as she explained, "I have to see you in daylight because, with the artificial light, my sight goes." I'd presented her with an impossible task, far too big in comparison with her normal patients and outside the better conditions of her workplace.

Video: Humbling – living with blindness in China

The blind masseuses lived at their clinic, sleeping on the couches used by their patients during the day, with their meals prepared by an "auntie". There were many advantages to living and working in the same place, but perhaps some limitations too – and not much chance to learn about cooking. Knowing this, Jack and I had planned a series of dishes that explored different senses, especially touch and taste.

Wan Lin's first challenge was the kitchen knife, and with instructions from Dillon and Tony she was triumphant to have cut two identical steaks. As he cooked them, Jack showed us the professional trick for testing steak that works equally well for blind people: the feel of the muscle at the base of your thumb becomes tighter as you fold your thumb and fingers. Therefore, thumb only = rare; thumb and index finger folded = medium rare; add folded middle finger = medium; add folded ring finger = well done. Bolder than me, Wan Lin succeeded in tossing the vegetable garnish in the frying pan too.

Video: Steak and testing how well it's done

Handling a potato peeler was another new experience for her as she shaved the "whiskers" from celery for a Waldorf salad (eat your heart out, Rich). Jack stepped in with a better peeler and sympathised: "When we first started cooking, we had to go through this too, even though we can see. So I understand." Wan Lin's response was typically determined, saying, "Yes, but because we are blind we have to try harder, to be more independent."

The salad was about touch too: mouth feel. Whiskers between your teeth aren't very enjoyable, whereas apple and celery nearly the same size as the walnut pieces gives balance to each mouthful. Together we taste tested. Too sweet or sour? Enough mayonnaise without overwhelming the fresh flavours? Presentation, gastronomic techniques or exotic ingredients all come second to food that tastes good. Just as Luis told me in San Francisco: less can be more.

Wan Lin was full of fun and confidence. I'm not sure even many sighted people would be so self-assured to undertake their first cooking experience with a foreign dish amidst top professional chefs in such a prestigious hotel. It certainly took nerve and courage.

Lisa stepped in next to make chocolate mousse under the eye of chef Frank. Whisking eggs and sugar was probably new for her but, with his encouragement, she gave them more strength and vigour. Heating the milk, he explained, "I don't use a thermometer because I have good experience, and because we know that things tend to boil at 96 degrees in CQ." I'd forgotten that the high altitude of the city could make such a difference to boiling temperature.

Lisa's petite stature and youthful looks have added to the challenges in her life, as she explained: "I wasn't borne blind as far as my family knew. We only found out when I was about seven or eight years old when, as children, we were playing with our hands and making a camera-effect with our fingers. When I was using the "camera", we realised that I couldn't see through my left eye. Therefore they took me to the hospital and they found I had a problem with a growth in my brain that was pressing on my optic nerve and took my sight away. I had an operation when they removed the top of my head to sort out this tumour. Since then, they have realised that I don't really have any sight. After my operation, they discovered I was very poorly, very weak in myself, so I wasn't able to go to ordinary school or the blind school because I could only do certain hours during the day."

As a result, Lisa couldn't start at the blind school until she was 12 and stronger. There she met Wan Lin and they graduated to massage school together. She did the training, but there were more challenges. "Unfortunately, I have a very young looking face," she told me, "and, being not so strong physically, people didn't have trust in my ability to massage. I couldn't get any work so I had to rethink what I could do. I started to make my crafts by myself. I am self-taught and found there was a place where I could take my craft to sell." She'd brought a sample of her work, a beautifully decorated case for a travel pass.

I recognised her determination in the face of almost insuperable barriers, contrasting starkly with the benefits I'd had in coping with sight loss. The privileges of university education and a naval career gave me a head start.

By chance, one day, I had learned that the Navy was looking to train the first female barrister and, without hesitation, decided I could do that. Three years later I emerged after academic training, bar school and pupillage with a natty wig and gown.

My first "legal" job was as the commodore's secretary at HMS Nelson in Portsmouth where we ran probably the largest "Magistrate's Court" in the Service. My tasks were keeping the establishment's administration on track, the trials fair and legal. I advised the prosecution and defence on the law, the commodore of his powers and responsibilities, while prosecuting and defending more serious cases at courts martial.

The sight in my right eye was already starting to fail and reading became increasingly difficult. By the time I moved on to become Staff Legal Adviser to Flag Officer Plymouth, the problems were worse. Referral to Moorfields Hospital in London gave me access to top specialists who diagnosed uveitis, almost certainly the same condition that had blinded James Holman centuries before. Treatment was huge doses of steroids and a drug usually used to prevent transplant patients rejecting donated organs. Within weeks, my body had blown up like a balloon, I could hardly walk, and had grown a mass of unsexy facial hair. It took 14 months and two emergency hospital admissions before I was well enough to get back to work. I'd given up on my right eye and hoped, in vain, that I wasn't one of the rare people who would have the condition in both eyes.

Without anything like such advantages, Lisa still had the entrepreneurial spirit that I'd recognised when supporting disabled people to become self-employed in the UK. Faced with employers' ignorance, fear and prejudices, starting one's own business can be the only route to work for very many people who don't want their health conditions to limit their lives. It was true for me too. Starting my Disability Dynamics company was the only way I managed to work after the Navy. Years of delivering our Work for Yourself programs convinced me that help specially designed for disabled entrepreneurs not only improved their physical and mental health, their work prospects and finances, but also rebuilt family, community and social relationships. Win, win!

Back in Chongqing, the hotel chefs almost certainly had no experience of blind people in their kitchens but were patient and empathetic, caring and courteous. I listened as the rapport developed between them all. They were completely immersed with their experience of each other. It was extraordinarily poignant to see how big hearty head chef Jack warmed to these young women. There was no need for me at all, so I stepped back and let them enjoy their cooking together.

It turned into a very long day, finishing in the early evening as the sky darkened. Knowing that moving around at twilight was difficult, I tried to offer the girls a taxi home, but Wan Lin firmly refused – more due to her concerns about car sickness than trying to be independent. But I did manage to compensate them for all the time when they would have been earning. The chefs had put together a parcel of our creations, and other examples of Western cooking, so that they could share their successes and experiences with their colleagues.

International Hotel recipes.

Dillon's Sichuan-style Kung Pao chicken.

Video: Kung Pao chicken

250g chicken breast, cut into 1cm cubes.
5g salt.
10g potato or cornflour.
Ground black pepper.
5g cooking rice wine.
Tablespoon oil.
50g leek, sliced.
10g fresh ginger, sliced.
10g garlic, sliced.
40g Chinese red pepper (like chili).
10g dry red pepper.
30g sugar.
10g vinegar.
5g soy sauce.
5g old soy sauce.
5g chicken powder (stock cube).
100g peanuts.
Spring onions, shredded.

Method.

Mix the chicken, salt, flour, pepper and rice wine. Leave for 5 minutes.

Heat some oil in a pan and cook the chicken mix for 3 minutes before removing.

In the same pan, cook the leek, ginger and garlic for about 1 minute.

Add the sliced pepper and dried chilli for a further minute.

Add the sugar, vinegar and soy sauce and continue cooking.

Add the chicken powder/stock and, if needed, another teaspoon of the flour to thicken the sauce.

Return the chicken to the pan, add the peanuts and shredded spring onions and serve as soon as they are heated through.

My tips.

Dillon made me two bottles of the vinegar, soy sauce and sugar mix because it is used so regularly in Chinese cooking. Base a mix on the proportions in the recipe, which needs just 6 teaspoonfuls.

Dillon's Cantonese braised belly pork.

Video: Cantonese braised belly pork

500g pork belly, cut into 1-inch cubes.
Peanut (or other light) oil.
5g cinnamon stick.
5g star anise.
10g fresh ginger, peeled and cut into thin strips.
10g garlic, peeled and sliced.
10g leek, cut into strips.
15g sugar.
30g thick dark soy sauce.

10g taro curd (preserved bean curd with chilli).
20g Chinese cooking wine.
10g oyster sauce.
800g water.

Method.

Heat a 1 teaspoon of oil in a pan and fry the pork until browned (about 4 minutes) and set aside.

Add more peanut oil to the pan and fry the cinnamon, star anise, ginger, garlic and leek for about 1 minute.

Add all the remaining ingredients and bring to a simmer.

Return the pork to the pan and simmer gently to braise for 1 hour.

Stir after 30 minutes. (My translation of his "Roll twice with a shovel.") Remove the cinnamon and star anise before reducing the sauce. (Again his words were, "Last, pick up the spices, the fire will drain the juice and then you can eat it in a pot.")

My tips.

Spring onion could be used in place of leek.

Tony's Lao Lan Ma or Sichuan-style braised spicy and hot tofu.

Video: Braised spicy and hot tofu

500g tofu, cubed.
1 teaspoon salt.
3 tablespoons (10g) sesame oil.
10g fresh ginger, peeled and finely chopped.
10g garlic, peeled and finely chopped.
10g garlic sprout, sliced.
50g beef, minced so fine that it is more like sausage meat.
20g doubanjiang (spicy, salty paste made from fermented broad beans, soybeans, salt, rice, and various spices).
1 teaspoon (5g) pickled peppers.
2 teaspoons (5g) blade pepper (possibly dried chilli flakes).
2 teaspoons (5g) lobster sauce (possibly black bean chilli sauce).
1 teaspoon chicken powder (stock cube).
1 teaspoon sugar.
1 teaspoon (20g) soy sauce.
2 tablespoons cornflour.
2 tablespoons (10g) Sichuan pepper oil.
20g spring onions, shredded.

Method.

Simmer the curd and half teaspoon salt in a pan of water for 5 minutes, then drain.

Cook the ginger and garlic in 3 tablespoons of sesame oil for 2 minutes.

Add the minced beef and cook until brown.

Add and sauté the chilli doubanjiang paste and pickled pepper over medium heat, stirring.

Add and sauté the dried chilli flakes and black bean chilli paste for 2 minutes.

Add 1 tablespoon of water and then the tofu and gently stir through in the pan for 1 minute.

Add the chicken powder and sugar and cook on a higher heat for 3 minutes.

Add soy sauce and cornflour to thicken.

To finish drizzle with the Sichuan pepper oil. Add a sprinkling of Sichuan pepper and spring onion tops.

My tips.

This is one of the recipes where some of the ingredients may have got a little lost in translation, but the direction is clear.

Waldorf salad.

Video: Waldorf salad

5 sticks celery, peeled and thinly sliced.
2 apples, cored and thinly sliced.
2 handfuls walnut pieces.
2 tablespoons mayonnaise.
Salt, pepper, lemon juice, finely sliced chilli to taste.

Method.

Mix ingredients, adjusting their quantities and the seasoning to taste.

Frank's chocolate mousse.

Video: Chocolate mousse

150g milk.
330g dark chocolate (at least 50% cocoa solids), broken into pieces or buttons.
30g sugar.
1 egg yolk.
150g whipped cream.

Method.

Heat the milk in a pan until boiling.

Remove from the heat and add the chocolate and sugar.

When melted, and slightly cooler, beat in the egg yolk.

When mix has cooled to 30C, fold the cream and chocolate together.

Place into serving dishes and chill.

My tips.

As I was writing this, I had just been taught a French version for 8 people that is even easier.

9 eggs, separated.

300g dark chocolate (at least 50% cocoa solids).

Method.

Heat the chocolate in a small pan with about 2 tablespoons of water (or in a plastic bowl in the microwave on defrost).

When the water boils and the chocolate has started to melt, remove from the heat and stir to complete the melting.

While the chocolate is cooling, separate the eggs.

Stir the egg yolks into the chocolate until smooth and well incorporated.

Whisk the egg whites to the stiff peak stage.

Fold one third of the egg whites into the chocolate mix, and then follow with the second and final thirds in two separate stages. Fold gently together until the mix is all the same colour.

Place in serving dishes such as ramekins and chill for 24 hours.

This recipe can be adapted to any number of servings. Allow 1 egg per person plus 1 for the pot, or 30g chocolate per egg and at least 10g for the pot. Follow the rest of the recipe method but reduce the amount of water as necessary.

Macerated strawberries.

15 strawberries, hulled and quartered.
1 orange, juice and zest.
2 tablespoons sugar.
2 tablespoons orange liqueur (for example, Cointreau).

Method.

Mix all the ingredients and allow to macerate in the fridge for at least an hour.

My tips.

This will cheer up out-of-season strawberries.

Chapter 13.

Out and about in Chongqing.

After the energy ravages of cooking in the hotel, I was grateful for a more restful following day: light recreational shopping in the morning, presentations in the afternoon and a spicy finale with the classic Chongqing hotpot.

It was way beyond the call of duty for Sam and another of his colleagues, Nicole, to take me around the local area of Chongqing. In the large square in the centre of the city, the Intercontinental Hotel dwarfs the "Liberty Building" in size but not in significance. Erected to celebrate the return of peace after the Second World War, the Liberty Building is an important symbol of courage and survival. During that war, Chongqing was made the alternative Chinese capital. Although the geographical position of the relocated national administration was easier to defend, the city was not unscathed. The network of mudstone caverns and tunnels became vital bomb shelters during the hostilities. Now the city square attracts tourists and shoppers. We meandered along a line of market stalls, where Sam plied me with samples of their local homemade biscuits – from sweet to spicy – then up and down stone steps, hearing the tinkling of a dragon fountain spewing water and past the famous statue of a female Buddha. Most satisfying for me was a huge drum that I could beat and hear the sound echoing from the stone walls and passageways.

After the recreational shopping, back to the hotel to join Julia and Maggie for an excursion to the International School. My first talk on risk-taking to several classes of multi-national and Chinese eight- to nine-year-olds was a true pleasure. They were an excellent audience, rapt and attentive with many prepared questions and much inquisitiveness. The second group were truly typical of older teenagers worldwide: laidback and laconic; determined that curiosity wouldn't undermine their carapace of cool sophistication.

But the evening brought the best experience of the day. Chongqing is famous for its hotpot, rather like an oil fondue but at the top of the chili Scoville scale. I was truly privileged to be the guest of the hotel chefs Jack, Dillon and Frank, along with the general manager Sharon, plus Australian super-chef Julie, who had oversight of about 90 kitchens across the hotel group in China. True to such a professionally distinguished cadre, they were highly selective in their restaurant choice. We drove some 10 kilometres out of the city to a simple wooden structure in the fresh air of the mountains. The distant landscape slopes around us were decorated with hundreds of red and blue shining lanterns. After a day of light rain, it was all refreshingly damp and cool.

In a private room, we sat around a big wooden table which held a centrepiece of a roaring butane gas burner heating a bowl of bubbling chilli oil. Within the oil was another boiling pot of stock – for the fainthearted who couldn't manage the fierce chillies. I dare not wonder how it would all go down with UK Health & Safety inspectors! Between us were different platters of thinly sliced mushrooms, beef slithers, squid, tofu sheets, vegetables and, most off-putting in translation, "various glands and offal".

Each of us had a personal can of sesame oil to mix in a bowl with chopped garlic, coriander, soy and oyster sauces. Having selected the sliced delicacy, it was submerged in the hot oil or stock to cook for a few seconds and dunked in the sesame oil mix before eating. Managing tiny slithers in the hot liquids seemed a chopstick too far for me. Julie came to my aid and delivered cooked titbits into my oil bowl. Undaunted by its reputation, I did try several cooked in the chilli oil. The first was fine but, after three, I couldn't feel my lips anymore so retreated to the stock version. There wasn't a great deal of food, but the intense flavours and the quantity of oils made it very filling. Probably a successful solution to food shortages in the past. We toasted each other with the light Chinese beer, but I was grateful to be driven back to bed and sleep in the hotel by midnight while the others hit the bar.

Next morning, there was ample evidence of the night before: although I'd been warned to wear an apron to avoid splashing oil, every stitch of my clothing reeked of sesame oil. The whole lot went off to be washed and I needed another shower and hair wash. Sharon laughed and told me the hotel laundry is in high demand for everyone who has experienced the Chongqing hotpot. A good income generator.

By lunchtime I was fit to be seen and smelt again, ready to perform my very first live cookery demonstration ever. I could have chosen a less prestigious and powerful audience than the International Women's Group featuring several Consuls General, plus others at the very forefront of Chongqing business and society – movers and shakers in heels.

Let me loose in front of an audience and I'm happy. I've been speaking to crowds since reading the lessons at assembly and chairing the debating society at school. There have been bigger audiences and more serious gatherings since post-nuclear war training for senior army and police officers to compering disability employment conferences. I can hear when some audiences hold their breath, watching if I'll fall off the stage. I need to hear them laugh and breathe to be sure they're still present and alive.

This was an impeccably polite, generous and patient audience that laughed in all the right places as I waffled my way through a simple raspberry Victoria sponge with the essential help of chef Frank. He and Sam did all the hard work. All I had to do was crack the eggs and turn on the mixer. I just tossed raspberries into the mix and let Frank carry it away to the oven. Hardly testing or high cuisine.

Video: Pleasing powerful ladies who lunch

Frank's riposte to my humble efforts underlined the difference between professional and home cook: his dessert for the ladies was a stunningly sophisticated dark chocolate stiletto shoe garnished with fruit alongside my humble little sponges.

But the positive response from the elegant audience did suggest that my talk had opened a few eyes and been persuasive that disability doesn't destroy capacity or ambition. I hoped I'd done justice to the latent capabilities of about a billion disabled people worldwide.

Next day I was on my feet talking again. This time to the British Consul General and her team, plus those from the Welsh Office and British Council – just a few steps away from the Liberty Building square. Back at the hotel, Sharon hijacked me for an impromptu lunch with a group of lawyers visiting from Hong Kong. She wanted to use every opportunity to increase awareness of blind people in Chongqing such as Wan Lin and Lisa.

Then a taxi drive to a modern apartment block a distance away in this vast city with Julia, Maggie and Toby. We had barely managed to get out of the vehicle before the driver sped off, and it took a few minutes to realise that my essential cookery bag was still in the boot. Many voluble and high-volume phone calls rapidly followed until he was persuaded to return. The bag was handed over, but I never heard my talking scales again. I suspect they had slid into the nether regions of the boot.

Meanwhile, I'd been blithely sitting on a bench in the sun, enjoying the neighbourhood walking, chatting, and playing amidst the expanses of lawn and gardens.

We finally reached Hanying's apartment. She was loaning us the use of her kitchen, and her friend, Wang Yi, had brought her aunt, Yinyishu, to demonstrate the devilish art of making Chinese dumplings. These baozi and jiaozi are nothing like the heavier suet versions that we see bobbing on top of a stew. They are delicate steamed dough encasing fragrant pork and vegetables, devoured by the Chinese people on their way to work.

Yi explained her aunt's role: "She owns a baozi shop. She has owned the shop for 25 years. She started making baozi at age 18. The dumplings are served only in the morning for breakfast, perhaps also with rice porridge."

We started with the baozi, a simple dough leavened with a little yeast and baking powder. In the warm room, by the time the lotus root, ginger and spring onion vegetables were chopped and mixed with the finely minced pork, the dough had doubled in size ready for shaping.

And then the problems started. Having rolled a sausage of the dough, a piece was pinched off, rolled into a ball that was then pressed flat. The resulting circle had to be rolled out all around the edge to create the dumpling "skin". It was easier for me just to flatten the edges with my fingers. A little filling was placed in the centre of each before crimping the edges together, rotating all the time to produce a tiny cylindrical "handle" for the dumpling. I simply didn't have the touch sensitivity or the dexterity to do it – and neither did anyone else. The whole group of us struggled to produce a rather mismatched heap of baozi. We hid ours in the steamer under Yinyishu's supremely perfect dumplings for the 10 minutes steaming.

Leek is the key flavour of jiaozi rather than spring onion, and their skins are much simpler because the dough is more like a pastry and the circles are folded over the filling. But they still had to be flattened all around the edges. When I asked if there was an easier way of making the dumpling skins, Yi just laughed and said, "Yes, we can buy them!"

But, thanks to Yinyishu's patience and sometime exasperation, I had learned the authentic traditional method – even though it had taken hours and dusk was falling by the time we finished. Yi explained that Yinyishu had her usual early start the next day: "They always get up at three or two thirty to make all the preparation, get them in the steamer and get everything done. Because, in China, people get up very early for their work and they need their breakfast at six or six thirty." We put her in a taxi as the fastest way to get her home to bed, with profound thanks for her time and much-stretched forbearance.

Next day, we were escorted by the indomitable duo of Julia and Maggie to the "Test Bed" project run by young local entrepreneur, Lee Bo, in a historic quarter of Chongqing (https://www.ichongqing.info/attraction/testbed-2-arts-center). He was supporting the preservation of some of the city's ancient character. The traditional flower and plant market is a gardener's dream: masses of exotic flowers, foliage and miniature gardens planted in individual pots that I could gently explore with my fingers. There was also a library with coffee shop, plus the craft shop amidst the ancient stone and brick buildings, alleys and stairways. It was comforting to be amidst architecture on a more human scale after the glitz of the modern high-rise buildings. People in China were realising that travellers from all over the world want to see and experience the charm and attraction of the city's history, to capture a sense of how it is evolving without losing its character.

I was particularly entranced by the ceramics, especially tiny tea bowls only a few centimetres wide. They are hand-thrown with a delicate touch, with smooth interiors and pleasingly unglazed exteriors showcasing the natural texture of the clay. They cost a few pence each, but only the last two were available. Julia took up the challenge of finding more and, nearly a year later, presented me with a full set nestling in their matching storage bowl.

A further element of the project was the "Garden Restaurant" where I was welcomed by head chef, Mr Dong, who presented a fusion of Sustuchan and Yunnan province cuisines. In his professional Chinese kitchen in full lunchtime service, the sound level was astounding. Not just the usual clatter of pans but multiple gas burners roaring like jet engines to heat the huge woks. With so much going on and one's senses confounded, it was best for me to keep well out of the way and aim to understand what he was doing rather than getting in his way.

Mr Dong's first dish appeared simple: a whole cleaned croaker fish chopped with a cleaver. Julia translated: "He's not filleting it but chopping it into four pieces at a slant." The Chinese like fish cooked on the bone to keep maximum flavour. Water sloshed around and cleaned the wok as it evaporated. Sitting atop a lump of clay to retain the heat, the wok quickly brought the oil to bubbling. Each piece of fish was dipped in a very light sweet potato flour batter and quickly fried, before being recaptured by a slotted spoon the size of a lacrosse stick. Mr Dong reconstructed the fish on the serving platter and dressed it with garlic, soy sauce, sesame seeds and shredded spring onions – a disarmingly simple dish that kept the magnificent fish centre stage.

He made equally quick work of prawns. The heat under the wok was alarmingly fierce, with flames licking the inside. A few quick additions of red onion and black garlic, plus fish sauce mixed with chilli, it was all delivered to the plate within seconds for the final garnish of chopped coriander stalks. Good ingredients simply cooked and not over complicated – the same principles espoused by Luis in San Francisco and many others since.

More dishes flew to our table from other chefs for a truly authentic lunch. And there was another special treat: tiny shallow bowls just three centimetres wide of "Pu Erh" tea from the Yunnan province, with the reputation of being good for the digestion. The leaves of this very expensive tea are either fresh or have been dry toasted in a wok before hot water is poured over them. Julia explained, "Chinese tea is like Western wine. It is a collector's item, and some teas improve the longer they are kept. Some teas cost tens of thousands of pounds." I confess that my palate just wasn't refined or experienced enough to recognise the uniqueness of this tea, but I certainly didn't have any problems with my digestion.

Yinyishu's recipes.

Video: Chinese breakfast dumplings masterclass

Filling for Chinese breakfast dumplings.

500g pork, minced.
Fresh ginger, peeled and finely chopped.
Lotus root, peeled and finely chopped.
Leek (jiaozi only), finely chopped.
Spring onion (baozi only), finely chopped.

Method.

Mix the pork, ginger and lotus root.

Divide the mix in half, add leek to one half and spring onion to the other.

My tips.

Carrots can replace lotus root in these dumplings.

Dumpling jiaozi or joaozinho (try pronouncing as jow-zee).

500g plain wheat flour.
200g cold water.
Pinch of salt.

Method.

Mix flour, water and salt in a bowl.

Knead dough on a floured board until soft and elastic.

Form a long sausage about 2-3cm diameter.

Pinch off pieces from the sausage and shape into a circle.

Using a rolling pin or your fingers, roll all around just the edges to make them thinner, maintaining the circle shape.

Place a little of the filling with leek in the centre and form the dumpling by rolling the edges of the round of dough into the middle over the filling with one hand, while turning the whole dumpling with the other hand. This seemed to form a crimped tubular handle!

Steam for a few minutes until cooked.

Dumplings baozi (try pronouncing as bay-ozee).

500g plain wheat flour.
250g warm water.
5g dry yeast powder.
5g baking powder.
5g sugar.
Pinch of salt.

Method.

Mix all the dough ingredients together and knead to form a dough.

Allow the dough to rise for about half an hour until increased in size.

Make the "skins" as above and place filling in the centre of the circle.

Fold the dough over the filling to form a semi-circular shape, pinching the edges together.

Mr Dong's recipes.

Battered yellow croaker fish.

Video: Croaker fish

Clean and gut the fish.

Taking a cleaver, cut off the tail and part of the head and then cut the remainder of the fish into 3 or 4 pieces. Cut right through the whole fish in 2 or 3 long diagonal cuts. Leaving the fish on the bone retains its flavour.

Mix a light batter. (In China they might use potato flour or other forms of starch rather than wheat flour.)

Heat your giant wok on a jet of burning gas.

Pour a little water into the wok and swirl it around with a bamboo whisk.

Pour out the water and let the wok dry on the burner.

Pour in a pint or two of oil and bring to a steady bubble.

Dip the fish pieces in the batter and then submerge a couple in the oil to harden the batter before removing.

Place the remaining battered fish in the oil and, after a few minutes, return the first batch. Cook until the batter is crisp and the fish has firmed to the touch.

Use a giant slotted spoon to remove the fish from the wok.

Place the fish pieces on the serving plate in their original configuration.

Garnish with roasted garlic, soy and sugar sauce, spring onions, sesame seeds and vegetables.

My tips.

Don't try to cook like this at home. The combination of jet-like flames, heat, noise and very hot oil seems just too risky!

Prawn dish.

Make a smooth sauce of fish sauce, chilli, soy sauce, sugar and some fragrant oil.

Add oil to coat the wok at a temperature that makes the oil crackle and the gas roar.

Add the prepared prawns and toss so they don't stick together.

Add sliced onions, dried chillies and whole cloves of black garlic.

Add the sauce and chopped coriander.

The flames will spread inside the edges of the wok so that everything caramelises.

Arrange on serving plate.

Publicity shot of First Officer Women's Royal Naval Service having become the first Navy woman called to the Bar – with the Old Bailey in the background (London, UK 1989).

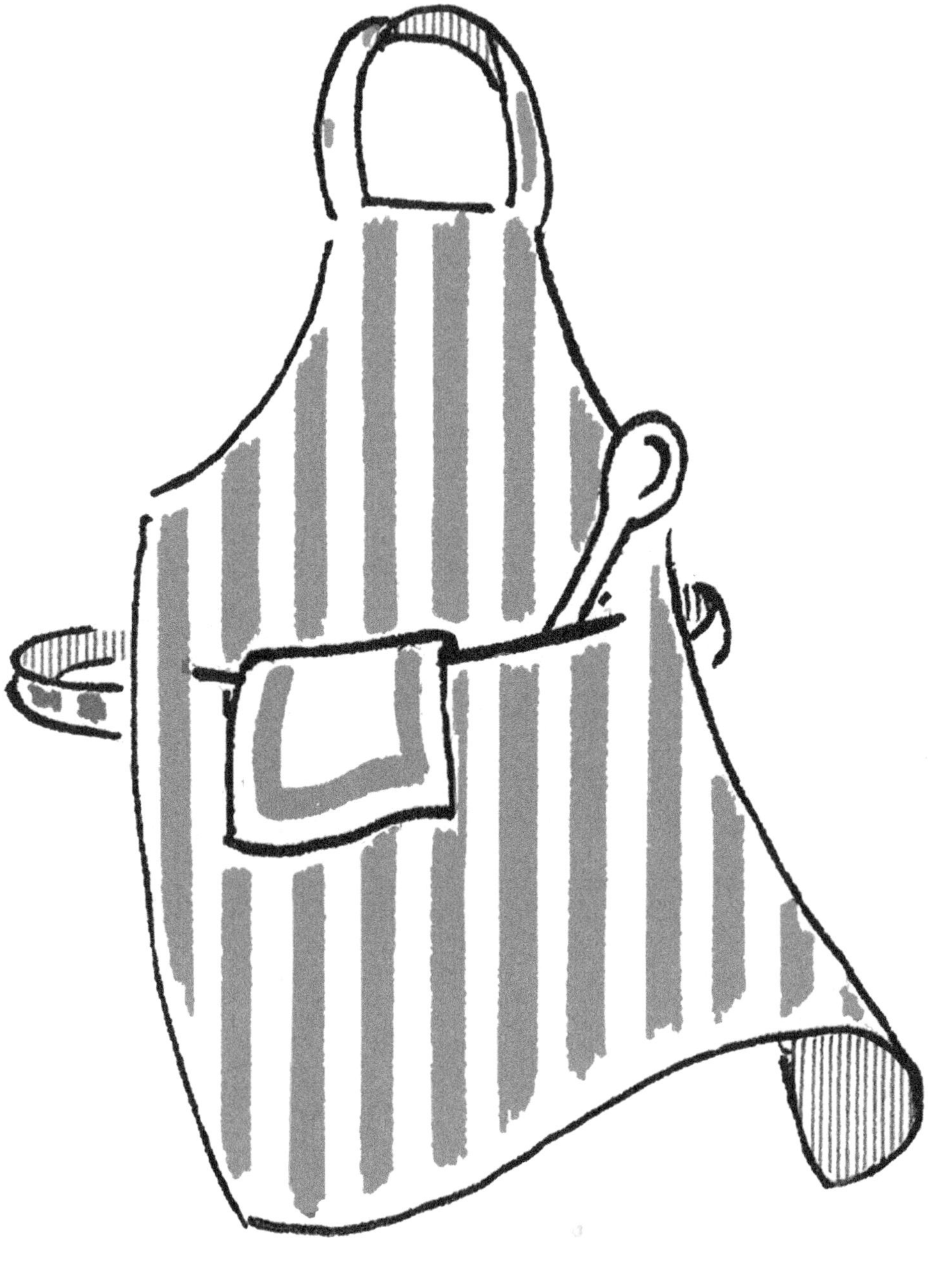

Toby's Baking Blind logo inspired by the aprons made by my mother (and which became the basis of the pewter apron "medals" I made and presented to thank the hosts, chefs and cooks throughout the tour).

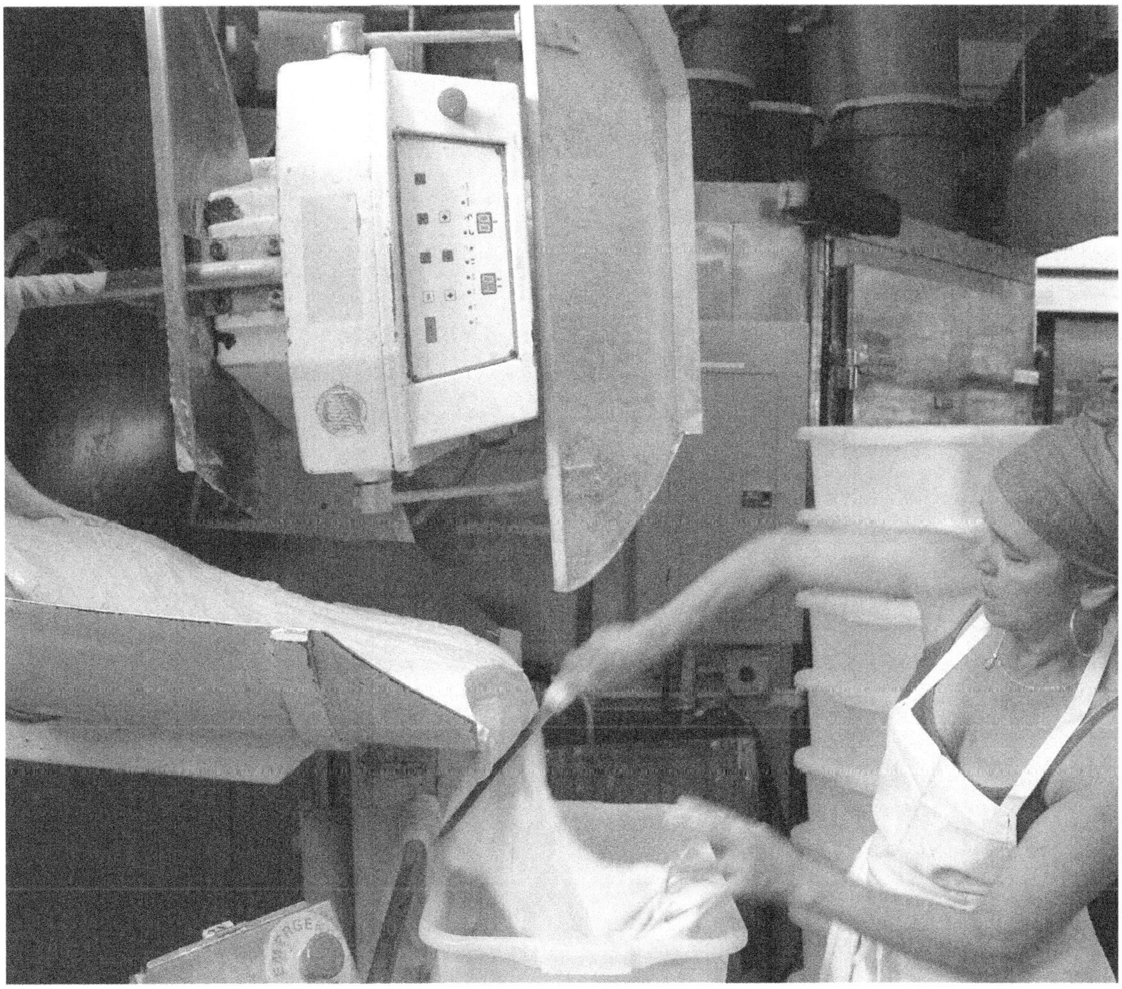

Tina making sourdough on the grand scale at California's famous Cheeseboard Collective (Berkeley, USA).

Noam in his original HIR fine dining kitchen, preparing to serve guests seated outside around the table amidst the rain-soaked jungle (Tamarindo, Costa Rica).

Celebrating 100 years of women in the British navy with some who served in the WRNS and others now in the Royal Navy (Virginia Beach, USA).

Toby's "Tower" illustration capturing impressions of Chongqing and other locations in China.

International School pupils laughing with strange ancient woman who is trying to tell them about cooking without sight (Chongqing, China).

Chef Fred explaining authentic indigenous bush tucker (near Seven Mile Beach, Australia).

Strange blind woman entertains local villagers with her odd cooking attempts (near Lilongwe, Malawi).

International music star, Lazarus playing his guitar (Lilongwe, Malawi).

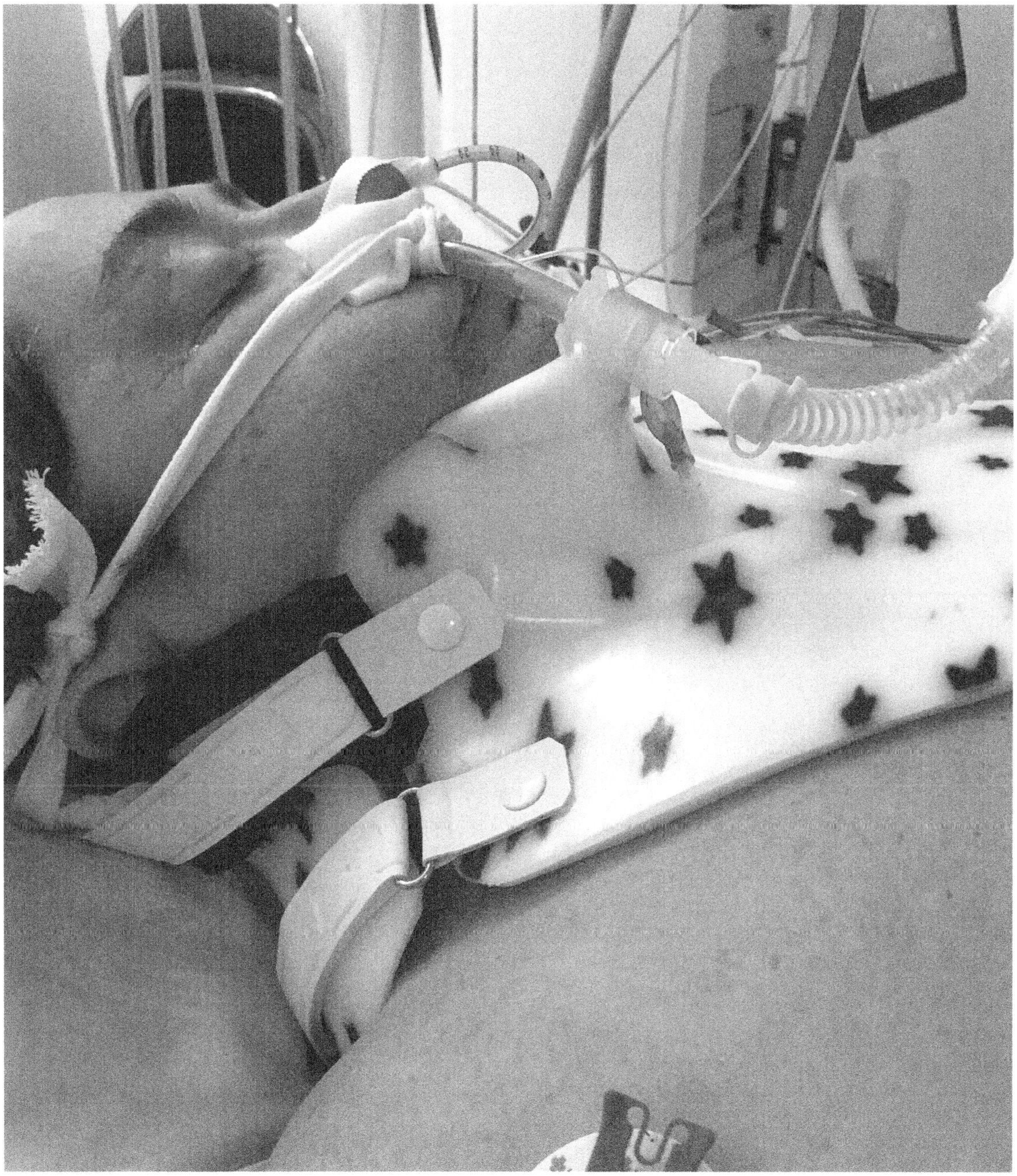

Surviving multiple fractures and other injuries in the Intensive Care unit, intubated and in an induced coma (Angers, France).

Addressing the great and good of California's business and voluntary sectors at the LightHouse gala dinner (San Francisco, USA).

Chapter 14.

The sounds of Chongqing.

Indomitable Julia was the great organiser and translator throughout our time in China. Her generosity was unstinting as she sacrificed a whole working week to us. Hence, it was especially good to get a better understanding of the architectural work that she and her husband, Matthew, had been undertaking in this city that is changing so fast. And the contrast couldn't have been starker. They took us to a building site on the very top of the Yangtse gorge, concrete, glass and steel rising from the ground as the city creates new work and living space. But underground was a different matter. We gingerly stepped through an old building in the early stages of redevelopment to discover hidden depths.

Over the millennia, the Yangtze River has deposited huge quantities of silt across the ancient flood plains, before cutting the new gorge channel through the resulting layers. Time has that mass of sediment into the mudstone on which Chongqing is built: crumbly and granular rock that forms the foundation of the city. Underground is a network of tunnels and caves dug into the soft rock that were used as bomb shelters by the citizens during the 1937-45 Sino-Japanese war. The Chinese capital was transferred to Chongqing during the hostilities, but still didn't escape attack.

I had some limited concept of how the life we know can be transformed by conflict. After Greenwich, I had moved on to my second job in the Royal Navy: war planning and home defence. We were still in the Cold War when nuclear strike was a real possibility. Along with the Army, police and other government departments, we were planning for the aftermath and how civil society might survive. I had my fill of surveillance facilities and underground bunkers.

In Chongqing, I was learning what life might have really been like as we walked down one of the tunnels, stumbling on the undulating floor, to reach a huge cavern where water dripped into a pool. At one time, this was a safe haven for hundreds, perhaps thousands, of terrified people. For me, there was a more positive experience: the echo which turned even my singing voice into mellifluous harmony. Matthew and I sang an impromptu be-bop duet that sounded fabulous. The first time in my life I had sung and enjoyed the sound! It was very difficult to leave and relinquish that moment of illusory magnificent vocal achievement.

But next step was Charlie's backpacker hostel crouched high on the very edge of the gorge. We walked down a narrow alley and branched off into another that wasn't wide enough for two abreast. I put out my hands to feel the mudstone on my right looming above us, embedded with the sinuous roots of trees growing on the surface way above our heads. On the left side there were the fences and gates to homes perched over the gorge, festooned with red painted slogans declaring people were in residence to dissuade house-grabbers.

Charlie's hostel is literally built on the side of the gorge. His living area and dining room were level with the alley, but steep concrete steps took us down to his kitchen tucked below, between the rock and the supports that prevented the whole edifice from tumbling down into the river. There was even a foot-high step in the tiny kitchen to accommodate the rapidly descending floor. His water tap was outside for washing up, and the kitchen corners were crammed with his ingredients. Charlie stood atop the step with his gas rings, while I humbly stayed below.

It would have been very easy to believe that modern Western style could have improved Charlie's kitchen. Perhaps an inside sink would have been more convenient; piped rather than bottled gas; a level kitchen floor and more. But all such standardisation and uniformity would have risked stripping away the patina of charm and originality lovingly built up over decades. In too many of the locations I visited there was such enthusiasm for the de-personalisation of steel and glass at the cost of lost personality, humanity and history.

Of course, a characterful cooking space needs to avoid sacrificing cleanliness, but this certainly wasn't the case here. Charlie explained his punctilious hygiene measures with the pork from his butcher: "I brought it home and washed the ribs twice in a colander under the running water. I marinaded the ribs in whisky for an hour, and then I washed them once more before placing them in the wok in a litre of simmering water." That wok was literally steam-cleaned before every use with a rinse of water evaporating over the hot burner. There was more cooking to follow, reducing the chances of any bugs surviving.

He was teaching me yet another version of sweet and sour pork ribs. After the simmering and another wok washout, he declared, "Some more fire!" and brought a little oil to sizzling point to brown the ribs. A good dash of vinegar was stirred through until that too had evaporated and the ribs were ready for what seemed to be light brown sugar. Charlie explained, "When you are doing this, you have to be very patient and you've got to turn the heat down when you put the sugar in." Sprinkles of salt and sesame seeds, plus a dash of his homemade vanilla sauce finished the dish. It bore no comparison with the sweet-and-sour pork I've experienced in the UK: battered pieces of meat with a fluorescently glutinous sauce. His ribs were tender but crisp, subtle and delicious – straightforward with a little time and care.

There were eight of us crammed into the tiny kitchen where Charlie stood atop his step, and I took up the suitably subservient sous-chef position below with the chopping board. For the next dish, I was consigned to slicing tomatoes and mushrooms, but did have time to do a short interview with local radio presenter Lancy. She aims to offer new ideas and wider horizons to her local listeners, and said, "My show is to introduce some interesting culture and interesting people (from within CQ, outside CQ and even outside China). We share music and culture together." Charlie was active in the cultural scene too, and his backpacker hostel, decorated by different artists, was the perfect alternative for anyone tired of super-sophisticated high-rise hotels.

Huwei offered a tip for the spare ribs: they should be more sweet than sour. Meanwhile, Charlie was combining some of the key Chongqing flavours of sesame oil, fresh ginger, garlic and star anise in a rich, succulent beef dish. Like any cook, he had his favourite gadget: his pressure cooker did excellent work in creating his "red-cooked beef" in minutes. And he too, like cooks anywhere, took care to find the best ingredients, saying, "I try to avoid buying beef that has a lot of water added to it. I can see that the beef has added water, because, when it is hanging on a hook, the water drips down. Although it tastes very soft, it isn't very good."

He was a marvellously generous, cheerful and thoughtful host. Toby and I were very touched when he presented each of us with a bracelet of simple wooden beads to remember our time together, Toby's carved, mine blessed by monks. A precious moment of a very special day when food transcended barriers of disability, culture, language and more. Once we were working together, it was easy to communicate our shared enthusiasm and experiences. A true meeting of minds and a language that goes beyond words.

We were a happy though weary group that filed back down the narrow alleyway in the falling dusk to the city lights and noise, leaving Charlie to the tranquillity of his home until his next group of backpackers descended.

The next day was just as packed with people as Mei and her British husband, Michael, invited us to a farewell lunch with their Rotary Club friends. And Charlie was there too – resplendent in his business suit.

I had hoped that I would be able to help Mei a little in her kitchen in the spacious apartment overlooking wide lawns and gardens – I could hear the expansiveness from the vantage point of their extensive balcony – but Mei was in full flight as she juggled all the pots and pans, meat and vegetables to create a lunchtime feast. Julia, as always the great translator, managed to snatch some of the activity and tastes for me. "She's doing a million things," she said. "I'll have to go stage by stage."

Those stages were fast and frantic: boiling water being poured over a whole duck; two types of mushrooms; steamed fish; fried aubergines; beef and purple sweet potatoes and more. I tasted one of the wood ear mushrooms and the mouth-feel was just as you'd expect from their name – rather damp, ridged, fleshy and flexible.

I was a little smug having recognised some of the Mandarin vocabulary when Julia said, "This is Mei's version of the spare ribs that you cooked with Charlie." Like any other busy home cook, Mei had an easy way to remember her ingredient quantities for 500 grams of spare ribs: "Two spoonful's of soy sauce, three spoonful's of Chinese yellow wine, four spoonful's of sugar and five spoonful's of vinegar and some orange zest." Her method was simple too. All the ingredients went into a wok with the lid on and cooked until all the liquid had evaporated before a final topping of sesame seeds.

I learned more about some of the key ingredients:

- **Huajiao or Chongqing pepper.** This is much more lemony, pungent, subtle and flavoursome than black pepper. It makes your tongue feel as if it is fizzing.
- **Huangjiu**. Yellow Chinese rice wine which is 10% alcohol.

And a tip for pickling ginger: peel and slice before placing in a jar with water, salt, Chinese yellow wine and, perhaps, a little Chongqing pepper.

Mei continued in a flurry of activity, darting between her preparation and cooking areas until every detail of each dish was perfect and ready to be set before her expectant guests. It was an amazing spread of Chinese cuisine offering so many different tastes and textures – even those strange mushrooms. We laughed and talked, told stories, exchanged gifts and made speeches. The ultimate delight was Mei offering an impromptu recital of operatic arias. Retirement hasn't dulled the power or range of her voice. It was a stunning finale to the lunch and our time in Chongqing.

On our final day all that remained was to gather our thoughts and memories of the visit, throw our belongings into bags and get to the airport in time for the late night flight to Australia. And that's where a problem arose. The UK travel company that had arranged Toby's Australian visa had entered the wrong birth date. By the time we had realised the cause of the problem, with the unfailing help and kindness of the Chinese airport staff, our flight had flown. We were stranded at the huge Chongqing airport, with very little remaining Chinese currency, in the small hours of the night with nearly a whole day before another flight was even possible. Our only solution was to return to the hotel where we could crawl back into our beds.

The Intercontinental concierge spent virtually the whole of the next day finding a solution and, throughout all the trepidation and worry, the support of the hotel, Julia, Andrew and Maggie was unstinting as we all attempted to get through the bureaucracy of a new visa, new tickets, revised arrangements in Sydney, plus a little sleep. Thankfully, by the evening, we were back at the airport, cleared by immigration and embarked for the next long flight south to Sydney. I had to just suck up all the extra costs and be happy we were only 24 hours behind schedule.

My final impressions from Chongqing were to forget any myths about life in China being grey, the people being unfriendly, or the culture being stifled. Here life, like the thrum of the traffic and the 24-hour construction work, never stopped. I experienced everything from the woman sitting alongside her pavement display of antique coins to the dynamic optimism of high-rise living. Even at night the city sparkled with drama. Vast collections of buildings lit up with the mystery of Chinese calligraphy to fish darting from tower to tower. The whole experience reinforced my conviction that a common passion can overcome cultural differences, language difficulties and so much more.

Video: Baking Blind in Chongqing, China

Charlie's recipes.

Sweet and sour pork (pork spareribs with a vinegar and sugar sauce: spare ribs tangxxu paigau).

1 kilo spare ribs, chopped to 3cm pieces.
10g white Western wine or whisky.
1 star anise.
100g dark vinegar (Chinese rather than malt).
1-2 tablespoons vegetable oil.
100g white sugar.
5g sea salt.
10g sesame oil.
Toasted sesame seeds.

Method.

Rinse the spare ribs twice in cold water and drain.

Place the ribs in a bowl and mix with the wine or whisky to marinade for 30-60 minutes at room temperature.

Rinse the ribs in water, drain and place in wok with 1 litre of water and simmer.

Skim off any scum and, when the liquid is clear, add one star anise.

Add the vinegar and keep the pork and cooking liquid simmering and moving until all the liquid has evaporated (about 30-45 minutes).

Only fat should be running out of the pork. Drain the pork in a sieve.

Clean the wok and return to the heat with a little salad oil.

Return the ribs to the hot wok to cook for a minute, moving constantly to avoid sticking until golden brown.

Reduce the heat and add the sugar.

Patiently stir and cook for at least 10 minutes while the sugar dissolves and coats the ribs and any remaining liquid evaporates.

Add the salt and sesame oil before serving, sprinkled with the sesame seeds.

My tips.

Charlie seemed to add more vinegar to adjust the flavour once the spare ribs had been fried and cooked until it evaporated. He also added his own vanilla sauce: a mix of vanilla, sugar and water.

Video: Charlie beef CQ

Red-cooked beef.

Video: Red cooked beef

At least 500g beef (I've guessed the weight and cut).
1 or 2 carrots, peeled.
A handful of green vegetables: cabbage, broccoli or similar.
2 tablespoons Chinese yellow rice wine (or whisky).
3-4 spring onions, peeled and chopped.
200g sesame oil.
1 clove garlic, sliced in half.
1 slice fresh root ginger.
2 bay leaves, stalk removed and torn.
1 star anise.
1 litre water.
1kg tomatoes, chopped.
500g mushrooms, chopped.
20g dark soy sauce.
10g salt.
500ml chicken stock.

Method.

Cut the beef (possibly fillet) into 3cm thick slices and cut each into 6cm strips.

Add chopped carrot and green vegetables to the meat.

Massage meat and vegetables in Chinese wine (although Charlie thought whisky would be better).

Add chopped spring onions.

Marinate overnight.

Next day, heat pan and add 200g sesame oil.

Add one whole clove of garlic, a slice of ginger, a couple of torn bay leaves and a star anise to flavour the oil and fry on a moderate heat until they can be smelled.

Increase the heat and add the beef and the vegetables.

Stir fry on a moderate heat (not sizzling) for about 5 minutes.

Remove from the heat and transfer only the beef and cooking liquid to a pan with 1 litre of spring water.

Simmer for 90 minutes or pressure cook for 12 minutes.

Meanwhile, chop up 1kg of tomatoes and 500g of mushrooms.

Return the beef and cooking liquid plus the tomatoes and mushrooms to the wok.

Cook for 5 minutes.

Add 20g dark soy sauce, 10g salt, 500ml chicken stock and bring all to a short simmer.

Chicken and prawn soup stock.

1 chicken carcass including giblets.
1 onion, peeled and roughly chopped.
1-2 carrots, peeled and roughly chopped.
1 stalk celery, roughly chopped.
Any other vegetable pieces or trimmings, roughly chopped.
10 whole prawns, peeled and de-veined.
1 tablespoon sesame oil.

Method.

Fry or roast the chicken carcass, giblets, onions and vegetables.

Cover with water and gently simmer for 4 hours to reduce the liquid.

Meanwhile, remove the heads and tails from 10 prawns, shells on but de-veined, and briefly fry in a little sesame oil.

Place the prawns in a pan and cover with spring water before simmering until cooked.

De-shell the prawns and blend the flesh with the cooking water.

Add to chicken stock as a good base for soups.

Chill in the fridge and reheat before using, or freeze for up to a month.

Mei's Chinese lunch feast.

Video: Chinese feast by Mei

Wood ear mushroom salad.

Eating the fungi felt like biting someone's damp ear. This should be a very simple dish and is prepared quickly. Note: I have had to estimate the ingredients for each dish but the methods are direct from Mei.

About 500g wood ear mushrooms.
About 2cm fresh root ginger, peeled and finely chopped.
Half a red pepper, de-seeded and finely chopped.
1 teaspoon Chongqing pepper, ground.
1 tablespoon sesame oil.
1 tablespoon oyster sauce.
1 tablespoon Chinese yellow rice wine.
About 1cm fresh root ginger, peeled and finely sliced.
About one quarter red pepper, de-seeded and finely sliced.

Method.

Wash the mushrooms in a little water and keep their shape.

Place the mushrooms in a bowl with chopped ginger and dress with finely chopped red pepper.

Place the bowl of fungi and dressing in a steamer and cook for about 7 minutes.

Remove any water from the bowl.

Heat Chongqing pepper, sesame oil, oyster sauce and Chinese yellow wine together in a wok and use to dress the mushrooms.

Garnish the mushroom salad with strips of fresh ginger and red pepper.

Marinaded and steamed beef.

About 500g fillet of beef.
1 tablespoon dark soy sauce.
1 tablespoon sugar.
1 teaspoon Chongqing pepper, ground.
2cm fresh root ginger, finely shredded.
2 spring onions, peeled and finely chopped.
1-2 tablespoons Chinese yellow rice wine.
2-3 tablespoons glutenous rice (or plain) flour.
Half teaspoon Chongqing pepper, ground.
500g red (or sweet) potatoes.
2 spring onions, finely chopped.

Method.

Cut fillet beef into chunks and marinate in soy sauce, sugar, Chongqing pepper (or a little chilli), grated fresh root ginger, chopped spring onion and a little yellow Chinese wine for at least 1 hour.

Lightly cover the mixture (especially the beef) with glutinous rice flour seasoned with Chongqing pepper (plain flour might replace the rice flour).

Place the bowl into a steamer for 2 hours.

The beef is then cooked with purple potatoes that are much sweeter than white potatoes (sweet potatoes might be used instead).

Serve with the beef on top of the potatoes, garnished with very finely diced spring onion.

There is not too much chilli in this dish so that the beef and potato flavours still come through.

Duck dish.

1 whole duck, plucked (head and feet removed for the squeamish).
2 tablespoons olive oil.
1 teaspoon Chongqing pepper, ground.
2cm fresh root ginger, roughly chopped.
1 tablespoon chilli sauce (preferably homemade).
2 tablespoons Chinese yellow rice wine.
3-4 tablespoons dried yellow soya beans, soaked overnight.

Method.

Pour boiling water over a newly killed and plucked duck then allow to dry.

Remove the intestines and organs from the duck and clean, then roughly chop the duck carcass into pieces leaving the skin on and the bone in.

Put olive oil in a large saucepan and add some Chongqing pepper, ginger, plus some homemade chilli sauce (quite sour and made by Mei's sister).

Heat the ingredients in the pan until the flavour can be smelled.

Add the duck pieces to the pan and fry for 2 or 3 minutes, until brown on all sides.

Remove the duck.

Place the duck pieces in a pan of simmering water with a little rice wine and dried yellow soya beans that have been soaked overnight.

The liquid just needs to cover the duck but add more water if it becomes dry.

Simmer for 2 hours – or longer if the duck is older – until duck is very soft.

Needle mushroom salad (jingzheng gu).

A different sort of white and rather stringy mushroom that is often part of a classic Chongqing hotpot.

About 500g needle mushrooms.
2-3 tablespoons chilli sauce.

Method.

Steam the mushrooms for a short time as they can cook quickly.

Serve the golden fungi with a sauce that is hot with peppers, quite sour and savoury.

Whole sea bass.

1 whole sea bass (at least 500g), guts removed.
3cm fresh root ginger, finely chopped.
1 cup Chinese yellow rice wine.
1 teaspoon fish sauce.
1 tablespoon oil.
1 teaspoon sugar.
1 leek, peeled and cut into fine strands.
2 tablespoons olive oil.
1 tablespoon oil.
2 teaspoons sweet potato (or corn) flour.
Drizzle olive oil.
Drizzle oyster sauce.
Sprinkle Chongqing pepper, ground.

Method.

Wash and remove the guts of the whole fish then cut slashes in the flesh.

Place in a bowl and marinade briefly in slivers of ginger, a good cupful of yellow Chinese wine and seafood-flavoured oil (like fish sauce in oil but rather sweeter).

Cover the fish with strands of cut leek.

Pour a little olive oil over the fish and leek.

Place the bowl in a steamer and cook.

Remove the bowl and fish from the steamer.

Heat some oil in a wok and add the liquid from the bowl.

Add a little sweet potato flour in water to slightly thicken (cornflour might be used instead).

Dress the fish with a little more olive oil, oyster sauce and more Chongqing pepper.

Pour the sauce from the wok over the fish.

Fried aubergines.

2 medium aubergines, washed.
2 tablespoons sweet potato (or corn) flour.
1 tablespoon sweet potato (or corn) flour for dusting.
Olive oil.

Method.

Cut the aubergines into irregular three-sided pieces with one side skin on.

Make a paste of red sweet potato flour dissolved in a little water and coat the aubergine pieces, giving them a sticky finish (plain flour might be the closest alternative).

Dust the pieces with more potato flour and a pinch of salt. (The flour prevents the aubergine soaking up too much oil when fried.)

Fry in olive oil.

Pork spare ribs.

500g pork spare ribs, chopped into 2-3cm pieces.
Half orange, zest only.
1 teaspoon Chongqing pepper, ground.
2-3cm fresh root ginger, peeled and finely chopped.
2 spring onions, peeled and finely chopped.
2 tablespoons dark soy sauce.
3 tablespoons Chinese yellow rice wine.
4 tablespoons sugar.
5 tablespoons vinegar.
2 tablespoons olive oil.
More sugar/vinegar to taste.
1 flat tablespoon sesame seeds.

Method.

Marinade 500g chopped pork spare ribs for 2 hours with zest of about half an orange, slithers of fresh root ginger, 2 chopped spring onions, Chongqing pepper, 2 tablespoons soy sauce, 3 tablespoons Chinese yellow wine, 4 tablespoons sugar, 5 tablespoons vinegar.

Heat the wok until smoking and add a little olive oil.

Add the ribs and marinade to the wok.

Bring to a gentle simmer and cover.

Cook until all the liquid has evaporated.

Adjust the sweetness/sourness to taste.

Decorate with sesame seeds.

Fatty pork (yan jianrou: a traditional Chongqing dish).

This pork is only 5% lean (the rest is fat) and nearly frozen so that it can be sliced very thinly (like bacon).

2 tablespoons olive oil.
2 teaspoons Chongqing pepper.
3cm fresh root ginger, finely sliced.
About 250-500g fatty pork, finely sliced.
2-3 tablespoons black fermented soya beans.
1 leek, washed.

Method.

Heat oil in a wok and add whole Chongqing peppers and ginger.

Mix in the meat to fry until it is brown, then add black fermented soya beans.

Cut long diagonal pieces (2 inches long and about half an inch wide) of the white end of a leek and even thinner pieces of the green part of the leek and add to the wok.

Continue cooking until the leek is just softened.

Chapter 15.

Hello, Kiama.

At last, after all the delays, we arrived safe and sound in Sydney and were met by Ken and Rosemary, our hosts for the first part of our Australian tour. She and I first met many years ago when she was working for the then St Dunstan's Organisation (now Blind Veterans UK). I was one of the UK's delegates to the European and World Blind unions, and she had rather madly volunteered to support me during an EBU conference week in Athens. That's another whole story, but it was a true meeting of minds over shopping, good food and great fun: peach schnapps, fish cooked in an anise liqueur, breakfast of Greek yoghurt topped with walnuts and dive-bombed with cherries, plus lots of leather (red shoes and handbags, a peach jacket for her and electric-blue cape for me), boxes and boxes of crystallised fruit dipped in chocolate for friends, and drinking coffee with the jeweller while a pair of earrings were being adjusted. The conference clearly made rather less of an impression, although I still play the CD of Greek music each delegate was given. We have kept in touch over the intervening years, and I'd briefly met her new husband, Ken, before she and I spent a week cooking near Perugia in Umbria, Italy – another story culminating with a huge tin of home-produced olive oil that I crammed into my suitcase.

Now was my first chance to visit their new home in Kiama, a couple of hours' drive from Sydney. This was a small seaside town where the 8,000 inhabitants are regularly expanded with the tourist seasonal influx.

Video: Hello Kiama

Ken and Rosemary had already made the trip the previous day to meet our original aborted flight and seen their meticulously planned schedule for our few days crumble. Rosemary's no slouch, but a woman of indomitable organisation: she promptly reshuffled all the players, our fixtures list and all her menus.

Ardent and practical Christians, she and Ken had specifically designed their new home to offer a recuperative retreat to ministers seeking a break from their responsibilities. Toby and I had our own bedrooms, bathroom and living room in a separate section of the house alongside the communal kitchen so that we all had separate spaces to work and relax.

The rest of that first day was spent decompressing from the drama of the flight from Chongqing. We explored the rocky coastline, where Toby was chilled to the bone swimming in a natural seawater pool, and I was thrilled to hear the thump and cascade of the great wave-driven water spout. Every minute or so, the waves drive under the rocks and are forced through a hole to spout a jet about 20 metres into the air. The sheer force creates a shuddering boom as the ocean strikes the land and, then, the high cascade slaps down onto the rocks to drain away. The original indigenous people have lived in the area for over 17,000 years and gave it the name Kiama (meaning "the place where the sea makes a noise"), reflecting the blow-hole sound that has continued throughout those millennia. It makes modern civilisation feel rather like a flash in the pan!

The name Kiama is lost more in translation when pronounced as "key armour" by the digitally electronic voice of my screen reader rather than the more correct "ky ammer." By the time I arrived there, my mispronunciation was so embedded that it was easier never to mention the town by name at all.

From their home on the outskirts, Ken and Rosemary were close to the lush undulating countryside. We walked through the green fields, fed friendly horses, and were amazed by huge, contorted trees. Beyond us, the landscape kept rising through more hills to the distant mountains. This was very much farming country, symbolised by the life-size and highly decorated fibre-glass cow in the town centre. The small houses, nestled amidst the peaceful pastoral landscape, were a stark contrast to the non-stop vibrancy and noise of the teeming Chongqing metropolis.

Thanks to Rosemary's careful arrangements, next day the delayed Baking Blind Show was back on the road with award winning cook, Jo, resplendent with medals around her neck, supported by Jennifer and Gemma, fellow members of the Country Women's Association of New South Wales – the Down Under version of the Women's Institute with equal reputation for home cooking. I was especially keen to learn all about Jo's "lemonade scones" for which, she explained, the CWA is famous: "I think that most people in Australia relate scones back to CWA. It just seems to be scones, jam and cream. CWA. If we're marching in a parade, they say, 'Where are your scones?' At the Royal Easter Show, which is our big agricultural show, there were up to about 53,000 scones that they'd baked between 10 days and two weeks."

The scones were simple in their ingredients: self-raising flour, cream and lemonade. She was even more adventurous, saying, "You can use any soft drink. You can go with Fanta, which gives it a slightly orange flavour and an orange look. Or you could use ginger beer for a gingery tinge. I've used Coca Cola or Pepsi. It's the carbonation that brings it to life and gives it a little flavour. It doesn't overwhelm the scones, it just changes the look of them."

Cooking alongside Jo was a delight. Her passion, knowledge and great sense of humour were exactly what I'd expect from a completely confident and super-competent cook. We laughed all morning and invented new recipes on the spot: How about beer in place of lemonade to make scones for a ploughman's lunch; I've since used sparkling wine to make a cream tea even more deluxe. The variations could be as endless as there are carbonated drinks in the world!

If the ingredients were simple, it was Jo's expertise that made the difference. Her understanding of how the dough should feel and be handled produced prize-winning results. It's the crucial step beyond just following a recipe by adapting to different ingredients, ovens, weather conditions and much more. She didn't even bother to measure out the cream, but added half the tub to bring the mix together before plopping it out onto the floured work surface. Some more flour on top and she gave me the next instructions:

"We're going to fold it in on top of itself and pick up a bit of flour at the same time. And keep doing that until it comes together. When you press your finger in now, it won't stick to the mixture. When you pat it down, if you haven't got enough flour in, it starts spreading. So, when it stays still, you know that you've got just enough flour. And you haven't worked it too much so it won't be a tough scone. It should be beautiful and soft when we cut them out. Because I normally cook them for show cooking, I want them to be presented quite nicely, so not to be falling over or looking like they've been chewed up and put on the tray."

We dipped the cutter in the leftover flour, cut out each scone with a smooth down-and-straight-up action, before peeling away the spare dough for re-use. After ten minutes in the oven, from being just under two fingers thick, they'd doubled in size. And Jo had her next prize tip: "Once I'd got the scones out of the oven, I popped them into the colander in a tea towel so that they'd stay nice and soft. They haven't gone hard on the outside."

Once the remainder of the cream had been whipped, the scones were ready for judgement by her CWA colleagues. It was even more daunting when Gemma revealed, "I've been a pastry chef for six years now." And Jennifer showed her expertise too, explaining, "Pull it in half. You shouldn't need to cut a good scone."

In addition to running her own business, Sweetwood Cakes, Jo's claim to fame had appeared in every home in her town of Milton: the front cover of the phone directory featured her and her classic basic chocolate cake, which was my next lesson. "This one is normally for birthday cakes," Jo said. "I use the cake for cake pops. It's like a little ball of cake on a stick that you cover in chocolate, and then you can put sprinkles and things on. Kids love them. And I use this recipe for cupcakes as well." Again, it was very straightforward: heating some of the ingredients in a pan and, once cooled, pouring onto the whisked flour and eggs before transferring the thick sauce to the baking tin and into the oven.

This CWA trio were far beyond me in terms of skill and experience, but unstintingly generous in sharing their time and knowledge. As they left, Jo promised me more recipes, which quickly dropped into my inbox. Great cooks just love to pass on their triumphs.

Jo's recipes.

Lemonade scones.

Video: Lemonade scones

670g self-raising flour.
300ml cream.
375ml lemonade.

Method.

Preheat the oven to 220C, Gas 7, 430F.

Sift the flour into a large bowl, add the cream and lemonade, mix lightly with a knife to form a ball of dough. Don't overwork the dough or knead it.

Turn the dough out onto a very lightly floured board and pat it out until it is about 2 fingers (2.5cm) thick.

Using a round 5cm cutter, press straight down and pull straight up for each scone. Cut several and then gently ease away the remaining dough for re-patting and cutting a total of about 20 scones.

Place the scones on a baking tray, fairly close together.

Bake the scones for about 10 minutes, until golden brown.

Remove scones from tray, brush off any surplus flour and place in a colander lined with a tea towel and fold the towel over them to keep the scones soft.

My tips.

I used half a bottle of sparkling Chardonnay wine instead of lemonade, with good results. I divided the dough in half and added a couple of tablespoons of horseradish sauce and lots of chopped fresh dill, plus a little extra flour to the remaining dough for savoury scones fit for a smoked salmon mousse or similar. These scones took a little longer to cook as they were slightly wetter. For all these scones, I cooked them at Gas 7 and rotated after about 10 minutes and then gave them another couple of minutes. Another alternative would be replacing the lemonade with beer, and perhaps adding cheese to the scones too.

Chocolate cake.

Video: Chocolate cake

240ml water.
120g sugar.
125g butter.
2 tablespoons cocoa.
Half teaspoon bicarbonate of soda (or baking powder).
180g self-raising flour.
2 eggs, beaten.

Method.

In a large pan, mix the water, sugar, butter, cocoa and bicarbonate of soda together and bring to the boil. Leave to cool.

Once cooled, add the flour and the eggs. Fold together until all ingredients are combined.

Pour into a lined 20cm round cake tin and bake at 180C, Gas 4, 350F for 40 minutes, or until a skewer comes out clean.

Turn upside down onto a cooling rack.

Caramel mud cake.

250g unsalted butter.
200g white chocolate.
270g brown sugar.
360ml water.
2 teaspoons vanilla essence.
3 eggs, beaten.
240g plain flour, sifted.
60g self-raising flour, sifted.

Method.

Place the chocolate, butter, sugar and water in a small saucepan over low heat. Whisk until sugar is dissolved and chocolate is melted. Allow to cool (at least 1-2 hours).

Preheat the oven to 165C, Gas 3, 330F. Lightly grease and line the bottom of a 22cm round or square tin.

Whisk in vanilla and eggs. Slowly mix in flours.

Pour into tin. Bake for 100-120 minutes. Place a loose piece of foil over the top to prevent browning.

Chocolate mud cake.

250g butter.
150g dark chocolate pieces.
240g white sugar.
240ml hot water.
70ml whisky.
1 tablespoon instant coffee powder/granules.
180g plain flour.
30g self-raising flour.
30g cocoa.
2 eggs, beaten.

Method.

Place all the ingredients (except the flours, cocoa and eggs) in a bowl and melt over a pan of boiling water, ensuring that the water doesn't touch the bowl.

Allow to cool for at least an hour.

Preheat the oven to 165C, Gas 3, 330F. Lightly grease and line the bottom of a 22cm round or square tin.

Fold in the flours and cocoa followed by the eggs.

Pour into the prepared 22cm tin and cook for about 90-120 minutes. Cover with a sheet of foil if cooking too quickly on top. As long as the cake doesn't sink in the middle when touched, it should be done.

Chapter 16.

High drama.

What could possibly go wrong? There we were, in a peaceful seaside town surrounded by bucolic countryside, and delightedly anticipating learning about indigenous bush tucker with chef Fred (www.fredsbushtucker.com.au).

It all started simply enough, as we bought a large snapper fish en route to the local scrubland park area to rendezvous with him. The picnic area had all the essentials: tables and benches plus the ubiquitous barbecue. All we needed was our star, who arrived full of mischievous laughter. He loped along, slightly one-sided due to a long-term back injury, with the support of his Blackwood stick gathered direct from the bush.

He'd brought an armful of plant material and said, "We wrap the fish in paperbark. Straight on the fish and it is going to stick to the skin while it's cooking. We use this like indigenous baking paper." But I think he was rather tongue-in-cheek when he explained its origin: "I got it up in Woolagong, near the steel works there, so it's going to have that extra smoky flavour through it." Of course, bark will tend to burn over fire so our first step was to give it a good ten-minute soaking, weighed down in the bucket of water with a handy stone. Paperbark is a bush material with many other uses, as Fred explained: "You can use it for thatchings on rooves because it's really waterproof."

He gave me a handful of leaves, confirming my guess of lemon myrtle from the citrus scent, saying, "It sure is. Now grind the leaf up a bit to get the oils out of it. Give it a good scrunch up and then have a smell. Amazing, isn't it? I'm going to put it into the fish. You can use it for anything you use lemon for." He added another handful of river mint to the cavity and the fish was ready for its paperbark wrapping.

Next came the outer layer of Guyanian lily leaves. These are huge, succulent boat-shaped leaves. One could easily contain the whole fish. I just needed to do a little trimming with Fred's handy axe, which meant everyone kept their hands well away from my swinging blade!

Tied up with strong strands of paperbark, the whole parcel would retain the smoke and moisture as the fish cooked for about 30 minutes on the barbecue.

While we waited, Fred showed me more wonders of his bush supermarket. I'd already heard of wattle trees and using their seeds in desserts, but didn't know that they could help catch fish too! "There are plenty of different varieties around," Fred said. "With one of the varieties, possibly like this one, you can grind the leaves up. If you've got a fish pond or a fish trap out in the river where the fish are gathered, then you can drop some of this stuff in the water. Then the fish all float to the surface. Not dead, it's not a poison, it just takes the oxygen out of the water."

Once you've caught the fish, you need a handy basket to carry them in, and Fred had just the plant: "This stuff's called lamandra. It's like a spiny grass. There are plenty of uses for this one plant." With three of the grass strands clenched between my teeth, he showed me how to plait them. Now I had a simple bracelet, or the beginnings of that basket, plus something to eat. "The succulent base of the grass is a bit like rhubarb," Fred said. "It's full of starch and carbohydrates." There was more food in the flower head. "When they're dried," he continued, "you can get all the seeds out and grind them down on a rock, or with a mortar and pestle, and you have flour." Mixed with a little water, the flour makes a simple flat bread to be cooked on a stone in the fire.

Banksia flowers help with the fire. The flowers are huge, providing high-energy sugar for birds, bees and humans. The dried flower seed heads are enormous, smooth and tactile, and packed with natural oils. "If you're the cook in the camp, and you've got to go to another campsite, you can put this in the fire. It'll stay cold and won't catch on fire. It will keep alight for two to three hours. Carry it to the next campsite and, that way, you don't have to light the fire up." With lamandra baskets full of your firelighter and the fish, you arrive at the next camp ready to cook a hot meal without a scrap of ecological damage or debris. And no hunting for two Boy Scouts to rub sticks together either!

"This is Tasmanian mountain pepper. You only need a little bit. It's a small berry," Fred then explained as he showed me something very similar to a familiar peppercorn. He was very emphatic that it wouldn't be too hot but, as soon as it was on my tongue, he laughed and said, "No, not to begin with!"

As an expert forager in his "bush supermarket" Fred cautioned: "With the animals, if it moves, you eat it. With the plants, you can eat a lot of them, but there's one way you can make sure of things, especially with berries. If people are unsure about which berries you can eat, there's a couple of rules. There's the colour: if it's red, that usually means bad. Although when you think of strawberries and raspberries, that rule doesn't count all the way. Another one is: if the birds are eating it, it's a pretty good sign you're going to be OK. And the next way is: if you grab the berry, you put a bit of juice on the soft part of your wrist. If it starts swelling up or it's itchy, don't eat it. If you're still not sure, put a bit on the inside of your lip and, if it starts swelling up or going numb, and if you want to go any further than that, run for your life."

While I'd been learning just the tiniest bit of his whole life's knowledge, the snapper fish had been cooking. It was a very large hot parcel for Fred to manhandle to the picnic table, and not without difficulty. On a campfire, it might have been slid out onto the adjacent rocks. The fish was triumphantly unveiled, moist and succulent, fragrant and flavourful. It proved that cooking "en papillote" succeeds in nearly any situation. Fred and I nibbled on the fish, sipped our cordial made from citrus-flavoured lilly pilly berries, and put the world to rights.

Toby and another friend sloped off after the busy morning to swim on the nearby beach and, once we had helped Fred clear up, Ken, Rosemary and I drove down to pick them up. As we came to a halt, a police car arrived, with the officer asking if we had called for help. We hadn't, but I had a horrible feeling I knew who was involved. More police cars were arriving as we stepped onto the boarded walkway over the sand, and it quickly became clear that there were two swimmers far out and in difficulty. The beach was deserted, so it didn't take long for Ken to confirm that the pile of clothing belonged to Toby and his pal. Rosemary assured me that she could see two heads above the water before she went off to get more information. This was Seven Mile Beach, and nearly deserted apart from a girl who had been walking her dog. She'd spotted the swimmers in distress and her father promptly called the emergency services.

More people were arriving. A total of four police cars with their crews, two paramedic units and two rescue surfers. It was clear to me that the last thing any of them needed was a blind person blundering around on the sand in their midst. I managed to give someone the basic details of the swimmers but, otherwise, could only stand and wait. Thank heavens for the man from Cumbria who came up to me as I was struggling to keep calm, clinging onto the handrail. There was no one else to give me a running commentary on the drama that was unfolding. I was surrounded by sounds: the crashing sea, the hubbub of the emergency people, the deep throbs of the first and then second helicopters arriving. I was horrified by the prospect of having to tell my brother, Christopher, if anything happened to Toby.

That anonymous commentator from Cumbria was invaluable. He described how the first rescue surfer was in the water and had reached the distant duo so that they could be supported by his surfboard. He was quickly followed by the second rescue surfer, who pulled one of the rapidly tiring swimmers onto his board and started back to shore. Meanwhile, Toby and the original rescuer were sitting astride their board and paddling towards the beach. Throughout, the helicopters kept station above, using their downdraft to blow the boards ashore and counter the sea currents. It all took about half an hour, but it seemed far longer, before two very cold swimmers were trudging up the beach, swaddled in towels and space blankets to recover their body temperatures. My lasting impression from the damp, goose-bumped skin protruding from their padded and foil-wrapped bodies was of a couple of oven-ready chickens.

Video: Bush supermarket plus near death

We all trooped back to the ambulances, where their vital signs could be checked, wet costumes removed and thankful hugs exchanged. It was quickly clear that they had been simply playing in the surf when a rip current had swept them out to sea, 300 yards in seconds, and they didn't have the strength to get back. Even in November, the sea was bitterly cold, and staying afloat had been difficult. Toby had been a star, using a buddy system to support his flagging companion, who had already experienced the warm welcoming stupor enticing him to end resistance to the fatal conditions. He recognised that within another few minutes he would have succumbed and drowned.

But we hadn't even considered the other key threat: the paramedics handed out shark attack images. The thought had never crossed my mind throughout that beach sojourn. A year later we heard that a man had indeed been attacked on that very Seven Mile Beach.

Video: https://www.abc.net.au/news/2018-11-17/shark-attack-at-gerroa-nsw-south-coast-man-hospitalised/10507750.

Toby and pal had managed a double victory although, a year later, we paid the price when a bill for over $500 from the emergency services arrived. They were worth every cent.

It was a cold, bruised and battered group that returned to the peace of Kiama for restorative hot showers and sleep. The huge irony was that, after all my efforts to promote the Baking Blind tour, it was the rescue that made the national television news that evening. Having previously linked up with the local media, a fleet-of-foot reporter had recognised us on the beach and captured the drama on video. The coverage helped us realise just how lucky we had been, how close to disaster, but that we could probably survive any future setbacks.

Fred's barbecued snapper recipe.

Video: Barbecued snapper

If you plan to use a river fish, first find the right type of wattle tree and collect the fruits. Create a fish trap in the river by damming it on either side of your fishing ground. Throw the wattle berries in the water and the fish should rise to the surface as the water becomes de-oxygenated. Scoop out fish. Or be rather more boring and buy from supermarket!

1 large snapper fish, cleaned.
Armful of paperbark (melaleuca).
2 large Guyanian lily leaves.
Handful of lemon myrtle.
Handful of river mint.

Method.

Soak the paperbark in water for 10-20 minutes.

Place the myrtle and mint in the fish cavity.

Wrap the fish in the soaked paperbark.

Using a handy axe, chop the lily leaves to size.

Enclose the fish parcel in the lily leaves and tie the parcel together with remaining paperbark.

Place the parcel on a hot barbecue and close the lid. Cook for about 15 minutes.

Serve hot on the perfectly shaped lily leaf platters.

Chapter 17.

Enabled cooking.

It was a rather subdued band that made the return journey to Sydney the following day. Emotional exhaustion, some delayed shock and bruised bodies all contributed to a less than high octane atmosphere. But we were due to spend the morning cooking with blind professional chef, Martin, who was inviting us into his home on a precious Saturday to demonstrate his recipes. The show had to go on.

The familiar rhythm of recording our recipes was comforting and soothing, much strengthened by the generous welcome from Martin and his family. We were there to do a job, fulfil our commitments and capture Martin's own achievements. And, as he described himself, those achievements were considerable: "By trade, I'm a chef. I was lucky enough for the last 25 years to work as a professional chef. But then I lost my sight and that's how I started on blind cooking." The result was his website to help anyone facing challenges in the kitchen (www.enabledcooking.com). "The whole mission that I have is that cooking is for everybody," he continued. " Enabled Cooking is exactly what it means: to enable people to cook. If you're visually impaired, if you're blind, if you're green, blue, yellow – it doesn't matter where you're from. Any chance to show people that cooking is fun, cooking is do-able and anyone can cook. To bring out some recipes, some tips about safety in the kitchen, how to organise the kitchen, how to set up. Just to give people confidence in cooking."

Not only was he trying to help others through the website, but he was working as a lecturer in a local college sharing all those years of professional experience. Martin had the same generosity of spirit as Luis in San Francisco, and so many of the other chefs and cooks I met. It seems that love of cooking brings out the very best in people.

I recognised the motivation that had kept him working when his sight failed. After the health issues with my right eye, I'd eventually got back into uniform as the secretary to Deputy Flag Officer Surface Flotillas in Portsmouth. But, within months, there were signs that the left eye was starting to fail. Driving was no longer possible, but I could still work on the computer with screen magnification. Most extraordinarily, I was still promoted to commander and spent a few months as the headquarters' staff commander. Usually "the commander" of a naval establishment strides around authoritatively carrying a silver-topped black cane. In my case, it was a white one.

I had a further couple of years in my last job in strategic personnel and manning. With the support of a superb warrant officer and screen magnification, my task was to redesign the appraisal report and supporting IT system for 37,000 naval ratings and marines. But neither my health nor my sight had improved: no chance of getting more good jobs or promotion; medical discharge was inevitable. My last day in uniform was in spring 1999, and my blindness was formally registered.

Losing the sight in my right eye was the most devastating. At that point, I was new to the idea of disability, blindness, working, living, coping, surviving. I became quite depressed but, with some no-nonsense counselling from a naval psychiatrist, realised I would manage. By the time my left eye was failing, I'd prepared for the new reality and lifestyle.

An easier transition than for some blind veterans coping with other major combat injuries and no time for adjustment.

My major worry was how I would earn an income, pay the mortgage and keep my home. But I hadn't been idle. The gift of the gab and networking meant that I started my new career as a paid disability consultant just two days after taking off uniform. Within 12 months I'd founded Disability Dynamics Ltd and went on to run the company for over 20 years.

I knew that it was far more than skill and competence that had kept Martin in his profession. Dogged resolve, entrepreneurial spirit and a vision beyond his own situation had been vital components. Fred had been the same, not allowing his own health problems to limit his heritage-championing business. And the similarities didn't stop there. Martin's first recipe with fish was an echo of Fred's paperbark-wrapped snapper of the previous day.

He explained, "It's a wholesome dish because we don't have to use any pots and pans. We just pack everything into a paper bag and bake it in the oven."

One of his top tips for other blind cooks was to follow the professional method of creating a "mise en place". In other words, having all the ingredients ready at the start, measured, peeled, chopped or whatever was needed so that they can be added when required. For both of us, the extra refinement is to have those ingredients lined up in the order they will be used. Sometimes this can just mean creating separate piles on a large chopping board. Other times, I put the ingredients into lidded boxes or plastic bags so I can't knock them over and make a mess. Martin was using a selection of spices and flavourings that he'd methodically measured out around the edge of a plate like the numbers on a clock so that he knew exactly what was where. Organisation is half the battle when you can't see.

Laying out and layering ingredients on a sheet of greaseproof paper really wasn't difficult with Martin's recipe. The only bit of skill was making sure that, when it was folded over, there was a good seal around the edges by folding them over three times. It was rather like crimping the join of a Cornish pastie. Once the parcels were made up, they could have been kept in the fridge for the day or popped straight into the oven. And the best way to serve is to slide them directly onto a plate so that the lucky recipient can open up the paper, savour the wonderful aroma and eat out of the parcel. Simple to prepare, cook and serve with hardly any washing up!

Next came his Middle Eastern-inspired lamb dish. He was using a rack of lamb, essentially a whole row of chops still joined together. Martin said, "I can sear it off with just one minute each side," as he put the rack, meat side down, into the hot pan with a little oil. Although I couldn't see if it had browned and caramelised for more flavour, I could use the techniques I'd learned from Jack in Chongqing by feeling how the meat had firmed up. While the whole pan went into the oven for 10 minutes, Martin prepared his garnishes. Even without sight, he was picturing the colours, textures and tastes as he designed a plate that would appeal. There was the dark, mellow baba ganoush of charred aubergines with tahini contrasting with white, sharp sheep's yoghurt, the crunch of dry-roasted pine nuts and almonds, the green freshness of mint, coriander and parsley, plus red pomegranate seeds and the sourness of preserved lemons.

Finally the lamb. After a five-minute rest out of the oven, it was straightforward to carve using a sharp knife cut down between the bones of the rack to separate each chop for its plate. Done and ready to serve. It was an outstanding plate that combined all the key flavours: sweet and salty, bitter and sour, with the lamb providing the savoury and meaty umami note. Any cook (or chef) could be rightly proud of both dishes that were quick and straightforward, delicious and true to their ingredients.

It was a calmer and happier group of people who left Martin and his family that afternoon for a whistle-stop drive to show Toby some of the Sydney sights. Even the drizzling rain didn't dampen our restored spirits.

Martin's recipes.

Baked fish fillet Asian style (en papillote).

Video: Asian-style fish en papillote

120g wombok, shredded.
Teaspoon sesame oil.
170g white fish fillet (hokey, snapper, cod, haddock etc.), skin removed.
Pinch salt and grind of black pepper.
100g sugar snap (snow) peas, trimmed.
20g shitake mushrooms, sliced.
15g enoki mushrooms, separated.
1 kaffir lime leaf, shredded.
2g fresh red chilli, finely chopped.
4g fresh root ginger, grated.
1 garlic clove, finely chopped.
2 teaspoons lemon or lime juice.
10ml fish sauce.
15ml sweet soy sauce.
5ml dark soy sauce.
5g fresh Vietnamese mint, chopped.
2g fresh mint, chopped.
5g flat parsley, chopped.
10g spring onions, finely sliced.
1 sheet nori seaweed, finely shredded.

Method.

Preheat oven to 200C, Gas 6, 390F.

Place a sheet of baking parchment on the work surface.

Create a bed of wombok on one half of the parchment, the same size as the fish, and pour over the sesame oil.

Remove any fine bones from the fish, place on the wombok and season.

Place the peas and mushrooms around the fish.

Sprinkle over the Kaffir lime leaf, chilli, ginger and garlic.

Drizzle over the citrus juice, the fish, oyster and two soy sauces.

Sprinkle over the mint, parsley, spring onions and nori.

Add a final grind of black pepper.

Fold the empty half of the parchment over the ingredients and tightly fold all around the open edges at least twice to make a parcel that will retain the juices.

Place the parcel on a baking sheet and cook in the oven for 10-12 minutes.

Serve parcels direct onto warm plates.

My tips.

If wombok is not available use pak choi or even very finely shredded cabbage.

It may seem daunting to use so many ingredients for one portion, but making several individual parcels ahead of time and storing in the fridge until later in the day is more manageable – and there's little washing up. Chilled parcels will need another minute or so cooking time.

Oven roasted Australian lamb rack with baba ganoush, sheep's milk yogurt and pomegranate.

Video: Roasted rack of lamb with garnishes

200g aubergines.
5ml olive oil.
20g tahini paste.
50ml natural Greek yoghurt.
15g garlic, peeled and finely chopped.
10ml lemon juice.
10ml extra virgin olive oil.
Salt and ground black pepper to taste.
Pinch ground sumac.
Pinch sweet paprika.

Method.

Preheat oven to 220C, Gas 7, 430F.

Pierce the aubergines with a skewer and brush with olive oil.

Place on baking tray and cook in oven until soft (50 minutes).

Cool for 15 minutes and then peel.

Place aubergine flesh plus remaining ingredients in a food processor/ blender and whizz to a smooth texture.

My tips.

In Eddie's version the following day, the aubergines were cooked over a hot barbecue, which created a stronger smoky flavour and he added walnuts to give texture. This is one of those dishes that relies on your taste buds to decide how much of each ingredient works for you.

Yoghurt dressing.

50ml sheep's milk yoghurt.
5g preserved lemon, finely cubed.
10g parsley, finely chopped.
5g coriander, finely chopped.
5g mint, finely chopped.
Salt, ground white pepper and lemon juice to taste.
15ml extra virgin olive oil.

Method.

Mix all the ingredients and check seasoning.

Rack of lamb.

1 rack of lamb (about 500g, 6 chops), French trimmed.
15ml olive oil.

Garnish.

20g pomegranate seeds.
5g almond flakes, toasted.
5g pine nuts, toasted.
5ml extra virgin olive oil to drizzle.
2 sprigs mint.

Method.

Preheat oven to 190C, Gas 5, 370F.

"French trimmed" rack of lamb needs the bones to be scraped clean.

Season the rack and rub in the salt, pepper and olive oil.

Sear the rack on all sides in a hot pan.

Place the rack in a roasting tray, meat side down, and cook for 10-12 minutes. The inner meat should still be pink and medium-rare. Cover and rest for at least 5 minutes.

Cut between the bones to serve portions.

Place lamb on plates with servings of baba ganoush and the yoghurt dressing and then sprinkle/drizzle garnish.

Preserved lemons.

Martin explained: "I slice up the lemons. I add a bay leaf, cloves and just salt. Mix it in a jar and keep it in the fridge for one or two weeks and it preserves. That's it."

Chapter 18.

Iranian barbecue.

It was still drizzling the next day as I woke to hear someone digging close to the bedroom window. There was lots of whispering and laughing alongside the sounds of a shovel.

This was to be a special day. Rosemary had arranged for me to help her neighbour, Eddie, and his very pregnant wife, Mika, to create an Iranian barbecue for a group of her local friends. We literally stepped across the lawn into the adjacent home and the rather damp garden.

First Eddie proudly gave us a tour of his handmade outside cooking equipment: the preparation table and barbecue. He described making the pizza oven: "It's very simple and cost me zero dollars. We had the materials in the backyard. It's basically an oil drum on the inside that I filled up one quarter with sand and then laid two tiles of concrete on the top. That gave me the basic platform. Then I covered it with layers of bricks and, on the top, concrete and rocks (to make it decorative). And there's a chimney at the front with the barrel laying all the way back. You light the fire at the back and the smoke comes out of the front."

My task was to prepare the doner kebabs, but forget anything as parochial as bamboo sticks. Eddie presented me with an armful of metre-long swords on which we would impale the meat. In the light drizzle, a plastic carrier bag was the practical answer for mixing the simple ingredients. I roughly chopped a good handful of parsley, while Eddie added chilli and ground pepper, explaining the meat proportions: "You're going to mix about 80% beef and 20% lamb for more flavour from the oil of the lamb." He thought that beef alone could be too dry. It seemed a vast amount as I squeezed and scrunched the 4kg of mixture in the bag.

Once the meats had started to blend together, I was ready for my next instructions. "We take some mincemeat about the size of a tennis ball," Eddie said, "just the size of your hand that you'll feel comfortable with. You're trying to make it into a tube-like sausage." The end of the cylinder was slid onto the tip of a sword and then up the whole blade. We wetted our hands (not difficult in the rain) and moulded the meat onto the blade, with Eddie warning: "The more you play with it, the oil will stick to the sword and will separate the meat from the sword. When you cook it, the meat will fall off." He carefully checked each of my efforts before the row of swords was placed over the hot coals on the barbecue. A turn to allow each side to brown and they were done, as the metal conducted the heat. While they sizzled, smoky barbecued aubergines went off to become outstanding baba ganoush mixed with tahini, crushed garlic and chopped walnuts to be served with the Lebanese flatbreads charring in the pizza oven.

With enormous glee, he led me to one side of the garden where, tucked between the house and a wooden fence, he started digging. I could hear a pickaxe and shovel cutting into the ground, punctuated by Eddie puffing with effort and determination. I remembered the sounds from the early morning when he'd clearly started what was his fire pit. Despite all the effort, it turned out to be quite small: "Not very deep and about 300mm by 300mm. We fill it up with wood now. Some fine wood – easy to burn – and then I'm going to put some logs on top. I've started the fire and I'll bring some more wood." He even added some broken wooden furniture on top of the kindling. I was somewhat curious as to whether he often made a fire pit in this rather closely packed suburban area. Eddie admitted that he didn't because "The neighbours would complain too much", but cheerfully announced that now Ken, Rosemary and others were coming for lunch, they wouldn't be able to object. I confess I had a lot of sympathy with the neighbours. The pit was creating masses of smoke and, more worryingly, was only a couple of feet from Ken and Rosemary's wooden fence.

With the burning wood topped with charcoal briquettes, the pyre was ready for a foil-wrapped parcel of lamb shoulder. At the bottom of the parcel, Eddie had added roughly chopped onion and tomato to add flavour and moisture, and to keep the meat from touching the foil. The meat went in next. It had been soaked in water and was fatty side down to protect the meat from the heat. In Persia, where foil was probably not available, the meat might have been wrapped in wet cloth and then large leaves. He topped the pyre with more charcoal and wood. Usually a fire pit would have been covered with more soil to insulate all the heat but, in down-town Kiama, it hadn't been possible to dig deep enough. It was going to take hours to cook.

Meanwhile, I slipped back to Rosemary's kitchen where she was chopping hard with her friend and food hygienist, Jill, to create an extravaganza of salads. Rosemary had been awake and beavering away for hours, while Jill had forgotten to set her alarm and slept through the dark morning. There was wild activity to catch up for lost time. Their multiplicity of complex salads featured roasted cauliflower and date; rocket, avocado and mango; beetroot and chickpea; watermelon and feta; lentil and kale. When you're Down Under, lettuce and tomato is far too pedestrian.

Jill offered useful tips about food safety. Watermelon is prone to listeria, and rock melon to salmonella. She recommends soaking the whole melons in a bowl of water with the juice of one lemon or a couple of tablespoons of white or cider vinegar. For those at higher risk, or if you have bought a piece of cut melon, sprinkle it with lemon juice before eating. On the other hand, Jill's dessert suggestion was rather simpler: strawberries with a dollop of Nutella.

Back in Eddie's garden, the drizzle wasn't dampening the fun. Other neighbours had turned out to welcome Toby and me, and to share the generous spread of kebabs, salads and baba ganoush. We all fell on the wonderful Iranian feast, amply washed down with excellent Australian wine.

Rosemary had also arranged for us to visit the local Silos Estate winery (www.silosestate.com). It was clear that the fire pit lamb wouldn't be ready for hours, so we made our excuses, leaving the neighbours to continue lunch, with promises to return.

At the vineyard, we met the owner, Raj, who was valiantly trying to educate us about his wine business while clearly concerned about the welfare of his wife. She'd just returned from the hospital after being treated for a tick bite. This was turning into another dramatic day.

As we sampled his various wines, Raj explained that, nowadays, making the wine is only half the job, as management and sales have become increasingly important in the ever-tightening market. "I probably do 20 or 30 hours of manual labour a week," he said, "plus 40 or 50 hours of computer work. Anyone can make wine, but not everyone can sell it."

The Australian wine producing structure is changing. Although the labels of previous small producers are still being used, many have now been gobbled up by the very large companies. Ten years ago, there were around 4,000 Australian wine producers. Their number has halved as a result of the financial stresses on wine production. Raj said, "The farm gate price for grapes has plummeted. In absolute terms, it's a 99.9% reduction in consumption. So selling is absolutely critical if you want to survive." The good old days of easy and profitable wine sales is probably over, and the producers have to diversify, consolidate and change to be viable.

Although his wine wasn't fully organic, Raj was making big ecological (and economic) strides by stopping all irrigation and reducing his fuel use by 90%. He applied a pragmatic attitude to wine: "I have people who come in here and they have six to eight thousand-bottle cellars and they buy a case of wine and put it away. They're in their fifties or sixties. If you drank a bottle every day for the rest of your life, you're not going to make it (drinking through such a big cellar). About three or four years ago, a very good friend of mine was killed in a car accident – his wife and daughters survived. I was reminded that there was some stuff that we were "going to do", but there is no "going to do", you just do it. So now I'll just go and buy an old wine if I particularly want it. You can't live every day as if it is your last, but you certainly live every day to its full."

Living that full life was very much how we felt after tasting his wines and returning to the neighbours' party. It was clear that they too had been imbibing a little, and the jollity had increased during the intervening hours. It was time for the great unveiling as the lamb was carefully dug out of its fiery grave after nearly six hours cooking. Eddie was a little uncertain as to the results, saying, "You can hear something bubbling, but I don't know what's in there." It was a distinct challenge to find and retrieve the hot parcel, but it opened to release a wonderful aroma. He carried it triumphantly back to the (late) lunch table and dispensed with any need for carving as the bones could just be pulled out. The hot and succulent meat was rapidly shared and devoured to a round of applause. All that time and preparation for just a few minutes of delectable deliciousness! The simplest ingredients, cooked in the simplest way, to make an unforgettable dish to end the long meal. Highly recommended if you have understanding neighbours or invite them to take part.

We were rather a weary and bedraggled bunch that trooped back to the house next door to prepare for the trip back to Sydney and flight to Melbourne the following day. But our work wasn't finished. Together, Toby and I sat editing a composite video to capture our Kiama adventures. Eddie too was still full of exuberance, and came knocking with the hope of enticing Toby away for a trip into town for some farewell beers. We felt like rather damp blankets in having to decline but knew that, only halfway through this leg of the world tour, every scrap of sleep counted.

Video: Kiama adventures

Eddie's recipes

Video: Iranian barbecue

Doner kebabs.

3kg minced beef.
1kg minced lamb.
Lashings of ground black pepper.
Handfuls of roughly chopped parsley.
Finely chopped chillies.
Small handful salt.

Method.

Thoroughly mix, pummel and squeeze all the ingredients together in a bowl or plastic bag.

Take a handful of the mix and form it into a sausage and spear lengthways onto a sword, pushing it up the handle and then adding more.

Damp hands help with the moulding around the blade, which should be kept to a minimum. Too much handling releases the lamb fat which can mean that the meat falls off during cooking.

Cook over hot charcoals, turning regularly and remove once the meat has browned.

Fire pit lamb.

First, find friendly neighbours and invite them to lunch.

Dig a 300mm-square hole in the garden away from anything inflammable such as a wooden fence.

Place dry kindling in the base of the pit and then cover with larger pieces of wood. Light the kindling and wait for the wood to catch fire, then add a layer of charcoal.

Take a large piece of kitchen foil. Place roughly chopped tomatoes and onions in the centre and place the lamb shoulder on top, fat side down and season. Wrap the foil securely around the meat and seal the parcel by folding the edges.

Place the lamb parcel into the fire pit, cover with more charcoal, wood and soil and wait for several hours.

Take care recovering the parcel. It will be hot and have hot liquid inside.

Remove bones and share the meat.

Rosemary and Jill's salads.

Roasted cauliflower.

A large cauliflower, broken into florets then sliced.
Garlic powder and sea salt.
Olive oil.
4-5 medjool dates, diced.
Handful pine nuts.
2 tablespoons fresh rosemary leaves, chopped.

Method.

Preheat oven to 200C, Gas 6, 390F.

Sprinkle the cauliflower with garlic powder and salt to taste. Drizzle lightly with olive oil and cook in the oven for 10-12 minutes until soft and browned.

Meanwhile, place the pine nuts and dates in a small frying pan with about 2 tablespoons olive oil. Sauté over medium heat, stirring constantly to avoid the nuts burning, until golden and the dates have softened, about 4 minutes.

When the cauliflower is done, toss together with the pine nuts, dates and rosemary. Serve while warm.

Rocket, avocado and mango salad.

1 large mango, peeled and cubed.
1 avocado, peeled and cubed
2 generous handfuls roasted and salted nuts (cashews, peanuts, macadamia, or whatever you prefer).
5 double handfuls fresh rocket, washed.
About 180ml salad dressing (see below).

Place the mango, avocado and nuts in the salad dressing. Pour over the rocket (arugula) and mix the salad just before serving.

Beetroot, chickpea and spinach salad.

100g small spinach leaves, washed.
400g tin chickpeas, drained.
250g cooked beetroot, cut in quarters.
Salad dressing (see below).

Method.

Mix the vegetables in a large bowl.

Add and mix in the dressing just before serving.

Watermelon, feta and mint salad.

Half a watermelon, de-seeded, skin removed and cubed.
Half lime, juice only.
Large handfuls mint, finely chopped.
100g feta cheese, cubed.
Salt and pepper to taste.

Method.

Mix all the ingredients, adding the cheese last to avoid it breaking up.

Lentil, kale and potato salad.

200g lentils.
About 15 new potatoes.
2 teaspoons olive oil.
1 clove garlic, peeled and minced.
1 teaspoon fresh thyme leaves.
A double handful of kale, chopped.
A large handful dried fruit (sultanas, raisins, cranberries or whatever is to hand).
A handful walnut or pecan pieces.
Salt and pepper to taste.
Salad dressing (see below).

Method.

Cook the lentils and potatoes separately by boiling or steaming until cooked but not too soft.

Cut the potatoes into quarters and sauté in the oil until crisp, then add the garlic and thyme.

Add the kale and cook until wilting.

Place mix with lentils in serving bowl and fold in dried fruit and nuts.

Season and add salad dressing while still warm.

Salad dressing.

There are endless variations of classic dressings, but the principal ingredients tend to be:

Acid (vinegar or citrus juice).

Oil (olive or other).

Seasoning (salt and pepper).

Sweet (sugar, honey, agave syrup etc.) unless using sweeter balsamic vinegar.

Flavouring (mustard is often used but more can be added such as garlic, herbs, chilli).

The following offers a basic dressing that can then be varied for each of the different salads above.

Tasting is essential to check that the balance works with each particular salad and your own preferences.

50g vinegar.
150g olive oil.
1 pinch salt and good grind black pepper.
Half teaspoon sugar.
Half teaspoon English mustard powder.

Method.

Simply whisk the basic ingredients together, check taste balance and, if preferred, divide into different portions and whisk in different flavourings.

My tips.

Dressing can be added to some salad ingredients early (such as mushrooms or tomatoes), but will tend to make leaves wilt. You can place the "hard" ingredients in the salad bowl and dress, top with the leaves and then mix all at the last moment.

Jill's melon hygiene tips.

- **Watermelon**. Bacteria is listeria. Soak watermelon in bowl of water with juice of 1 lemon, or 2 tablespoons of white or cider vinegar, for 3 minutes contact time. Drain and then use.
- **Rock melon**. Bacteria is salmonella. Same treatment as for watermelon. For ease when out, wipe a paper towel wet with white or cider vinegar over surface of melon before cutting it up.
- If you are in an at-risk group, she suggests checking bought melons are still fresh and sprinkling lemon juice over cut pieces to kill any remaining bacteria.

Chapter 19.

Melbourne Cup.

A short internal flight from Sydney and we were wheels down in Melbourne (pronounced Mel-bun) at nearly exactly the time their famous horse race began – perfect for avoiding traffic. It was a major public holiday, with most of the population holding Melbourne Cup parties. Sociable Colin had given up his holiday and the festivities to collect us from the airport. He was another Royal Navy connection through my brother Martin. They'd both been caterers before their officer training, promotions and successful careers. As a retired commander, Colin, his wife Jane and their family, had emigrated to Australia where he embarked on his next public service career at a local town council.

My last visit to Melbourne had been years earlier as a UK delegate to the week-long World Blind Union conference. Back then I'd had a superb time visiting the galaxy of riverside restaurants. My strongest memories were fabulous towering water features spaced along the riverside walkway, 10-foot tall concrete obelisks with corrugated sides down which the water trickled. At night, gas flames erupted with amazing whooshes from the tops of the towers. It wasn't just one quick burn, but the whole line of water features would come to light in series and patterns – magical sensations of the sound and heat. Nearby there was a pavement water feature, and again sequenced jets of water squirted into the air and children squealed as they ran through the spouts. There had been a huge garden party with sheep shearing and indigenous Australian didgeridoo demonstrations – later I'd spent hours in the garden at home trying to play a borrowed one (instrument, not sheep). Another wonderful memory was the night-time boat trip down the river to "see" the small penguins nesting on one of the rocky outcrops. The skipper clearly believed that getting closer to the penguins would improve my vision – sadly it didn't, but I could hear them much better.

Melbourne retained small town charm amidst a great cosmopolitan city. Food predominated. The city has the highest proportion of cafés and restaurants per head of population worldwide.

Colin drove us through the suburbs to their home, a seemingly endlessly expanding bungalow in Oakleigh. It was only much later that I discovered he and Jane had given up their own bedroom to make the accommodation more accessible. No greater generosity hath hosts than when they give up their en suite bathroom!

That evening they introduced us to Oakleigh's vibrant multi-cultural nightlife. We meandered along the streets in balmy evening air, redolent with different languages and wafts of international cuisines. Our supper in the Greek restaurant, run by a Turkish entrepreneur, sitting alongside an Asian family, gave just a tiny flavour of the area and the economic benefits of real diversity.

Next day we were back to the cooking schedule with a vengeance. Our hostess, Maribel, welcomed us to her apartment and introduced her musician partner Harry, composer of the *Tarka the Otter* film music for the book by his father. She and I had been corresponding for months as two passionate blind cooks, but she already had her first cookbook to her name. Maribel had been a huge advocate and ambassador for the Baking Blind visit, supporting Colin in finding other local cooks to take part and helping publicise our efforts through Vision Australia. Now, at last, we could meet in person, and her welcome of champagne and superb savoury pumpkin seeds (pepitas) started the day on a perfect footing. I was touched to receive gifts from her: Australia-emblazoned oven mitts and a shopping bag that were put to good use.

Maribel explained a little of her own story: "I love to cook for my family. But what I do as a career is I'm a writer and speaker (www.maribelsteel.com). write all about visual impairment and how to cope. I write for Vision Aware America. I love gardening, travelling. I have a travel blog called Touching Landscapes."

Once I'd navigated her kitchen enough to be useful and safe, Maribel talked about her recipe. "I'm going to show you a beautiful recipe that my mother did for us just about every Sunday. It's called eggs à la flamenca. It's got that beautiful rich flavour of Spain with the chorizo sausage. We start with the Spanish sacred holy trinity: onions, garlic and capsicum – you call them peppers."

I recognised her tactile approach: "I'm just running some extra virgin olive oil into the pan without burning myself," she said. "Just feeling, which will frighten people, with my hands in the pan. I love this low frying pan which gives me lots of space and I can feel around. It's what I love about cooking as a blind person. It really is about feel." I do exactly the same.

We both have ways of keeping pans safe on the hob. I usually use a set-back gas burner, while Maribel had a guard rail surrounding each burner, explaining, "My partner has built these very sturdy trivets. Now I've got a big pot and there's no way that it's going to fall off." We agreed that electric induction hobs were even more difficult as pans can slide when being stirred. I'm sure that designers are more concerned with sleek looks than practical use. They don't realise that small digital controls aren't good enough for fast professionals, or anyone with less dextrous hands or sight limitations. It's that old chestnut: making design inclusive at the outset gets the best market share.

Like any two women, we talked about clothes and Maribel said, "Apparently, we are both wearing red." She speculated that many people might think colour is irrelevant for blind people. "They do feel surprised that we like colour. Why would we want to wear colour? Actually, it makes a big difference." And, of course, it wasn't just about clothes, as she proudly produced a dish that matched our outfits, saying, "It's a red polka dot bowl." I countered with my matching red luggage in our coordination one-up-ship. Since then, I've gone one better and now have a red cane too. Who wants a boring white one?

Once her ingredients had simmered, the mix was divided into individual dishes that were like little boats, pointed at each end, and Maribel was delighted by their nautical links to me and James Holman, saying, "Now we are going to dish up the mixture of our eggs à la flamenca into our Holman dishes. It's lovely and rich. The flavours of Spain. Then we do the cracking of the eggs. These are beautiful farm-fresh eggs that I bought at the market the other day. I've just cracked an egg over the top and it's wobbled off. Here we go with our flotilla of eggs à la flamenca into the oven."

The dish was just like Maribel herself, full of vibrant authentic flavours and colour. We sat on her balcony eating, sipping wine and luxuriating in the sunshine, while she and Harry regaled us with one of their songs: "Don't worry, be happy; everything's going to be alright", which is exactly how we felt.

It was a wonderfully glorious morning of like minds, like experiences, and like tastes.

Video: Surviving blindness by Maribel

Maribel has since published her memoires and appeared on Australian television and radio talking about her philosophy for living with blindness. "When I talk about the seven secrets of coping with vision loss, number one is acceptance. If you can't accept what it is that you've got to cope with, then nothing's going to happen. At some point, we all have to deal with the loss, the tragedy or whatever it might be, but it's accepting that'll allow you to move forward.

"Number two is collaboration with others, or allowing team work. It's not a weakness, it's actually a strength. I love delegating." For me, too, the right help at the right time is hugely welcome and opens up new relationships with new people. It is one of the great benefits of blindness.

"Number three is developing a good sense of courage. It takes bravery and courage to be able to get out there and try to do things. So you might need to take on some new training, get a guide dog, learn orientation. Just understand that it does take courage.

"Number four is organisation. To cope with vision loss, you need a super-organised manner in the house, the kitchen. If you are living with a sighted family, I like to say these are my kitchen rules. That's the way of coping.

"Number five is having a good sense of humour, expressing yourself, saying what you need. It's always funnier when you retell the story.

"Number six is a sense of intuition. Following your gut feelings. If I'm in a room and not feeling completely safe, or I'm not feeling comfortable, I might make my way out of the room. It's knowing your own energy levels and what you are going to tackle on those days." I feel exactly the same. If it's not a good day, if I'm not feeling confident, then I just do the boring things and don't make decisions. I'm not going to do anything hugely challenging as my brain's not going to be in the right place to be successful.

"Number seven is using all your senses. Being visually impaired, I feel that I'm more open to the touch and smell of life." Again, I completely agree. Lots of people don't appreciate the joys of being blind. They think we are in a miserable world of perpetual black darkness. In reality, my life is spent in constant gentle light, like an early summer's day, which makes life seem bright and positive. Because I'm endlessly physically in touch with other people and am sensitive to the nuances of their voices, it can be easier to have rapport and relate to them. Then there are huge landscapes of smell and sound that are lost to people focussed on what they can see. Life truly isn't that bad when you are blind. "Don't worry, be happy; everything's going to be alright."

Suitably refreshed, we piled into central Melbourne, where Maribel had some shops to share. I was particularly entranced by the spice shop, which seemed to offer every example you can imagine and then more. There were racks upon racks, from floor to ceiling, of individual containers of herbs, spices and other flavourings. It was all self-service, so we could open each container to smell the different delights within – an aromatic world tour. The variety reflected the city's communities, as Maribel explained: "What I love about Melbourne cuisine is that it is so multi-cultural. You can walk down the middle of Melbourne and find just about every flavour of the world, from Asian dumplings to Polish sausages, and Italian minestrone and pizzas to Spanish and French cuisine. We've got a great multi-cultural population here. It's the correct thing to do to embrace other cultures."

Following a frenetic day, it was good to return to the peace and quiet of Jane's kitchen, where she set a trend of perfect, simple and elegant suppers. Even though our naval careers hadn't overlapped, Colin and I could swap stories about mutual acquaintances, compare memories of Army vs Navy rugby matches and, as Navy-speak would put it, "swing the lamp" with tall tales of our military lives.

The horse-racing festivities were still continuing the following day as we visited the catering students at the Holmesglen College (www.holmesglen.edu.au). They were so busy in the catering kitchen that tutor Renée and I de-camped to a quieter space.

She said, "We are in our storeroom. We have a lot of fascinating ingredients in here ranging from all our spices, dry goods, everything that we need for the chefs to create amazing food. Oaks Day is a magnificent race day after the Melbourne Cup. A lot of ladies come out to get dressed up and celebrate and, instead of going out to the racetrack, they're coming to our fabulous campus. We are catering for about 140 people. Our menu today consists of ceviche of snapper and salmon on an avocado salsa with a lovely tiger milk dressing. We are also doing a smoked beef, which is sliced thinly and has cured egg yolk horseradish foam, Italian crisps and a parsley puree – and it's divine." And the ladies-who-lunch were out in their full finery from frothy hats down to their stylish shoes.

The college was also renowned for providing the hospitality and catering training for members of the Australian defence forces. This took us back to the naval theme of the Holman Prize, my and Colin's own military careers, and his links with the college.

Tight security meant that we couldn't video any of the military trainees, but their tutors were fair game. The first was demonstrating emulsification, warm in a hollandaise sauce and cold in mayonnaise. He explained how to transform the latter into Caesar salad dressing: "This is my base mayonnaise with nothing in it. It's quite bland. The second one is a touch thinner and I can taste the garlic but not the anchovy or parmesan cheese." Not only was he showing them the technical aspects, but also the importance of taste and texture.

Meanwhile, chef Michael was introducing a more senior class to the complexity of filo pastry as one of the final units of their course. His tip was: "It's all about making a nice wet and stretchy dough to start. You always stretch it from the inside to the outside." I remembered making filo years ago, rolling it on a damp tablecloth and then stretching it out with the backs of my hands to cover the whole table. Nowadays, I confess that shop-bought is easier and quicker.

Our visit concluded with me standing at the front of their lecture theatre talking to the military students about my own service career. They were probably somewhat bemused by this old blind Pom who must have seemed a million miles distant from their own experiences.

Video: Australian defence force catering training

But the time with those young military trainees took both Colin and me back to our own careers. We talked little about those weighty matters of defence policy, service strategy or military readiness, but concentrated on the truly important topic of naval life.

Army vs Navy rugby matches at Twickenham were very close to Colin's heart, but I was a somewhat poor contributor on the subject. I had been to only a few of the famous matches, but with virtually no recall of ever seeing a ball. In those days, it could be a very swish affair. Wardrooms would hire a coach for their officers and equip it with everything for an appropriate luncheon: tables, chairs, full linen and cutlery, picket fence to mark off the area, plus a pair of sentry potted bay trees. Naturally, there would be a cook to provide a three-course hot meal, plus stewards to serve it – all decorously set up in the car park. Pre-luncheon drinks would have started on the journey (immediately outside Portsmouth) and continued to and at the destination. Typically, we would perambulate amongst the other coaches and crowds of colleagues, rather pitying those who had no more than a "bag-meal" (sandwiches and other sad elements of a cold collation presented in a paper bag). Following our genteel and liquid lunch, there would be a general amble to the stands. One whole half would be filled by uproarious Navy officers; opposite sat a desultory selection of Army types. Hip flasks of sloe gin meandered along the rows and, somewhere, whistles were blown. Post-match, we would regather for redundant celebratory cakes (the Army always won), and further compensatory libations. It was a thoroughly relaxed crew that slumped into the coaches home unless, as on one occasion, it had already departed. A fellow lawyer and I managed to hitch a ride on another, having first ascertained the adequacy of their onboard stocks.

Maribel's recipes.

Eggs à la flamenca (Huevos à la flamenca).

Video: Eggs à la flamenco

2 tablespoons olive oil.
2 onions, peeled and diced.
3 cloves garlic, peeled and chopped.
Green pepper, de-seeded and sliced.
2 handfuls green beans, chopped.
10cm chorizo, sliced.
Handfuls flat leaf parsley, roughly chopped.
Two tins chopped tomatoes (with basil and garlic if available).
120g pitted black olives, halved.
240ml beef stock or water (amount needed will depend on liquid in tomatoes).
1 egg per person.

Method.

Preheat oven to 160C, Gas 3, 320F.

Heat olive oil

Gently sauté onions, garlic and pepper for 5-7 minutes.

Add the remaining ingredients (except eggs) and bring to a gentle simmer for about 10 minutes, until the beans are cooked.

Divide the mixture between individual serving bowls and break an egg into each (keeping the yolks intact).

Place in oven and cook for about 10 minutes until the eggs are firm.

Serve with crusty bread and salad.

Pepitas.

Pumpkin seeds.
Sweet dark soy sauce.

Method.

Place the seeds in a heated pan and dry roast until they start popping.

Stir in a few tablespoons of soy sauce and keep on heat, stirring until the mix is drier and starting to stick together.

Cool and separate seeds. Serve with aperitif or as a topping for salads.

Chapter 20.

Three gastronomettes.

Three women at the very top of their game within the food industry, fizzing with confidence, competence and the sheer joy of their spectacular successes. Over the next two days, our time was entirely devoted to these most talented women cooks. Dani was a renowned food writer and author. Charlene had impressive Cordon Bleu qualifications and international networks; Dré was one of the top pastry chefs and entrepreneurs in Melbourne. What fabulous expertise and experience!

First came Dani's home kitchen with her nifty demonstration worktop, an ordinary sturdy table that we lifted onto concrete blocks for the extra height. It's a simple idea that anyone can use to increase their work area in a tight space. She explained her 20 years of passion: "What I love about food is the way it connects me with people from all different walks of life. I think that food is the best way to dive into culture." (www.danivalent.com)

She showed me her "Four-minute bread" from one of her recipe books for the ubiquitous Thermomix. I'd heard about this hugely popular but hideously expensive piece of kit throughout my time in Australia. Essentially, it combined a food processor, weighing scales, steamer and cooker all in one piece.

Dani said, "One of my editors asked me to write a story about chefs and the gadgets they wanted in their professional kitchens. They all said Thermomix."

But our first step was choosing which version of the equipment we would use. The latest one was all sleek and smooth, easy to clean with a useful carrying handle but totally inaccessible: no tactile controls and a digital display. Luckily Dani still had one of the older classic TM 31 versions, sturdily heavy in metal with manual buttons and knobs. Within minutes I'd mastered it, except the digital weight display. Oh, for just a little audio chip and speaker, it would have been perfect. I despair sometimes when designers make decisions that exclude so many of us from great products. Don't they realise that disabled people make up 20% of the market? There are many more people who might cook more with the right equipment? And that professional cooks want equipment that's easy to operate in the rough and tumble of their kitchens? With smart speakers all over the house, designs will surely include more audio in and outputs. I can't wait!

The bread itself was the simplest possible. Just two minutes heating to activate the yeast and another two minutes machine-kneading before it was ready to shape. As Dani explained, "I make a sort of flower shape where I've got one central roll and six around the outside." The Australian heat meant the dough rose in about half an hour, ready for 20 minutes baking in the oven with a flick of water to crisp the crust around the light fluffy bread.

At home, I use a simpler bread machine. The tactile buttons were easy to learn and, keeping all the ingredients in one pan throughout, everything is so much cleaner. Even if you can see, avoiding a fine haze of flour on every surface is worth it.

Dani also introduced an ingredient that may be impossible to buy. "Kefir is a fermented milk drink that is very popular in Eastern Europe and lots of parts of the world," she told me. " Basically, you put these little lumpy grains, as they're called, into milk and leave it for a while at room temperature, and it ferments into this beautiful potion that is apparently very good for our tummies. No one knows where the first kefir grains came from. People who have moved from country to country would carry them like precious heirlooms because they needed to make their kefir. In Australia, we have a lot of refugees and, for a lot of these people, it's traditional for them to make these fermented products. Some of them have been fermenting things almost in hiding. They'd be doing it under sinks or beds because that was part of who they were. There are little fermenting hubs where you can buy these kinds of things, but really they're passed from hand to hand." She stored the kefir grains, like small pieces of soft, wet cauliflower, in a jar with milk, explaining, "It's like having another pet: you have to feed them. I've cultured some cream with the kefir and then whipped that into butter."

We spread it, with the tang of yoghurt and hint of vinegar, on the hot rolls before topping off with her fig jam made with lime zest and juice for extra pectin set. Dani was unapologetic, saying, "I've buttered it as I would have done in private, which is a lot. My grandmother lived to 101, and she had her butter an inch thick, so I feel that's my permission to have as much as I want, whenever I want."

Video: Thermomix and kafir

With mouths still full of those delicious flavours, Colin packed us all into his car for the trip to a development in the countryside on the outskirts of Melbourne. Just completing her Cordon Bleu Master's degree in Gastronomic Tourism, our hostess Charlene (www.charlenetrist.com) was one of only a handful of people to represent Australia at an international symposium in Copenhagen, rubbing shoulders with the restaurant industry elite and progressing her ambition as a multimedia culinary destination scout. Next time you need a foodie setting for a film or television series, Charlene's your woman.

That morning she had turned her husband and children out of the house to give us space for filming. Welcoming us with a glass of wine, Charlene emphasised that she wanted our cooking experience to be relaxing, sensual and sensuous. "Too often we simply rush at cooking," she said. "It is understandable in a modern world where the pace of life is constant speed. But sometimes we need to take time out and thoroughly appreciate the food we are cooking, the ingredients and the work and lives that created them. It is part of the respect for the food, the producers and, ultimately, the people we are feeding. Taking time is part of the joy of cooking."

Colin, with the practicality typical of any naval officer, quickly departed to purchase something more mundane: emergency rations of wraps and sandwiches. We could foresee that cooking lunch was going to take hours, and we would need to stave off the alcohol and hunger pangs. Disaster struck as Toby was setting up the fixed wide-angle camera: it slipped off the work surface, and it was only much later that we realised we'd lost all this footage and had to rely on the close-ups.

Meanwhile, I was immeasurably touched by the thought and care Charlene had given to the cooking of her ravioli as she explained, "We are using raw smoked eggs which have been smoked in a hot smoker. These eggs come from a free-range farm (https://smokedeggs.com). They wanted to utilise some of the cracked eggs that weren't suitable for retail sale. It took them two years of testing and trialling different combinations of smoke intensity, of heat and length of time in the smoker. They look like eggs that have had a suntan."

The resulting eggs had absorbed the bitter smoke tannins in their shells, leaving the contents with the taste and fragrance of wood smoke. "I like to use food as a way of connecting to the world around me," Charlene said. "One way I can do that is by thinking of the journey that the ingredient has been on before it arrives in my kitchen." I had to laugh a little at the eggs' journey: approximately 70 kilometres which, in Australia, was local!

Making the pasta wasn't that tricky, but all about touch and taste, smell and sound, adding the cool aromatic eggs onto the warm soft flour as Charlene described, "Feel how beautiful it is to break through the yolks and how the texture changes as you start to incorporate the flour. Recipe books often give you a static recipe. But there are so many variations that can happen: the humidity in the air, the size of the eggs, the type of flour. We must rely on our senses to guide us on whether it needs more flour, to firm up the dough or whether we need more liquid." Her approach was very different to the earlier Thermomix dough experience, but both have their place in a cook's life.

We used a little of her local grass-fragrant olive oil to moisten the dough for kneading on the bench, transforming it from the feel of linen through cotton to silky smoothness with a couple of sprays of water to achieve the perfect spring-back speed from a firm finger press. Stored in a plastic bag inside a paper bag, the dough needs to rest in the fridge for a couple of hours but, protected from drying out and light, it can sit in the fridge for a few days before using. Practical as ever, Charlene produced one that she had made earlier. As I came to rolling, I'd learned long ago that those fancy pasta machines are far too tricky. Hand-rolling the dough feels much more authentic and in tune with the ingredients, even if the results are less than perfect.

As I kneaded and rolled, Charlene talked: "I have a Maltese heritage. My grandparents migrated from Malta to Australia. With them they brought all the typical European customs, such as sharing a meal as a family and growing our own veggies. That was a very elementary introduction to food for me, but things got interesting in my pre-teens when I was having a really difficult time at school.

"I was very shy and introverted. I was the victim of a little bit of bullying. I found making friends quite difficult. My mum picked up on that and one day she bought me a ***Woman's Weekly*** cookbook of very basic recipes. My very first recipe was a basic version of Singapore noodles using cup noodles, some soy sauce, some curry powder and some frozen vegetables. It really was amazing. They applauded my efforts, and I felt great about it and felt successful.

"From that moment I became addicted and tried to do everything I could to learn more about food. I cooked at every opportunity and, before I knew it, this sense of connecting through food just overtook me. I got to about Year 10 and did my first home economics class. In the kitchen I felt super-comfortable because I'd done so much research, and I'd practised heaps, and I said this is what I can do, this is me. For the first time in my life I had my peers begging the teacher to pair with me. I was always left last in school sport, last to pair in drama, but, in the kitchen, I had found my place. It took me completely by surprise. I connected food with connecting with people, and then my self-confidence started to bloom."

Charlene had even worked out the detail of constructing the ravioli for me: a handy pastry cutter around which to pipe the pumpkin and goat's cheese mash, into which the separated smoked egg yolk could be placed – without breaking it. Then a spray of water, and another sheet of pasta placed on top, and gently pressed down to remove the air but without squashing the filling. My final task was to find each mound of filling under its pasta blanket and cut through with another pastry cutter. Everything depended on my sense of touch.

It took me a very long time to produce just one nearly successful ravioli, so imagine the hours to create plates of three. Topped with smoked egg meringue and toasted hazelnuts, this is definitely a dish for solo suppers because, when perfectly cooked, the egg yolks should still be runny, meaning a spoon and apron are vital for a clumsy consumer. I recommend this as the ideal dish to make and eat for anyone who wants to share the challenges of dining in the dark! The smoked egg made an outstanding pasta dough, but I'd try something very much simpler in my own kitchen.

By the time we had sampled our creation, we had been cooking for hours, were exhausted, and Charlene's husband had been ringing to know whether he and the children were allowed home yet. She, and her whole family and kitchen, had been thoroughly disrupted, and it was definitely time to get out of their lives. It had been a superb experience with Charlene. A special opportunity to understand how cooking can be life-changing.

We were a very tired group that Colin drove home for another of Jane's stunningly simple suppers and early bed. Tomorrow was going to be another long day.

But a fresh dawn brought new energy, and considerable anticipation of learning from Dré at her very upmarket patisserie and restaurant. It felt more like entering a fashion boutique, which was probably right for the fabulous temptations on offer.

We were ensconced in a distinctly chilly preparation room, where my task was to complete one of her trademark eclairs. But first Dré gave me the tips that might have saved the disastrous profiterole experience of Virginia Beach. She explained that once the butter and flour are mixed in the pan it needs cooking much longer than you'd expect. "Cook it out like a roux," she said. "You continue to cook it until it starts to catch on the bottom. Then you cook it for about another minute. It becomes quite dry in the pan, almost like a pasta dough."

Once the eggs had been beaten into the dough (off the heat), Dré's second tip was to let the mix rest. "We never pipe on the same day, so all the gluten has the time to relax. It's easier to pipe the next day because it's firmed up," she explained. She didn't think that choux pastry needed piercing after baking to release steam as her method made it dry enough.

The next meticulous step was to place a thin rectangular biscuit on top of the piped éclair. "It's basically a shortbread that has been rolled really thin," Dré said. "It keeps the shape because it is a bit of weight on the top. And, even better, you can get really creative and flavour the shortbread." Both biscuit and choux pastry are baked together and, to my horror, most of the biscuit is then carefully cut away, leaving a neat rectangular opening into which the filling is piped, surrounded by a little residual crunch and flavour. I couldn't believe all the precious time and effort dedicated just to control the shape of an éclair, but that's professionals for you. It was somewhat reassuring to learn that all those delectable biscuits were devoured during the staff coffee breaks.

Under Dré's expert direction, I managed to fill a piping bag with her caramel bavarois. The easiest method is to drop the narrow end of the bag into the bottom of a tall jug, open out the wide end and fold it over the sides of the jug. Once filled, she showed me how to gather together the top of the bag and use a long strip of clingfilm to tie around it. Now there was no chance of the mixture spurting out the top when piping from the other end. I could then hold the bag like a pen to pipe the first layer of filling into the éclair.

Dré's team had prepared Rice Krispies coated in more caramel and chocolate that I sprinkled on the bavarois for crunch before the next layer: stronger-flavoured caramel butter cream to give yet another texture, temperature and mouth-feel.

Now we were ready to start the decoration, but, first, I had to practice piping the spiral of caramel mousse set with chocolate. Dré made it sound so easy, saying, "Even pressure and spiral slowly with just your wrist." Imagine the fun of doing this blindfolded, holding the little soft squidgy éclair in your left hand while trying to line up the nozzle with the top, squeezing the bag and keeping those wrist rotations going! I just had to guess if the mousse was still on the top or sliding down the sides. Her verdict: "It's uneven, but you've got the spiral." I claimed it was "artistically interpretative".

And the decoration wasn't finished. The mousse had to be impaled with exactly five tiny shards of tempered chocolate and wisps of real gold leaf.

This was the sparkle that marked out Dré's ambitions. "We always have to have bling," she said. "This is the extra little bit of luxe and finesse that we want to offer." She handed me the tiny book of 23 carat gold leaf, so fine that the delicate sheets were interleaved with rice paper. The concept was that I should take miniscule pinches from one sheet and artistically scatter them across the éclair, but the gold leaf was too fine to feel between my finger and thumb. Dre had the answer, suggesting, "Try the back of your hand." She was right. The skin and little hairs had just enough sensitivity that I could find the super-fine gold leaf and pinch off small scraps.

Finally enclosed in a patisserie case of card and paper to protect its delicate finery, the éclair was done – probably not up to standard for sale, but certainly ready for devouring. It was a sublime variety of temperature, tastes and textures that deserved as much time in the eating as the preparation.

All of this had taken hours in the very cold pastry kitchen, so it was a great relief to get back into the hot Melbourne sun in her garden restaurant. We talked more about her plans for the future during lunch and, months later, Dre delightedly told me: "Big news! We actually sold the businesses last year, both Chez Dré and Bibelot, and we've opened a bakery called Q Le Baker. I've also had another little girl, Kiara, so I've definitely got my hands full." Dre's latest venture is in the world of ice cream where business is booming (www.icecreamco.com.au).

These last two days had been a fitting finale to our time in Melbourne. Gastronomically diverse, the city showed that great cooks and chefs aren't constrained by issues of race, nationality, ethnicity, disability, gender or other false barriers. Instead, food is all about generosity, sharing, learning from each other, crossing culinary borders and using the best ideas and ingredients, whatever their source. Melbourne is rightly famous and world-eminent for food. It was a privilege to get behind the scenes with some of the people at the forefront of the industry.

Walking along the riverside, there was another entrancing experience when I was introduced to a kid goat. It wasn't obvious why someone had decided that this was the place to gather a selection of animals, but that kid made my day. The menagerie was clearly aimed at children, but we disabled people can do things that other adults might find too demeaning, too embarrassing, too silly. Instead, I had the joy of feeling that small, warm and wriggly body through its soft wool, that wetly cool tongue lapping my hand, all wrapped in the sun-heated smell of goatiness.

Video: Baking Blind in Melbourne

We were moving on to new adventures in Africa. Heartfelt thanks and farewell to Colin and Jane's home sanctuary as we took the first step, flying up to Perth where airline schedules meant a 24-hour stopover. We desperately needed the break.

Perth was a joy. Not having to cook, getting more of a sense of the outback Australia we imagine, and meeting Lynda after probably 30 years since we were both serving in the old Women's Royal Naval Service. We met up in a hotel deemed by the travel company as "accessible". One day I'd like to insist that all their "advisers" actually attempt to negotiate tiny bathrooms and miniscule bedrooms with their eyes closed. They might have a better perspective of the treacherous rooms they blithely sell. But the bar/café was a treat. Food straight from the hotplate and fryer amidst predominantly male fellow customers whose talk seemed smattered with "digger", "cobber" and "mate". Just minutes from the airport, we felt as if we were on the frontier with the real bush; although perhaps there is less and less of the "authentic" Australia that I imagined from Nevil Shute's *A Town Like Alice*?

Lynda's local knowledge was perfect for exploring a wildlife park and, while I felt my way through a staggering range of craft products, one of our team escaped into the real bush to find wild kangaroos. We moved on to a gallery celebrating indigenous Australian art and crafts. Being able to touch and smell the different pieces, their shapes and materials was just right. We were even able to talk to one of the artists before buying his picture – a sinuous snake captured on canvas in thousands of tiny paint dots. The French impressionist, Seurat, is one of my favourites and used a similar technique, but may not have known that another culture had got there, probably millennia earlier.

While I'd been starting to work in pewter at home, the delicate terrapins and tiny lizards created and cast in metal by these artists were far beyond anything I could imagine producing. It was rather humbling to appreciate how such an ancient culture could produce a heritage of such excellent and living art so closely in tune with the natural life around them.

Back to the hotel, purchases packed and farewell to Lynda, before getting to the airport for the night flight to Africa. But the best laid plans go awry and the plane had been cancelled. We were luckily accommodated in one of Perth's top hotels for another 24 hours before the battle of trying to get a seat on the next flight. I unashamedly took advantage of the full pathos of being a disabled person to get those fast-disappearing seats: a pronounced white cane, a body-weary limp, the stooping shoulder and even the suspicion of a drool.

It might have worked in Perth, but there was no chance during the transfer in Johannesburg. We were rather taken aback by the aggressive approach of the airport staff. The last time I'd been in South Africa was for another World Blind Union conference in Cape Town. The highlight had been the arrival of the then president, Thabo Mbeki, who swept in accompanied by a rendition of the national anthem, Nkosi Sikelel' iAfrica, sung by his choral retinue. While his words of welcome and wisdom have faded, for a gathering of visually impaired people he couldn't have made a stronger or more memorably impressive entrance.

Dani's four-minute bread.

Video: Thermomix four minute bread

300g water.
1 teaspoon dried yeast.
500g bread flour.
10g salt.
1 teaspoon olive oil.

Method.

Mix all the ingredients and allow the yeast to become active, ideally with some gentle heat.

Knead in a mixer or similar for two minutes.

Divide the dough into 7 equal portions and roll to create balls with good surface tension.

Place on a baking tray lined with oiled baking parchment.

Place tray in oven at lowest temperature possible for 45 minutes to rise.

Increase the oven temperature to 240C, Gas 9, 460F.

Flick a little water over the rolls and cook for 15-20 minutes.

My tips.

This cooking temperature seems very high. I would tend to heat the oven to the temperatures given by Dani but turn the heat down to Gas 7 during the actual cooking.

Charlene's recipes.

Pasta dough.

Video: Smoked egg pasta dough

200g durum wheat flour plus extra for dusting.
2 (smoked) eggs at room temperature.
1 tablespoon olive oil.
Quarter teaspoon sea salt flakes.

Method.

Place the flour and salt in a circular mound on a clean work surface.

Make a well in the centre of the flour and break in the eggs. Use fingertips or a fork to break the yolks and combine them with the whites.

Still with fingertips, gradually blend the flour around the well into the eggs until all is combined into a dough.

Check the consistency of the dough: not too dry and crumbling; kneadable without sticking to your hands or the work surface. Too dry: spray on a little water. Too wet: add a little more flour to the surface.

Knead the dough for 6 minutes. Hold the dough on the surface with one hand and push the dough away with the other hand. Fold the stretched dough back on itself, give a half turn and repeat.

You will feel the dough change texture from cotton through linen to silk. Test it is ready by gently pressing a finger into the dough. It should spring back quickly.

Divide the dough into two equal portions, place in plastic bags and chill in the fridge for at least 30 minutes for the gluten to relax and make rolling easier.

Ravioli filling.

Video: Smoked egg ravioli

800g (jap) pumpkin.
300g soft goat cheese.
Quarter teaspoon freshly ground nutmeg.
Quarter teaspoon freshly ground black pepper.
Quarter teaspoon sea salt flakes.
12 raw smoked egg yolks. Reserve the whites of two eggs.

Method.

Preheat oven to 220C, Gas 7, 430F.

Slice the pumpkin into 6 equal portions, rub with olive oil and bake for 1 hour or until softened. Allow to cool/refrigerate overnight.

Mash the cheese and add the pumpkin (skin removed) plus other ingredients (except the eggs) until smooth and mixed. Place in a piping bag and chill.

Sage beurre noisette.

125g butter.
12 fresh sage leaves.
50g hazelnuts.

Method.

Heat a frying pan until hot, add the butter and heat until melted, then add the sage ensuring it is well coated in the butter. Keep the butter and sage on a high heat until the butter turns to a caramel colour and smells "nutty". Add the hazelnuts, then reduce the heat to keep warm until serving.

Garnish.

Grated parmesan cheese.

Soft smoked egg white meringue (egg whites whipped to soft peaks at the last minute).

Constructing the dish.

Roll out the pasta using a rolling pin to make two rectangles about 2mm thick. If using a pasta machine, laminate the pasta by rolling through the widest setting, folding in half and re-rolling, and repeat until silky. Then roll through the machine working up to the number 6 setting.

Cover rolled pasta with a damp tea towel to prevent it drying out.

Pipe 12 4cm diameter circles of pumpkin puree on one of the portions of pasta, leaving about 4cm space between each pumpkin circle.

Gently place a smoked raw egg yolk into the centre of each circle.

Using a pastry brush or spray of water, moisten around each circle. Uncover the second portion of rolled pasta dough and gently lay it over the first.

Use your fingers to gently press over and around the filling to remove trapped air and bond the pasta together. Cut out the ravioli using a 5-6cm circular cutter and place on a lightly floured tray. Refrigerate until ready to cook

Prepare the beurre noisette.

Bring a large pan of salted water to a simmer and carefully slide in the ravioli and cook for 1-2 minutes until the ravioli float to the surface and are cooked.

With a slotted spoon, remove and drain the ravioli and slide into the pan of beurre noisette. Baste quickly with the butter and place on warm serving plates, top with more beurre noisette, the sage leaves and hazelnuts plus the garnish. Serve 2 or 3 ravioli per person.

My tips.

Spray water on rolled pasta and only roll out what you can manage at a time as pasta dries very quickly.

Ordinary eggs will work if smoked ones aren't available, but the flavour of the dish will be different.

Dré's recipes.

Video: Caramel eclairs

Choux pastry.

200g milk.
5g sugar.
5g salt.
100g butter.
8.5g egg, beaten.
150g plain flour.

Method.

Bring the milk, sugar, salt and butter to boil in a pan.

Add flour all at once and cook out excess moisture from the dough, stirring constantly.

Once a film develops on the base of the pot, cook for a few more seconds before placing dough in a mixer to allow the steam to escape while mixing.

Mix in eggs in small increments to make a smooth, elastic choux paste.

Place into a piping bag and refrigerate overnight. Pipe with a plain tip nozzle onto baking parchment.

Cook the choux pastry eclairs or profiteroles in a preheated oven at 190C, Gas 5, 375F for 7 minutes. Turn down to 170C, Gas 3, 340F for 28 minutes.

Croustillant (shortbread crunch on top of choux).

143g butter.
113g sugar.
113g plain flour.

Method.

Combine all ingredients with paddle in mixer.

Roll between two sheets of parchment paper with rolling pin.

Cut 12cm in length, 2cm wide. Store in freezer.

Place on top of choux pastry before baking.

Caramel bavarois.

325g milk.
325g cream.
162.5 sugar.
2g vanilla paste.
130g egg yolks.
45.5g gelatine mass.
325g cream, semi-whipped.

Method.

Heat cream and milk, not too hot.

Make a dry caramel with the sugar, deglaze with liquid and vanilla.

Pour over yolks and cook "anglaise" to 84°C. Add gelatine mass and strain.

At 30°C, add whipped cream.

Whisk before using.

Salted caramel buttercream.

900g sugar.
450g cream.
15g salt.
2.5g vanilla paste.
37.5g butter.
700g butter, softened "pomade".

Method.

Make a dry caramel. Deglaze with hot cream, salt and vanilla. Add butter.

Cool caramel down to 40°C before adding softened butter pomade.

Pour mixture into a mixer and add butter slowly until just incorporated.

Set in the fridge. Bring to room temperature before using.

Caramel Chantilly.

250g sugar.
1420g cream.
385g Criolait 38% (milk chocolate).
150g butter.
8.5g salt.

Method.

Make a dry caramel with the sugar. Deglaze with 500g cream.

Add butter and salt.

Pour over chocolate and make a ganache.

Mix in remaining cream and set overnight.

Constructing the dish.

Cut small slit in the top of the éclair choux.

Pipe in some caramel bavarois with a piping bag.

Pipe in some caramel butter cream (at room temperature).

Sprinkle and push down some of the chocolate-coated Rice Krispies (optional – these were made by Dré's team).

Whip the caramel Chantilly until just starting to firm up.

Pipe the Chantilly with a star nozzle onto the éclair in a coil shape.

Decorate with shards of broken dark chocolate and gold leaf.

My tips.

Dré's advice could have avoided the disastrous profiteroles I'd made in Virginia Beach: "Once the butter and flour for the choux pastry are mixed in the pan, it needs cooking much longer than you'd expect. Cook it out like a roux. You continue to cook it until it starts to catch on the bottom. Then you cook it for about another minute. It becomes quite dry, almost like a pasta dough."

Chapter 21.

The warm heart of Africa.

After the long and difficult journey arriving in Lilongwe, capital of Malawi, was a huge relief. Our November arrival coincided with the hottest time of the year and, while the temperature wasn't overwhelming, I could foresee that cooking in a kitchen was likely to be difficult.

Video: Baking Blind in Africa

Coming from the UK, completely surrounded by sea, it felt quite strange to be landlocked and distant from any ocean. But Lake Malawi running down the side of the country was an intriguing alternative. This "lake of stars" (according to explorer David Livingstone) supported the local fishing industries that were central to the older parts of the capital and still fed the people.

This was a fast-developing country, and the many roadside signs announcing the funding support from all over the world were described to me. The Carlsberg factory was perhaps one of the most unusual, the original factory and distribution plant being the only one in Africa. The internet and mobile phones were improving communications, while road and building construction was strengthening the economy. Blind people were benefitting too as I was to learn.

But the country's rural heritage remained strong. Many of the Malawian people still grow much of their own food in land around their villages and in their city gardens. Fruit and vegetables, such as mangoes, onions, cucumbers, lettuce, beans, carrots and, especially, the tomatoes that featured in nearly every dish, were picked fresh and reach the kitchen without the complexity and cost of supermarket logistics and infrastructure. If you are growing vegetables such as cassava or pumpkins, then you can eat the leaves too. Making use of every part of a plant justifies all the time and effort of growing it.

People had to think about food in a different way. If electricity and refrigeration wasn't available, then they needed a safe preservation method. Dried fish and air-dried okra and bean leaves were typical.

Just like the grits I tried in San Francisco, maize was a good carbohydrate alternative to potatoes, pasta or rice – essential when you have a busy and physically active life. In Malawi, the staple food is nsima, which is like porridge made with the ground maize kernels (that we'd eat as sweetcorn). The nsima came in two versions: the basic brown, or white, when the husks have been removed before grinding. Other carbohydrates included sweet potatoes and flour made from raw groundnuts (which we eat as roasted and salted peanuts). Locally grown rice was equally valuable but, like the dried okra leaves, first you have to pick out every tiny stone, tough twig and unknown leaf.

As in most parts of the world, protein tended to be more expensive and eaten more sparingly. But a freshly killed, plucked and cooked chicken that has had a free-range life was worth savouring, and often made a celebratory meal for guests or that special family occasion. Being landlocked, Malawi imports seafood, but the fresh waters of the rivers and Lake Malawi offer a bounty of fish, particularly the famous chambo – a tilapine cichlid fish.

Cooking outside was more comfortable in the hot climate and, where there wasn't electricity or gas on tap, a basic fire on the ground was the answer. A strong terracotta or metal pan perched on a couple of bricks around the flames made economic one-pot cooking. And forget your food processor: you stand with a long-handled pestle and grind cassava leaves in the mortar at your feet. Although some of the methods and ingredients were different, the principles of creating good nourishing food from local produce were very familiar.

We were lucky to be hosted and sponsored by the renowned Latitude 13 hotel (www.latitudehotels.com) where Jessica, Toby's sister and my niece, had worked a few years earlier. She had been involved in the eclectic interior design of the hotel's individual apartments that celebrate handcrafting and recycling. She went on to create giant papier maché globes for the lighting of more of the Latitude hotels in other countries. Back in Lilongwe, we were ushered into spacious accommodation: a kitchen and living area with two bedrooms and a bathroom above. The space was beautifully tactile, with smooth refurbished pipes creating the bannisters around the landing, and the recycled wood of the furniture contrasting with the sleek lines of the modern bathroom. But the stairs, without any outside handrail, seemed highly perilous. Without hesitation, the general manager, Mehul, came to the rescue, and by the next day he had vacated his own accommodation and I was installed in a rather more accessible but equally well-appointed environment.

Over the years, I've realised that many are nervous around disabled people. They are worried about saying or doing the wrong thing, embarrassing me, or even worse, themselves. Interactions work better if I take charge and put them at their ease, tell them what is needed and how to do it. A few painful knocks have also taught me not to distract them with other conversation: they are already coping with new responsibilities and risks; they don't have the capacity for idle chit-chat.

And the cooking commenced. Again, the hotel staff had gone to great pains to make the experience as comfortable and easy as possible. Rather than being confined to the heat and noise of his professional kitchen, boisterously cheerful and generous head chef Cephus had set up tables and a portable stove under a huge shady tree alongside the swimming pool. We were cooler in this airy setting, with our labours punctuated by the joyous shrieks of the children and the splashes of them romping in the water.

Cephus's first step was to measure my head, concluding, "I think that your head is large." And I couldn't disagree. A few deft moves and he presented me with my own adjustable paper chef's toque, open at the top: more hygienic and the air could circulate. He talked a little about his background: "I love cooking. I've been doing it for close to 15 years. There is love in cooking." He was clearly inspiring his team as sous-chef Emily shyly giggled with me saying, "I am enjoying working here and I'm learning from him."

We started with an apparently straightforward halloumi salad, but it reinforced the differences in life when the amenities we take for granted are not available. Hence, washing the lettuce wasn't just a matter of running it under a tap. Where there may not be refrigeration between farm and kitchen, and where natural manure feeds plants, more rigorous measures are needed. Our simple lettuce had to be soaked in a purple solution of potassium permanganate for 10 minutes before Cephus was satisfied that it would be bacteria-free for rinsing and shredding. He cautioned me, "It can stain your hands," but also reassured, "It doesn't change the flavour at all."

He was proud to use another mainstay ingredient and said, "The halloumi is locally made, right here in Malawi. It's a cheese made from goat and sheep and, sometimes, cows' milk. It is processed in such a way that its boiling point is very high, so it's easy for you to grill or deep fry it. It's a very good source of calcium."

Our meticulously served mixed salad was topped with the crusty fried cheese plus homemade beetroot, carrot and butternut squash crisps for extra crunch and eye appeal. "I'm arranging it beautifully. Seeing is also part of eating," he said. The crowning glory was his cooked dressing using the inner pulp of passionfruit (granadillas is their local name), and there was absolutely no trace of the permanganate left.

Cephus explained his hallmark menu: "Halloumi comes from the Middle East countries, so we have incorporated it into our menu so that we have different food coming from different regions and continents. In our cuisine, we have mixed fusion. There's Italian, French, Malaysian. Different types of cooking are put together to accommodate everyone who comes to visit Latitude 13." In one of the most prestigious hotels in the capital, he was catering for discriminating multi-national, multi-racial and multi-faith guests. Sitting in the poolside restaurant, we could be rubbing shoulders with national politicians, local socialites and representatives of international charities. I was a long way down the pecking order!

By the time we moved on to his bestselling dish, Cephus was very relaxed about cooking with me. "We are going to make risotto with butter-fried prawns. It will be a wonderful time, you and I making this dish together. We will share this fun. It is difficult for us to get seafood because we are landlocked, so most of our seafood comes from Mozambique." But other ingredients were home-grown: "Chopped oyster mushrooms are grown locally within our neighbourhood here."

As he stirred the pan and gradually added the stock, Cephus talked about changes. "Malawi used to be a one-party state," he explained, "but, this time around, it's under democratic rule. Things have changed a lot. We should start with communication. With the internet, it's easier to communicate with other people. It's made a difference in the sense that, a long time ago, we could only use letters to communicate with people who were far away. Having these networks and a lot of communications equipment has made our lives easier. There are road networks which are being constructed. It's changing the entire economy of Malawi just because people are engaged in business and they are able to move, they've got transport, that means everything is going well economically." He said that standards of living were improving and that people were happier: "We can see construction of buildings, more hotels being built. It is making our lives better."

He told me how blind people are benefitting too: "In Malawi, the government is supporting them a lot. There are schools where blind people can go. They've got their own writing – you call it Braille – that you can feel with your fingers. They are giving them opportunities to do some piecework, like knitting. When they knit, they can feel it and produce a certain jersey. The support is helping them move towards work."

Like any great chef, Cephus was adapting his past experience of cooking in an Italian restaurant to his current dishes and use of local ingredients. "I like this dish so much. The risotto rice has the same qualities as our staple food in Malawi. Nsima, which is made from maize flour, is also high in carbohydrates. So someone having this dish will have a lot of energy to work throughout the day. Polenta flour and maize flour look similar so, instead of cooking the nsima flour the way we normally do, I twisted it and used it in dishes where I would normally use polenta." Typically, he'd make a firm polenta-style cake with nsima that could be sliced to accompany a dish.

It was a successful morning creating two great dishes which we devoured hungrily alongside the pool and the chattering children. The combination of more familiar European-style food with Malawian ingredients and cooking techniques was an excellent introduction to the country's culture. Everyone had been immensely kind, generous and enthusiastic. No wonder Malawi is known as the "warm heart of Africa".

Cephus's recipes.

Halloumi salad.

Video: Haloumi salad at Latitude 13

Tomatoes, halved.
Clove garlic, peeled and finely chopped.
Drizzle of olive oil.
1 beetroot, very thinly sliced.
1 handful butternut squash shavings.
Oil for frying.
1 head lettuce, roughly chopped.
1 bunch rocket leaves, roughly chopped.
1 small onion, peeled and sliced into thin rings.
1 carrot, peeled and cut into matchsticks.
Half avocado, peeled and cubed.
120g halloumi cheese, cubed.
About 1 tablespoon plain flour.
1 orange, peeled and segmented.
Drizzle passionfruit dressing.

Method.

Sprinkle the tomato halves with finely chopped garlic and a drizzle of olive oil then place in the oven. Cephus: "I leave them in the oven overnight at 100 degrees Celsius (210F)."

Cook the butternut squash and beetroot crisps. Cephus: "We first peel our beetroot from raw and then slice it into very thin slices. We rinse it in a little water and dry it again to remove a little of the colour just because it might get in our oil. Then I medium fry it at about 60 degrees Celsius (140F), slowly because, if you fry at a high temperature, they will get burnt." He used the same method with the butternut squash crisps.

Wash the lettuce and rocket. If using potassium permanganate, soak the leaves in the solution for 10 minutes, then rinse thoroughly and pat dry.

Mix the lettuce, rocket, onion, carrot and avocado.

Heat a little oil in a pan. Gently roll the halloumi in the flour and then fry until brown and crisp on each side (about 2 minutes per side).

Place the cheese on the salad with orange segments.

Drizzle with passionfruit dressing before topping with beetroot and squash crisps.

My tips.

Storing the halloumi cheese in brined water helped it keep for 5-6 days. It was washed and dried before being rolled in flour to create the crispy crust when fried in a little olive oil.

Passionfruit salad dressing.

3 passionfruit, pulp from interior.
300ml olive oil.
300ml white balsamic vinegar.
1 lime or lemon, juice only.

Method.

Simmer all the ingredients in a pan for about 5 minutes until reduced and thickened, stirring frequently.

Sieve and discard the seeds.

Cool the dressing and adjust acidity and seasoning.

My tips.

In Malawi, Cephus could get tinned passionfruit pulp.

Risotto with butter fried prawns.

Video: Risotto with butter-fried prawns

1 onion, peeled and finely chopped.
2 cloves garlic, peeled and finely chopped.
1 tablespoon olive oil.
200g risotto (arborio) rice.
1 glass/120ml white wine.
2 large handfuls oyster mushrooms, chopped.

1 litre fish, chicken or vegetable stock.
2 large handfuls prawns, heads and shells removed, de-veined.
Tablespoon butter.
1 garlic clove, peeled and finely chopped.
1 lemon, zest and juice.
Salt and pepper.
3 tablespoons parmesan shavings.
1 tablespoon balsamic reduction.

Method.

Gently fry the onion and 2 cloves garlic in olive oil until soft but not coloured.

Add the chopped mushrooms and cook on low heat.

Add the rice and continue frying while stirring.

Pour in the wine and increase the heat to let the alcohol evaporate completely, leaving just flavour, while stirring.

Add a cup of the hot stock to the rice and stir, allow the rice to absorb the stock before adding a further cup and repeat over about 25 minutes until the rice is cooked. Cephus: "Now I have to add some of my stock, slowly, slowly, a little at a time until the rice is cooked, but it mustn't be cooked to a porridge stage, just to be al dente."

Meanwhile, sauté the prawns in butter with more finely chopped garlic and lemon zest, season and add lemon juice to taste.

Place risotto on two plates, top with prawns and their buttery garlicky lemony juices. Sprinkle with cheese and drizzle with the balsamic reduction. Serve immediately.

My tips.

You can use homemade fish stock or stock made with cubes. Cephus's stock was "made from the carcass of the chicken with vegetables simmered a long time in the pot."

Chapter 22.

Cooking under the African sun.

Next day we were closer to the people of Malawi. Thanks to Cephus, Mehul and sous-chef Mphatso we were visiting a nearby village to learn more about local food. All the residents had turned out en masse for us, demonstrating their strong social culture: the women with the younger children sitting on one woven straw mat, other girls on another, while the male elders sat on chairs in the shade as befitting their age and status. Like any teenagers, the young men lurked around the edges being determinedly bored with the whole spectacle.

The backdrop was the line of circular-shaped homes built of handmade bricks under rough render. Baking the bricks over open fires helps with construction, but brings the risk of carcinogens. The basic thatched rooves were doubtless cooler in the hot climate, easy to create from local vegetation and, with waterproof liners, kept them snug and dry. The whole design was for outdoor community living with cool, airy sleeping quarters. The structured village culture was impressive. In a place without electricity or running water, everyone and everything, down to the communal latrine, was immaculately neat, tidy, clean and orderly. There was a strong sense of peace, order and positivity. I could hear the fresh washing flapping on the line in the distance, the villagers chatting and the children laughing.

Rather than cooking in the traditional clay pots over fires on the ground, Cephus and Mphatso had set up a sort of field kitchen in their midst where I could try to be entertaining and repay the villagers' hospitality. There was general hilarity as I stood pounding leaves in the mortar at my feet lacking any finesse. One of the local women kept a very sceptical eye on my attempts throughout the morning as she was clearly keen to ensure that I did justice to their traditional recipes.

In reality, Cephus and Mphatso did everything and just let me do the odd bit of stirring and tasting. He explained, "That's our vegetables: cassava leaves mixed with groundnut powder (flour made from raw ground peanuts) and tomatoes. You have to scoop a little bit and test. You've taken too much!" The chopped leaves were simmered for 5-10 minutes before adding chopped tomatoes, the nsinjiro flour and seasoning. It was an excellent accompaniment to the fish, dusted in flour and fried crisp in groundnut oil, served with a little lemon juice. "Our vegetables will be going with the sema and the fish. That's chambo that you can get fresh, because Lake Malawi stretches from the northern part of Malawi to the southern part. There are a lot of fish, but this one is very famous and is similar to the telapi fish in Lake Malawi – catfish and butter fish."

The ubiquitous nsima was made like a porridge, more and more of the rough-textured maize flour added to boiling water until it formed a slowly bubbling and blooping mass that could be spooned onto the plate. The combination of chambo fish protein, vitamin-rich vegetables and maize carbohydrate is a classic Malawian meal, all the local ingredients delivering all the nutrition needed while tasting wonderful in that wide open space.

Mphatso taught me a sort of banana steamed pudding: three chopped bananas mixed with two cups of maize flour and a teaspoon or so of bicarbonate of soda. The mix was wrapped in banana leaves, tied with a strand of a spare leaf and steamed for 20 minutes.

Meanwhile, while we worked over the burners, Toby was a huge hit with the young men and children as youthful exuberance transcended any language barriers. Mehul had sent the hotel driver off to buy sweets, drinks and treats for them, and the plastic bottles were clearly as desirable as their contents. He was planning ways in which the hotel could support the village, and clothes, bedding and many other spare items were destined to make that simple lifestyle a little easier.

Having shared out our cooked dishes, we and the whole village trundled a few miles across the rough terrain to a large open space flooded by the sun's heat. A noisy crowd drawn from the locality had gathered to celebrate their chieftain, who stood tall and proud in a formal business suit before his people. There were wildly exotic costumes and masks worn by the dancers, and much foot-stomping to the sound of cheers and singing. They were all having such a wonderful time that the hotel driver couldn't keep still but jumped out of the car to join the dancing. I felt a bit left out of it all, sitting on rather a throne-like bench on the side-lines while everyone else was having a great time.

This was one of the most striking days of the whole tour. I had been very concerned that we might seem rather voyeuristic in the village: distant Europeans having an "experience". It was humbling to appreciate what positive lives were possible amidst such simple and basic circumstances. I came away with considerable respect for those villagers, who were maintaining their traditions, bringing up their families, and celebrating their society. Externally, everything seemed so different, but the life essentials were reassuringly familiar and strong.

Video: Cooking and dancing with Malawian villagers

Driving back through the centre of Lilongwe, we stopped to visit the Remembrance Memorial, a massive construction marking all those Malawians who died in the two world wars and other conflicts. I ran my fingers across names carved into the great stone monolith, and descended the long steps to give them a naval salute. Perhaps we don't pay enough attention to all those who fought alongside us in the past. But it did strike the chord of how military service binds us together, from those who were commemorated there, through James Holman, to my own career.

Chapter 23.

Ghosts and spirits.

There are about four thousand people with albinism in the 70 million population of Malawi. More prone to skin cancer in that land of hot sun, their eyesight is often affected, meaning many have significant levels of visual impairment. Their lack of pigmentation results in paler skin and hair, which means they stand out from their fellow Malawians. Many of them have a very tough time. As has happened in so many places around the world, people who look different have been treated differently. In parts of Africa, those pale people with albinism had been believed to be ghosts or spirits.

Some, especially in rural areas, faced more problems. Women giving birth to a child with albinism have been accused of infidelity and abandoned by their husbands, making life and finances even tougher. People with the condition have struggled to be integrated into their communities, with disastrous consequences on their education and employment prospects. Most sinister are the physical attacks. Tione from the Association of Persons with Albinism in Malawi told me that over 20 people with the condition had been killed over recent years – and three during the previous 12 months. But death wasn't the end of it. Some bodies were dug up, and there was trade in their bones for use in ritual magic in other countries. Disability has many drawbacks, but nothing compared to the deadly discrimination some still encounter.

But there was clearly progress in Lilongwe. We spent a day with Tione, her daughter Samantha, and the association, a self-help group that shared some of their experiences (www.actiononalbinism.org/page/c6cd5zzky9qtvx7viqtw0o1or). Like so many other people with disabilities, they had the motivation and determination to succeed in the face of, in their case, almost insuperable barriers.

We drove through the busy, noisy streets of Lilongwe to a gated compound enclosing a productive garden plot, accommodation and a separate room set up for dining. The garden produced food to eat and sell, as Tione explained: "In here there are three beds. The bean vegetables were here. I just pulled them up and sold them yesterday. These are pumpkin leaves and, in the other bed, are potato leaves." There was also a small orchard growing pears, mangoes, guava and five types of bananas.

The members of the albino group and their supporters were very excited to explain the enormous range of food they had bought at the local market for our cooking session. Maize flour featured again. "There are two types of flour," Tione said. "This one is called giewa. It is the one prepared with just the maize, you don't take anything out. Then you have the white one. This is where we take the husk out. We will have two different types of nsima. They taste somewhat different because we soak the white one in water."

There were more bags of ingredients stacked on the table. Tione explained, "We have two different types of mangoes (the local yellow mango and the green hybrid version). Then we have cucumbers, onions and two types of dried vegetables: dried bean leaves and dried local okra leaves. We have the rice, locally produced. We have two types of fish. The fresh one is chambo and the dried smoked fish that we call sepa. And then we have the vegetable, the leaves coming from the pumpkin. Then we have the groundnut flour, the tomatoes and the peaches, which we wash and eat like apples."

We already had enough for a feast, but one key live ingredient had nearly been overlooked: "We have the chicken we just bought from the local market and, as we were carrying it here, we saw an egg. This is going to be real traditional food."

Sitting on the wooden veranda, my first task was to assist Cecilia to prepare the pumpkin leaves. Each long thick stalk has fine strands that have to be stripped away, rather like the stringy bits on celery. It was difficult to feel all the strands, so I managed the obvious ones, while Cecilia, who had a little vision, finished the job. Although she was so shy that she could hardly talk to me, she certainly managed to communicate her derision at my very pathetic attempts. I moved on to bean preparation – easier for a novice.

Virginia, another member of the albino group, was more encouraging about my efforts to chop the pumpkin leaves. As a schoolteacher, she knows how to encourage those who aren't doing so well! She talked about her job in Lilongwe: "I teach English. The ages range from 10 to 18. It's a girls' secondary school." She enthused about the capital's travel improvements: "The access to facilities. If you want to visit the market, the clinics, the hospitals, as with your visit here, it doesn't take much time. Just some minutes instead of maybe an hour." She also gave me more insight into the consequences of her medical condition: "The challenge of having albinism in Malawi is the skin pains. The heat from the sun, the skin reacts with pain. We appreciate that our government has now shipped in the sun screen cream that protects us from the sun." Ordinary sun lotion isn't sufficient protection, and the only other alternative is to cover up: "We put on long-sleeved white clothes that reflect the heat and need a hat – none of which is comfortable under the hot sun."

Video: Malawi Albino Party Part 2 Draft 2

Virginia knew that others often have little understanding of their situation, such as the sight consequences of albinism. She said, "I can see things that are close to me. Reading and writing are very difficult." Moving around the busy and, sometimes, chaotic city is also challenging: "We take someone close to us who will tell us if there is danger ahead." Other pedestrians, who realise the situation, will read street signs and directions or "When there's a danger ahead of us, they are able to explain: let's use this way; wait a moment there's a danger; wait there's a car ahead of you; let's now cross." But not everyone is so understanding. "Human beings have different mindsets. Some people are not kind. If they see something that is dangerous, they just pass by. They don't care and mind their own business. If they understand more and have more information about us, I believe that they would act more positively towards people with albinism."

With all the preparation completed, it was time to start cooking. This was the authentic Malawian style: several small fires on the ground surrounded by bricks on which the different pots sat. Virginia explained the method with the pumpkin leaves: "We boil the water first. Once shredded and put into the boiling water, the pumpkin leaves don't take long to cook, about five to ten minutes. Then we add chopped tomatoes and stir them with a stick. They cook for some minutes and, when they change colour, they are tender." There was very little water in the pot, so it was more like steaming spinach than boiling cabbage.

The smoke-dried fish with a completely unpronounceable name was simply fried, while the fresh chambo was cooked with vegetables: "The fish has been cut into two pieces and we have put it in the pot. We have just added some water to it and added tomatoes with a little oil and onions."

In the UK, when we open a supermarket pack of ingredients, we expect it to be ready for cooking straightaway. We have probably forgotten the extra care needed to prepare home-grown food such as the dried okra leaves, gathered into a handy bag from a pile at the market. "This is another little dish called osma," Virginia explained. "These are just the okra leaves, which are dried under shade not in the sun. Once it is dried, then you can keep it for a long period of time. The first step is to remove anything that is not the okra leaves. Then we can start the process of making it into tiny pieces. You put it in between your hands. The hand-rubbing makes the leaves disintegrate, before being added to salted boiling water with bicarbonate of soda that helps break them down further. You put in the okra then you cook it into a paste and, after some time, you put in the groundnut flour and some tomatoes."

The rice was tossed in a sieve as it also needed all the extraneous debris and husks removed before cooking: "This is a local rice. We are checking for the stones and for everything that is not necessary." Our unanimous agreement was that this is not a job to leave to a blind person.

Nsima was, of course, also on the menu, and I learned that it has to be stirred hard to create the right consistency, like Goldilocks' porridge, not too thick and not too thin. Tomatoes were the other common theme, appearing in nearly every dish including the beans, carrots and onions.

Meanwhile the chicken had been removed to a discreet location for despatch. Dipping the carcass in boiling water helped with removing the feathers and, once the plucked bird had been washed again, it was simply simmered in water. It had never crossed my mind that hens have a whole series of developing eggs within their bodies. Some did not yet have their shells and had been boiled alongside the bird.

As all the elements of the meal were progressing, I talked with another member of the albino group who was also working hard to support his family. Lazarus was a one-man-band street musician. Beer bottle tops strung on wire around his ankle formed a sort of tambourine, and his heel beat the simple drum wedged under his stool to complete the rhythm section. He played the tunes on his donated guitar, but it was his voice that transformed simple songs into evocative and memorable music. He had composed many of the songs which were often inspired by the Gospels because, he said, "God is King."

Life and finding work wasn't easy for him due to his albinism. It took long hours of playing around Lilongwe to earn enough money to feed his young children, Josephine and Elijah. His body was starting to suffer from the repeated foot drumming, his fingers sore from the strumming, and his back was feeling the strain of long hours playing. But he was making progress and was endlessly cheerfully upbeat, although painfully shy. His ambition was to open a shop so that his wife could work too.

And it was time to eat. A huge feast was spread before us all and prayers were said in thanks for the plentiful bounty. Normally their meals were rather simpler: "Usually nsima, some vegetables and some protein – fish or meat."

Our prayer of grace over the meal was followed by boisterous cheers, toasts of bottled water and much laughter about my hopeless efforts with the pumpkin leaves. Lazarus serenaded our happy chatter and laughter.

Appetites satisfied and each different element of the meal tasted, we all waved and said our farewells. The noise of the city, its traffic and voluble throngs of people, plus the constant sounds of new construction were reminders of the activity and progress surrounding the more tranquil compound.

It had been a day of learning more about struggles with health and disability, plus their consequences on social integration and financial survival. Just tiny genetic changes had so much impact, and yet people are still resilient, ambitious and motivated. Our equality concerns in the

UK pale into insignificance compared with the terrors that some have faced in Africa due to their colour.

But there was good news in the following months: Lazarus was taken under the wing of popstar Madonna, a film about his life and music was produced, and he has a growing presence on social media and the internet (www.lazarus-malawi.com). He has also been featured on the BBC World Service doing what he does best. Who would have guessed at the start of this simple cooking adventure that I would meet Lazarus and many others who match the success of James Holman? Triumphs of resilience and talent overcoming more difficulties than most of us can imagine. There is no end to the surprises and abilities of people all over the world.

Video: Virginia talking about life in Malawi and Lazarus

And so our time in Africa came to a conclusion, more grateful for what benefits life offers and more respectful of what others achieve.

Video: Baking blind in Malawi

Chapter 24.

By the skin of my teeth (literally).

The next bit of this story is difficult for me to write for reasons that will soon be clear. There wasn't a great deal of time for relaxation when we got back to the UK. All that unpacking, washing, sorting out heaps of correspondence, catching up with domestic tasks that had languished for months, preparing for Christmas on top of the follow-up actions from the tour, bills, claims, thank yous and more.

The annual Christmas Fair in Portsmouth Naval Base was the perfect chance to showcase a location that would have been well-known to James Holman (much of his early Navy career was within a short boat ride) and my own experiences. He would have recognised the old Naval Academy, where I'd been responsible for the university units and, later, changed the performance appraisal system for over 37,000 people. He too probably walked along the narrow dockyard roads, between the mellow brick buildings and beside the rope walk (www.historicdockyard.co.uk). I was less confident that he'd have heard anything like the modern renditions of sea shanties, and the backdrop of modern warships would have been a wonder. For me, this became a special video, as it captured experiences that day that I've lost due to the amnesia of subsequent events.

Video: Naval history still inspires

But, at the time, it was glorious to be sleeping in my own bed again and, within a couple of weeks, I was packed and en route to France, prospecting for European cooking opportunities and new adventures.

I know that I flew to France from Southampton airport, and cooked a little for a staff Christmas lunch during the following week. I remember going to a restaurant for my birthday lunch, but not what we ate. I was in a car, an alarm buzzing due to a bag on the back seat. Then, a massive bang and waking, mouth full of teeth chips. Sure we had been hit, I managed to suggest taking photos. Unable to move, and the passenger door wouldn't open. But I had the clear impression of an open door on the right, the invitation to pass through it to the comfortable light-filled space beyond. It took a resolute decision not to slip away but to shout as loudly as I could, mainly to reassure myself that I was still alive. The last recollection was the sound of the firemen cutting off the roof of the car.

Six weeks later I regained consciousness in a hospital in Angers, still unable to move, tubes up my nose, surrounded by beeping machines and absolutely furious that my hands were tied to the bed's side rails (www.chu-angers.fr).

Over the next days, weeks and even years, I gradually learned what had happened: a car crash with one man killed and others injured. I've never discovered whether an air ambulance moved me to the hospital, although it seems I arrived first. Apparently it was easy to locate me in the emergency bay – something to do with loud stentorian demands for help with my bladder.

The car airbags had saved me, but there were still fractures to my spine, sternum, all the ribs on my left side, plus other head and body trauma. The biggest threat was the C2 neck vertebra fracture. Paralysis from the neck down was a real possibility, even if I survived. The medics abandoned surgical repair. Turning me facedown was too risky, as the broken ribs wouldn't support my weight. The only solution was to encase my neck and upper chest in a sort of fibreglass brace to prevent any movement and allow the bones to fuse back together naturally. Along with some internal bleeds and other injuries, I wasn't breathing too well either. Heavy sedation kept me still while bones mended, and tubes down my nose delivered food and oxygen.

I wasn't alone. Toby, brothers Martin, Peter and Christopher, plus friends Joan and Sue all travelled over to France to visit during those first six weeks in the Intensive Care unit. Apparently I was a little lucid with some of them. I have no memory of weeks before the accident, or those visits, but friends and family did feature as the heroes in the nightmares I was experiencing. I was living a vivid life of drug addiction, captivity and rescue, like starring in my own thriller psychodrama with a chorus line of French nurses. What is said and done around people who appear unconscious still seems to penetrate their minds.

As I became more conscious, I understood why my hands were tied: I'd tried to feel the nasal intubation and terrified the medical team that I might pull the tubes out. Reinsertion would not have been possible and, without the tubes, I'd have died. Looking back, and after much help with the post-traumatic stress disorder, I can now be more grateful and less furious.

I wasn't their easiest patient in other ways too, blind and unable to talk due to the tubes. Martin had written up common phrases that would help them with English vocabulary that had escaped their classrooms. "I'm going to wash your private parts" made me laugh, even at the time. In turn, my French was from ancient schooldays, and more complicated due to the tubes. Writing seemed to be the answer, but there was much hilarity when I asked for "la plume de ma tante" instead of a pen. The solution was to develop a whole language of bi-lingual sound effects, while my French comprehension rapidly improved.

The Intensive Care doctors and nurses were utterly superb and empathetic. A team of at least six was needed several times a day to turn, wash me and make me feel human again. It was a routine that emerged in my dreams, but had been transported to a stylish Belle Époque apartment in Paris. Even unconscious, I was doing interior decorating.

All this time, and for weeks to come, my neck and chest were held rigid in the brace. Being kept completely still allowed the broken bones to slowly mend, at the cost of pressure sores on my head and chin. Longer hair is needed now to cover the scars on my head and, while hopefully not too visible, I'm very conscious of the changed feel of my face.

My room in the Intensive Care unit seemed to have become a drop-in centre for staff gossip and laughter. I was improving enough to choose the colour (red) of a new, smaller neck brace that allowed the pressure sores to start recovering. Two physiotherapists began working on me, initially sitting and gradually progressing to the upright. When I first managed to stand, with much help and a metal support frame, there were about a dozen of the staff crowded in, cheering me on. I was determined to show them what their work and care had achieved.

There was still a very long way to go. After two months of intensive care, I was loaded onto a stretcher for transfer to the Capucin rehabilitation hospital, still in Angers. I remained confined to brace and bed for another month while the critical cervical vertebrae slowly fused back together, although permanently displaced. Physiotherapist, François, got to work on me straightaway, and I started learning to move my legs and arms again, using the electric bed transformed into a massive chair to relearn sitting, cycling on a bed pedalo to start rebuilding wasted muscles. My first "shower" in the big en suite wet room was thrilling. Transferred onto a special trolley by nursing assistants Bernadette and Claudette, the sides folded up to form a waterproof enclosure – my "petit bateau". I was wheeled into the wet room and the shower jet applied – utter bliss to be clean again, top to toe. And the joy of losing the catheter after all those months, once I could prove to the echograph that I was capable of emptying my bladder independently! I had quickly learned that privacy was a thing of the past. I'd also been promoted from the hard neck brace and could even remove the foam version in bed – the pleasure of fresh air on skin once again.

Video: A twist of fate interrupts Baking Blind world tour

The time eventually came for my first venture out of bed for months. That move is seared in my memory. Rolled from side to side into an enormous bag, the handles attached to a ceiling hoist, the electric pulley activated. I was terrified that if the bag didn't fail, the ceiling would. But the shrieking bundle was successfully deposited in an electric wheelchair – new freedom to move, but only if one could see to steer with the joystick. With help, I was able to leave my room and explore the hospital and its grounds. I could venture outside, nervously clinging to the chair as my muscles and balance struggled to cope with slopes and kerbs. I could even visit the hospital café to sit alongside real, undamaged people for a hot drink in a more congenial environment.

But François wasn't letting me relax. Trundled off to one of the enormous gyms, I had my first contact with other patients, some determinedly trying to walk, others who had been in the hospital for several years, simply enjoying a different place to chat. He placed me in front of a set of parallel bars, with instruction to get out of the wheelchair. It was just impossible. I returned every day that week, and wept each time I failed. Over three months in bed had banished the strength of my arm and leg muscles. Faced with this challenge, my mental resilience evaporated.

Video: Walking wounded

Wall bars were the salvation. A sloped stool under my knees gave me the confidence that I wouldn't slide to the floor, and I pulled myself upright using the bars. The parallel bars that had seemed insuperable became my supports as I staggered up and down, gradually holding on less and less. I began to realise there would come a time when I'd be walking the long distance to the gym rather than using the wheelchair. It seemed an impossible goal but, day by day, over two months, my walking improved, the parallel bars became easy, a walking frame was made redundant, and I could manage with a supporting arm and my white cane (rescued from the accident).

Even when I could get from the bed to the walking frame by myself, independence was still out of my grasp: I needed someone else to guide me to the wheelchair and, eventually and to the sound of trumpets, to the loo. It was a huge sense of freedom after so many months prone. Eventually I could use the walking frame like a white cane to feel my way around, and the nurses had marked the grabrails in the bathroom so I could locate myself. I could even manage a solo shower using the high chair in the wet room, but drying my feet was still too challenging for my poor balance.

Another triumph was relearning stairs. By then I was managing the corridor with the walking frame, and persuaded the physiotherapist to take me to the main staircase to "experiment with the balance of lifting one foot onto a step." It was a ruse, as I was completely determined to do better and be independent. Pulling myself up with the bannisters, I grunted my way up to the first landing. It felt miraculous, but proved rather easier than the trepidation of going back down. Taking one foot off the step, and hoping it would connect with the next step down and not give way, was a matter of mind over body. That staircase became a joy for me as the weeks passed and I could progress from one landing to one floor and then more. Most delightful was the wonderful echo of the stairwell. The nurses thought I was quite mad when they heard me singing "I am a mole and I live in a hole" with all the rumbling resonance.

The staff learned to tell me when they entered and left the room, and who they were, so I wasn't talking to an empty space. Everything was arranged to the millimetre: I could (usually) find the call button, a drink or my audio book; I could use my laptop without disconnecting the charging cable. But it wasn't always straightforward. Although I'd learned the layout of the room and wet room, I still needed a guide to move anywhere else, and the staff were often too busy to help. Losing the call button was so simple, but a major setback. One day I'd dropped my phone. Rescuing the situation meant putting on the neck brace, struggling out of bed, using a foot to find it on the floor, bending to pick it up – impossible. I often had to wait for hours until someone came to sort out the latest disaster.

The staff explained the meals and cut them up so it was easier to eat when my left arm was still immovable. Typical hospital fare, never more than warm and a stranger to salt and pepper, let alone anything more interesting. A visitor brought in a glorious Thai curry, steaming from the microwave, as a special treat.

Like our own April Fool's Day, April 1st is celebrated in France with the "poisson d'avril" – a paper fish pinned on the victim's back. The hospital staff were determined to make us smile too, and one of the male nurses doing a drag impression woke me to deliver a special Easter croissant. Another day, I was woken by two nursing assistants singing silly French songs, with the nurse adding a chorus. These were typical of their efforts to break the monotony of hospital life, lighten our days, bring a smile and reconnect us with life in the real world

Emotionally I was on a roller coaster and could verge from tears and misery to joy at the flick of a switch. The medication was contributing, plus all the effort of trying to recover as fast as possible and getting frustrated. Painful daily injections of blood anti-coagulants weren't much fun either for someone who is needle-phobic. Alongside, I was realising that my memory and word-finding abilities had taken a hit – it was depressing to discover that my mind had been injured too. But, at least, every day passed quickly with the routines of meals, ablutions, physio, visitors and sleep. Time was passing and I was healing.

Bernadette helped me with the first shower on the wet room high chair. Fabulous, but the downside was discovering two lumps on my breast. The possibility of cancer on top of everything else was daunting, and the news quickly spread throughout the medical team. There was a distinct atmosphere of tension and worry as everyone knew, but not what to say. Fortunately, within a week, three burly ambulance men kitted out in fluorescent surcoats (I could hear them rustle) trolleyed me for scans. Thankfully it seemed that the lumps were no more than blood clots caused by the accident rather than cancer, but it took more checks over many months for the specialists to be finally satisfied.

Video: Penny in Les Capusins

The Baking Blind project had never been far from my mind throughout. All those months of work and hours of videoing around the world, all the media interest that had been created and, most specially, all the people who'd given their time, interest and energy without seeing any result. I posted a couple of videos from my hospital bed, just to explain why there had been a deafening silence for so long. The wonders of modern technology enabled a live radio interview with the BBC in the UK. A casting company contacted me for an advert promoting olive oil, but I wasn't surprised to get no response to my rather shaky audition video shot in the hospital family room. But that was a location that became very special when I managed my first time back in a kitchen. Simply sitting in the wheelchair, chopping for a fruit salad, was a milestone.

Eventually, five months after the accident, I was able to get home to the UK. Even that return was bitter-sweet. While I was in hospital, a burglar had stolen my handbag collection and the designer costume jewellery I'd gathered over more than quarter of a century. None of it was wildly valuable, but completely irreplaceable because, even if vintage pieces were on the internet, how could I find them? On top of the insurance claim describing each piece, there were all the legal consequences of the accident, plus the efforts to rebuild both my business and Baking Blind. Alongside, I was embarking on years of physical and mental recovery. The PTSD nightmares and travel anxieties, the continuing need to rebuild my physical strength and mobility, the speech therapy for a voice damaged by the tubes and neck braces, coping with the injury to my concentration and cognitive skills – all of this and more amidst permanent exhaustion. Leaving the safety and security of the hospital made me recognise how institutionalised I'd become: content with familiar faces and routines; less able to cope with the great outside world.

But it was fabulous to be home again with friends visiting and supporting. Co-cook Jon arrived with boxes of frozen homemade meals that were a complete lifesaver when I was still struggling to move and manage seemingly permanent exhaustion.

Video: Home sweet home

Brother Martin and his wife Julie travelled from Plymouth to create a spectacular homecoming supper to mark all the support of family and friends during the last five months. His Italian ragu reflected both his professional expertise (previously the Royal Navy's fleet catering officer) and his unstinting care.

It was certainly one of those dishes that had to be cooked from the heart: chopping vegetables so fine that they virtually disappeared; hours and hours of stirring and gentle simmering; two types of minced meat with just the right balance of lean and fat; the weird but successful addition of milk; lashings of wine to evaporate.

He used red onions, but this was clearly a recipe open to variations as he said, "You could use white onions, although for some reason I have never tried them. I prefer the slightly sweeter red onion. You can play with the quantities of onion, carrot and celery. I experiment, and might do a bit more of each. Lots of garlic. I would normally use at least four cloves, but it depends on how much you like. I will usually add more tomato paste to give a deeper richer tomato flavour to the sauce, but be careful not to add too much."

He was more exacting about the vegetable chopping: "I have a philosophy on the chopping of the vegetables to make my sofrito, in that I want the individual cut pieces to be no bigger than the individual morsels of the beef and pork mince. So, I spend quite some time cutting the veg into brunoise size cubes (about 3mm square). This is time consuming, but the end product is very pleasing and reaps rewards in the texture of the sauce." He gave the same care to cooking the vegetables, saying, "You don't want to be frying the veg per se, but letting it sweat in the oil and the natural fluids of the veg itself."

Adding milk seemed odd until he explained: "This coats the meats and protects it from the harshness of the red wine later. If the celery is particularly green then you might find everything takes on a slightly green tinge at this time, but this is nothing to worry about. This is not blue string soup you might see in a Bridget Jones film!" The long simmer was just as painstaking, although a slow cooker could be a good option. Martin described the result he wanted: "This is the deep cooking process that intensifies the flavour and renders the meat and vegetables into a true ragu sauce. It should darken and release the oils/fats from the meat etc., and will mean there is a dark golden oily layer on the top. This is normal and shouldn't be removed. It's part of the dish."

With such rich unctuousness, anything more than simple plain pasta would have been overwhelming. This was definitely not a meal for the faint-hearted or cholesterol-conscious. For someone who'd been living on rather plain hospital fare for months, it was a distinct shock to the system, but gloriously indulgent and heart-warming. What a wonderful welcome and huge incentive to get back into the kitchen.

Martin's Italian ragu recipe.

Video: Italian ragu

4 cloves garlic, peeled.
2 large onions, peeled.
3 large carrots, peeled.
3 good size sticks of celery, trimmed.
6 tablespoons olive oil.
A large knob of butter.
1kg beef, minced (at least 12% fat).
500g pork, minced (high fat content).
1 pint full fat milk.
750ml good red wine.
2 tubes of tomato puree.
500ml passata.
Ground nutmeg.
Salt and pepper to taste.

Method.

Finely chop the vegetables to 3mm cubes, keeping the onion separate.

Heat the oil and butter in a large heavy-based (cast iron) pan and sauté the onion until transparent.

Add the garlic, carrots and celery to the pan and continue cooking on a medium heat, stirring to allow the vegetables to cook gently.

Gradually add the minced meat, breaking it up, stirring and cooking until it has changed colour to light brown.

Stir in a few large pinches of salt to draw out the meat juices.

Stir in the milk.

Bring the mixture to a simmer to evaporate the milk and other fluids, continuing to stir regularly and feel that the mix is soft and uniform in texture.

Stir in the wine and continue to simmer until it has nearly all reduced, before adding the tomato paste and passata.

Season with salt, pepper and a good pinch of ground nutmeg.

Very gently simmer the pan, uncovered, for at least three hours, stirring regularly.

My tips.

This is a careful and long-winded though not complicated recipe that is likely to take most of a day. Perhaps the chance to listen to a good audio book while you meticulously chop and stir? Martin suggested serving with "a flat-style pasta – linguine is lovely – but it probably should never be served with spaghetti or any of the round, long pastas. Add Parmigiano and seasoning. On the side serve focaccia bread."

Chapter 25.

Hampshire home cooking.

Back at home was good, but the physiotherapy and other treatments continued: coaching for my voice; exercises and aqua therapy for my body; psychology for my brain. At the same time, the Baking Blind project continued to be my main concern. Toby and I started to edit the masses of world tour videos. It was slow progress, as over 100 episodes needed scripting, voicing and finalising while I felt permanently exhausted with a brain working only part time.

Before the accident I had persuaded some local Hampshire blind people to cook with me. It had been surprisingly difficult to make the contacts and then our sessions had been delayed for months. Now, even though the standing and moving was still painfully difficult, I wasn't going to miss these opportunities. The Southampton Sight organisation had lined up three innocent volunteers and Toby was on hand to capture our performances (www.southamptonsight.org.uk).

Steve set the standard with his Sri Lankan beef curry. He was one of those precise and meticulous cooks who I try to emulate, getting all the ingredients prepared first and then cooking easily without making a mess – so important for anyone. He explained his technique for identifying different ingredients: "I've got enough vision that, with some sort of visual aid, I can still read the labels on the spices. I use a magnifying glass and smell also helps."

He gave me more practical tips. Emptying a tin of part-solidified coconut milk can be a spill hazard for anyone, so Steve wisely stirred with a fork first to avoid a huge lump splashing out. His method of searing meat worked too, placing the pieces in the pan clockwise so that, once he'd completed the circle, the first were ready to turn.

It was an excellent curry, fragrant with cinnamon, sharp with tamarind, and not too hot as he'd been cautious with the chilli. My first experience of Sri Lankan flavours and I was sorry that my tube of tamarind paste had languished, unloved and neglected, in the cupboard for more years than its "best before" date could bear. I was thoroughly inspired to make my own curry spice mix to use with chicken thighs and create a new regular favourite.

While Steve's curry was gently simmering, Kate showed me her chicken, leek and pancetta pie and described her own visual impairment: "I'm classed as registered blind even though I'm not completely black-blind. I have a little bit of light and dark and the tiniest little bit of shadow. If I'm walking along a path on my way to work and there's a lamppost or something in the middle, I may, if I'm concentrating, just see something enough to move out of the way."

Kate had been running cooking classes for the members of Southampton Sight and had brought a gadget to test with me, explaining, "Basically, it's a mini chopping board on the end of a pair of scissors. It's a very sharp blade to help you cut meat or vegetables." We both tried that strange piece of equipment, without success. There are so many gadgets that promise so much and deliver so little. These scissors were hopeless and, laughing derisively, we consigned them to the bin. Together, Kate and I proved that a simple sharp knife can work best.

Carefully selecting off-the-shelf mainstream products can be simplest and cheapest. Years ago, I had an audio alarm designed to sit on the rim of a mug and beep when boiling water reached the right level. But now there's a super water heater that will boil and dispense exactly the right amount with one button press – on sale anywhere – which is much safer. I must have been given at least three talking jugs that never got used. They take up too much space, are too fiddly and too slow. It's easier to remember that 100cl of water weighs 100g and use the talking scales instead.

The trickiest part of making Kate's pie was spooning the hot filling into the dish without knocking over the pie funnel. We rescued the situation, but it took quick work to get the pastry in place, glazed and into the oven before it all started melting over that hot filling. This pie was one of my favourites and I've cooked it many times, with or without the pancetta or leeks, and sometimes with a small glass of white wine to ring the changes.

Sue was the next volunteer, sharing her all-in-one method for rich coffee cake, slathered with butter icing and walnuts. All the tastes to take you back to childhood. She explained: "I don't have any sight at all. I use Braille labels on all my spices and all the ingredients. I decant things into containers so that I don't get unnecessary spillages from packets of flour etc." She had brought her containers of flour and sugar, identifying which was which with the flick of a finger.

She showed me a Braille recipe book, saying, "I like to follow it step by step." One of the drawbacks was the bulkiness of Braille "translations". Her volume was one of the five needed to capture just one standard printed cookbook. Not only was the paper much thicker to take the tactile impressions, but each letter or number may need its own symbol. The Braille books have other drawbacks in the kitchen when they get sticky – blind cooks are using their hands all the time. Sue said, "I'm constantly washing my hands so that I don't get muck over them."

She told me: "I learned Braille when I was about 14 years of age. I went away to a special school. It is much harder when you get older. It's something you develop, so the younger you start, the better." Fingertip sensitivity needed for fluent Braille reading reduces with age. The over fifties will have difficulties. But the majority of people losing their sight are already older, meaning that most will never use Braille. Instead, we rely on other ways of "reading": screen magnification and screen readers on computers; audio labels read by barcode readers; something as simple as stick-on raised letters. I use them all. My tip is that basic Word documents are most flexible for Braille printers, for large print, for other adaptive software.

Nearly a quarter of a century ago, I did try a Perkins Braille machine. It was like a very old-fashioned shop till needing the keys to be smashed down to make the tactile indentations. There are more technological versions nowadays but, even that long ago, it felt like returning to the Stone Age after life with computers. I just didn't have the patience for such time travel.

Sue had her first experience of using a food processor, whizzing the cake mix and then the icing in minutes. Those deft fingertips were in action as she tested the cooked cakes, saying, "They need to be springy to the touch." We were in a rush to finish, so the cake had to cool in the fridge to avoid the butter icing melting as we smoothed it over. We'd saved the most challenging part to the end: spacing walnuts on the top evenly is a very difficult thing for a blind person to do.

Gary was another Fareham blind cooking enthusiast. We discovered we both used the same local butcher-cum-greengrocer and shared tips on his best produce. Even more of a coincidence, his father had been a Navy chef, responsible for creating the spectacular chocolate galleons presented at the annual wardroom Trafalgar Night dinners at my Portsmouth military alma mater, HMS Nelson. A fleet of those galleons would be paraded shoulder height around the packed dining tables, sparklers ablaze and hidden pyrotechnics firing a gun salute to the traditional sound of "Hearts of Oak", played by a Royal Marines band in the minstrels' gallery above our heads. The wardroom would be packed with officers be-decked in their mess kit, medals sparkling, and me with a set of golden aiguillettes on my shoulder.

But enough of my memories and back to Gary. He was one of about 1,000 people in the UK to have Bardet-Biedl syndrome, which can result in extra fingers and toes, other physical drawbacks and, commonly, gradually deteriorating sight. He explained: "With the condition, some people have kidney problems, some are extremely large, some have impotency, some have diabetes."

He'd been born with extra tiny digits that were removed within a few months, and had no idea that he had the syndrome or that it might affect his sight. Like many others, he was progressing through life with a busy and successful career with one of the big High Street electrical retailers. "I started losing my sight in my mid-thirties, although the condition had been there since birth. It first started as I was driving home and it was uncomfortable with glare and lights."

He took the obvious step of getting his eyes checked by an optician, which progressed to years of investigations by various specialists at different hospitals. He even started his own research. "I went to a library and found some books," he told me. "One book said I could be cured; a second book said there was no cure, and that's what I have. There is no cure for my condition. At first, I put my head in a hole. I wanted to bury it. But, after a few months, I dusted myself down and got on with life, which is what we all have to do. You have two choices: you sink or you swim, and I'm not going to sink."

Describing his sight, Gary explained, "I have peripheral vision. I have no central vision. I can see about three foot in front of me. I go through life thinking that my wine glass is half full. It's the only way that anybody can deal with things. I've had lots of ups and downs in life."

While no longer working, Gary's enthusiasm and motivation remained undiminished: he was active across the local community of blind people, led one organisation and supported others. He was doing his best to reduce the condition's other physical consequences, explaining, "I go to the gym and fitness train, which keeps me agile and a bit fit." He summed up his approach: "Life's a bitch but, heigh-ho, we get on with it."

Cooking was another of his passions, which meant he could contribute practically at home. "If you don't cook, you go hungry and, if the wife cooks, she'd probably kill me. Or alternatively we'd have the fire brigade in, dampening down the kitchen." He taught me his own dish, rather disturbingly named "Roadkill", a mutation of risotto, paella and pilau made with basmati rice so truly international! It was a one-pot wonder of a warmer, chicken, herbs and spices made colourful with tomatoes. By including the rice in the pot as it cooks in the oven, this dish was easy on both the cook and washing up. He also asked me to make an apple crumble dessert based on his own version using sultanas soaked in whisky. Inevitably, I made my own adaptation: raisins soaked in brandy, reminiscent of the French tarte a l'ancienne with an oat-based crumble topping and Bramley apples that were dropping from my garden trees like bombs. He probably needed quite a bit of gym work to counteract all those carbohydrates.

Steve's Sri Lankan beef & tamarind curry.

Video: Sri Lankan beef curry

2 tablespoons ghee (or butter).
1kg beef (skirt or blade), cubed.
2 onions, peeled and chopped.
4 garlic cloves, peeled and finely chopped.
5cm piece fresh ginger, grated.
2 teaspoons turmeric.
1 teaspoon crushed red chilies.
4 teaspoons Sri Lankan curry powder.
7.5cm piece cinnamon bark.
1 teaspoon sea salt.
4 to 5 curry leaves.
1 teaspoon tamarind paste, dissolved in 8 tablespoons hot water.
1 tin coconut milk.

Method.

Melt the ghee in a large saucepan, seal the beef on high heat and set aside.

Reduce heat to moderate and sauté the onion, garlic and ginger until onion is transparent.

Add turmeric, crushed red chilies and Sri Lankan curry powder, and cook for 1 minute, then add the beef again together with the cinnamon, salt, curry leaves and strained tamarind water. Mix well and cook for 10 minutes.

Add coconut milk and continue cooking on a low simmer, uncovered, until meat is tender (adding more water if the pan is drying out).

Sri Lankan curry powder.

Grind together 100g each of coriander, cumin and mustard seeds, plus 2 tablespoons ground turmeric, plus 1 tablespoon each of fenugreek seeds, ground cinnamon and 10 cloves. Store in an airtight jar.

Kate's chicken, pancetta and leek pie.

Video: Chicken, pancetta and leek pie

4 chicken breasts or boneless thighs, skinned and cut into 1cm slices.
A handful of pancetta, cubed.
A knob of butter.
A dribble of olive oil.
2 large leeks, trimmed and thinly sliced.
150g button mushrooms, trimmed and sliced.
1 heaped tablespoon plain flour.
300ml chicken stock.
A few sprigs of fresh thyme, leaves only.
2 teaspoons made-up (or ready-made) English mustard.
1 heaped tablespoon crème fraiche.
Half teaspoon fresh grated nutmeg.
1 sheet of pre-rolled puff pastry.
1 egg, beaten.

Method.

Brown the chicken and pancetta in the butter and oil in a large pan.

Add the leeks and mushrooms and cook on a medium heat until the leeks are softening.

Stir in the flour, followed by the stock, thyme leaves, mustard, crème fraîche and nutmeg.

Stir well and season with salt and pepper.

When the mixture has just started to thicken and simmer, spoon it into an ovenproof dish.

Cover with the pastry, tucking in or trimming the edges, and brush with the beaten egg.

Cook in a preheated oven at 200C, Gas 6, 390F for about 20 minutes until the pastry is golden.

My tips.

I prefer to add the chicken later in this recipe, after the crème fraiche. If the pieces are small, the temperature of the sauce as it heats up, plus the time in the oven, will be enough to cook it.

If using a commercial stock, don't add more salt until you have checked the seasoning.

Move quickly when placing the pastry on the pie. It will start melting so needs to be in the oven quickly.

Sue's coffee cake.

Video: Coffee and walnut cake

3 eggs, weighed.
Same weight butter.
Same weight sugar.
Same weight self-raising flour (or plain flour plus a teaspoon of baking powder).
1 teaspoon baking powder (optional).
Coffee essence/flavouring to taste.

Method.

Weigh the eggs and then measure out the same weight in butter, sugar and flour.

Place the butter and sugar in a food processor and whizz until mixed.

Add all the remaining ingredients and whizz until light and fluffy.

Place the mixture into 2 sponge tins.

Cook for about 20 minutes at 180C, Gas 4, 350F.

My Tips:

This is essentially the same cake mix I'd made in Costa Rica and Chongqing with a hand-mixer but here using a food processor and a little more baking powder. Now, I would tend to whizz in the eggs one at a time, with a spoonful of flour, and only add the final flour for a couple of pulses at the end to fold in.

The amount of coffee flavouring depends on your taste and what you are using. A tablespoon of coffee essence can be replaced by instant or other coffee dissolved in a little boiling water. Avoid using too much water as it will change the proportions of the mix.

Coffee butter icing.

110g butter, softened.
220g icing sugar, sifted.
Coffee essence/flavouring to taste.
Walnut halves to decorate.

Method.

Whisk all the ingredients until soft and fluffy.

Ensure cake has cooled.

Using half the icing for each, cover the top of each sponge and place one on top of the other.

Decorate the top layer with halved walnut pieces.

My tips.

Walnut pieces, chopped small, could be folded into the cakes with the flour for more flavour and texture.

Gary's "roadkill".

Video: Chicken "roadkill"

1 large tin chopped tomatoes.
1 teaspoon smoked paprika.
1 teaspoon turmeric.
Pinch of saffron (optional).
1 teaspoon mixed herbs.
1 teaspoon dried herbs de Provence.
2 chicken stock cubes.
150g butter.
2 mug-fulls basmati rice.
3 large chicken breasts, skin removed and cubed.
3 rashers bacon, de-rinded and cut into strips.
200g chorizo, diced.
2-3 slices ham cut into strips.
2 green peppers, de-seeded and diced.
2 medium onions, peeled and diced.
500g mushrooms, trimmed and sliced.
4 cloves garlic, peeled and finely chopped.
1 tablespoon tomato purée.
250ml red wine.
Salt and pepper to taste.

Method.

Place the tinned tomatoes, spices, herbs and stock cubes in a large lidded ovenproof stockpot (over 2 litres) and start heating on the hob.

Meanwhile, melt the butter in a separate pan and sauté the rice until it is starting to brown before adding the rice to the stockpot.

Lightly sauté the chicken, bacon and chorizo before adding with the ham to the stock pot.

Sauté the peppers and onions followed by the mushrooms and garlic before adding to the stockpot with the tomato puree.

Deglaze the sauté pan with half the wine and add to the stockpot with the rest of the wine.

Stir the pot well and season to taste with salt and pepper.

Put the lid on the pot and place in the preheated oven 180C, Gas 4, 355F and cook for 15 minutes.

Remove pot from oven and stir before returning for a further 15 minutes.

Remove the lid and stir the pot, returning to oven for a final 15 minutes or until the rice is cooked.

Apple crumble.

Video: Apple and rum-soaked raisin crumble

Handfuls of raisins.
Brandy.
Bramley apples, peeled and cut into chunks.
220g porridge oats.
110g butter.
110g hazelnuts, roughly crushed in the food processor.
110g soft brown sugar.

Method.

Soak the raisins overnight in enough brandy to cover them. It is worth keeping a jar of them in soak for future dishes.

Fill an ovenproof dish with sufficient apples, plus generous handfuls of the raisins.

Rub the butter into the oats, nuts and sugar.

Top the apples with crumble mix and cook in a preheated oven 180C, Gas 4, 355F for about 45 minutes.

My tips.

The proportions of this crumble mix are two porridge oats to one each of butter, nuts and sugar. I keep a bag ready in the freezer for topping any fruit for a crumble. Try mixed fruit including pineapple and banana, rhubarb and crystallised ginger, apple and Christmas mincemeat, or apple and raspberries.

Chapter 26.

On my travels again.

Life was still tough as I continued to grapple with recovery. A hernia stopped the very basic Pilates; the coma nightmares were receding, although trepidation about car journeys still loomed; and my energy and physical activity continued at the pitiful level. For someone with a dentist phobia, the misery of extensive work to repair the tooth damage was only possible with good doses of sedation. By the time I'd managed all the treatments each week, a little video editing and rested each day, time was rushing past.

But there were many wonderful high spots, including a Royal Garden Party arranged by the Not Forgotten Association. I had been to the palace before, and each occasion had been special. This time was a triumph of mind over matter as we walked in from the taxi drop-off at the Albert Memorial. It felt posh walking through those great gates, past the police officers and sentries. The path through the outer and inner courtyards was lined with impeccably uniformed serving military men and women, welcoming us veterans. Then up the red-carpeted steps, through the palace and down more steps to the gardens.

By that stage I was exhausted, and plopped onto the nearest chair. We simply turned the "Reserved Table" sign over and sat nonchalantly as if we were in exactly the right place. Delicate plates of finger sandwiches and tiny cakes were collected from the refreshment marquee. The woman who joined us had served at Bletchley in the Second World War, and was still going strong and full of fun. After tea, we strolled around gardens so extensive that even the sounds of the military bands disappeared amongst the trees. Back with the congregation, sitting on a stone bench, plied with strawberries and cream, the afternoon concluded to the notes of "Beat Retreat" and the National Anthem. A memorable day.

Another outstanding event in the midst of all the recovery efforts was being awarded an Honorary Doctorate by Middlesex University of London. My long-term and highly trusted taxi-driving friend and co-cook Jon drove me to the ceremony. We were received by distinguished academics for lunch, after which I was robed in an academic gown and topped off with an arcane but jaunty cap, complete with dangling tassel. Amidst the procession of the great and the good, I stumbled my way onto the stage before a huge audience of new graduates and their families. My little award was very much the sideshow to the students' own achievements, and I managed to distribute their degree scrolls without dropping any. It was reminiscent of my time as Chair of the Learning and Skills Council for Hampshire and the Isle of Wight, me juggling scrolls and handshakes with a procession of achievers, trying not to bungle their special moment in the spotlight of success.

Then my first public speaking experience for months. Not at all easy due to the physical and mental injuries. Thankfully, those graduates were already an excited and enthusiastic audience, bound up in their own delight and achievements, so that I could probably have read an Argos catalogue and they would have politely applauded.

A return to San Francisco was the next challenge: managing the long flight; giving a Baking Blind World Tour presentation to the gala dinner; other events marking the conclusion of the inaugural Holman Prize year.

Not all flights are without incident. Even the best trained cabin crew can forget the obvious. On one long-haul flight, I managed to adjust the seat to the prone position with my legs neatly inserted into the tunnel under the seat ahead. But both I and the crew had failed to clarify the use of the touchscreen controls to reverse the situation or, more importantly, buzz for help. Amidst a darkened cabin of snoozing fellow passengers, I thumped on the bulkhead to get attention

But the next disaster was discovering that I only had the clothes I'd travelled in. I was marched to Macey's, one of the famous chain of American shops. Just a few waggles of the trusty white cane and I had more help than I knew what to do with, two shop assistants scouring the department while a couple of willing fellow shoppers were plying me with their own recommendations. Even better, it was sale time, meaning there was no need to hold back. Result: an eclectic selection for bargain prices. And my triumph was undiminished on returning to the hotel to find all those missing garments had been unpacked during jet-weariness and hidden in the depths of an obscure cupboard. Soon would be the fun of getting it all into the suitcase home.

It was another delight to meet up with Luis and hear of his cannabis cooking for TV. When he wasn't creating mind-bending desserts for the small screen, he had returned to his passion for teaching.

There was more time to experience the city, visiting Fisherman's Wharf and Pier 39, and sampling the clam chowder served in a loaf (delicious and not too touristy). The sea lions were the absolute joy. Great groups of them snoozing and sun-bathing on large wooden rafts. I could hear them barking, snuffling and breathing; even more distinctively, smell their salty fishy odour.

A boat across the bay with those heroes Ben and Blanche took us for a reunion lunch in Solselito – calm and peaceful after the tumult of San Francisco.

Another new experience: the famous trolley cars pulled around the city on a network of underground chains. The outside bench was perfect for me, hearing the clanging bell, the street sounds and feeling the air moving through my hair. The return trip made other passengers giggle: the steep inclines made me slide up and down the polished wooden benches. The movement was so subtle that I didn't realise until I'd concertinaed a crush of bodies.

I had heard about the numbers of homeless people in the city on the previous visit, a large encampment in one area, and people sleeping on the pavement on the main street. Most jaw dropping was that it seemed acceptable that homelessness extended to many people using wheelchairs. There was some kerfuffle on a bus as the passengers cleared space for a man in his "chariot". A supermarket trolley had been cut in two, half attached to the back of his wheelchair, and the other at the front carried the remainder of his worldly possessions and his dog. He sat defiantly, propped against his folded mattress, displaying a sign that castigated the political system that had failed him. Yet other passengers seemed to accept his situation as an everyday occurrence rather than evidence of social breakdown.

On a more positive note, it was good to catch up with fellow Holman Prize winners. Ojok had succeeded in training more blind beekeepers in Uganda, and Ahmet had achieved his kayak crossing of the Bosporus. The local coastguard had briefly closed the busy shipping lane for his transit, but the downside of boat-loads of enthusiastic supporters was that his special navigation system was inaudible. The result was that his crossing was guided by his mobile phone app!

While it was disappointing that LightHouse hadn't been able to drum up any media interest in our adventures, the hundreds of excited guests at the gala dinner proved an avid audience. We three had been bidden to turn up, booted and spurred, a couple of hours before the reception in order to practice our moves. We sat on chairs at the back of the cavernous hall, while people milled around setting up the tables, chairs, cutlery and sound tests. Someone had decided that we needed a long ramp to get to the lectern on the stage, helpful despite a rather wobbly handrail, but the large hole at the top promised a precipitous descent. We pitched into the reception to meet as many guests as possible, drawn from the affluent great and good of California, the tech industries of Silicon Valley, and other LightHouse supporters.

Amidst the chatter and movement of guests taking their seats, the first screening of the LightHouse video that had taken so many days to capture over a year earlier was rather lost. But the noise level subsided as the $200 per head meal was served and I was more confident in negotiating the ramp, the now-resolved hole and the lectern to present my own short video to that large crowd. With just a few allotted minutes, a still squeaky voice and not the best memory, I'd been worried I'd make a mess of the big moment. I managed the introduction.

Video: Speaking at gala dinner in San Francisco

But the main story had been more of a problem. Toby and I had worked hard to capture the high spots of the world tour, and the best audio moments to create a "soundscape" for many blind people in the audience: the helicopters from the air/sea rescue, the Chinese opera diva, wildlife in the jungle, and even the awfulness of me singing in the hospital.

It was wildly energising to be standing before a gathering of over 500 whooping and cheering guests, getting them excited and responding.

The preceding Happy Hour may have played a part, but I felt back on familiar and happy territory in front of a crowd.

Video: A sound of the world

The dinner guests were utterly enthralled as Ahmet and Ojok told their own stories too, each tale littered with mishaps and triumphs. Throughout the evening, the attendees had been cajoled, encouraged and pressurised to donate towards LightHouse by a wildly enthusiastic professional fundraiser. It was a revelation to hear her drive up contributions and galvanise the crowd to fund rebuilding a holiday camp destroyed by forest fire. My own donation was three days accommodation and cooking experience for two back in Hampshire (to which LightHouse had added the flight tickets). I confess that I was secretly smug when it raised the charity auction top bid (more than a guitar signed by Queen's Brian May).

Next day, I was privileged to spend a little time talking with George, the originator of the DAISY audio book system, and his wife. George has probably made more difference to the lives of blind people worldwide than anyone since Louis Braille. As links with LightHouse were ending, I couldn't resist a chance to share ideas about the potential for the Holman Prize with Bryan, the chief executive. With huge, dedicated endowment funding, and hundreds of entries from across the world each year, there was the opportunity to create a network of some of the most ambitious and able blind people globally – and extend through their own connections too. Involving mainstream media could have taken the whole concept further than just blind people talking to each other, opening up the minds and attitudes of policy makers, employers and communities.

Many months and much physiotherapy later, I was welcoming that madly generous auction bidder, Jennison, to Hampshire for his cooking days with me. His lack of sight hadn't held him back either: co-founder of Global Accessibility Day and LinkedIn's accessibility evangelist, he was driving change across the whole spectrum of disability (www.globalaccessibilityawarenessday.org).

Thoroughly embedded in the world of high technology, it was quickly clear that Jennison was far less comfortable working in a kitchen. Comparing just our hands, it was obvious that his were designed for keyboards: quick and dexterous, soft and smooth. In contrast, after years of holding knives, kneading bread and grappling with ingredients, mine are strong and hard, with the odd knife and burn scars.

But Jennison was undaunted in tackling his first-ever experiences: "I've not been known for chopping my onions. Ever. It's out of my comfort zone. I don't walk around with dreams of paring vegetables and fruit or even cooking." I wasn't sure how he managed to feed himself at home. "In Silicon Valley, I go out a fair bit," he said. "At least three or four nights a week into either San Francisco or eat locally. And the other nights, I'm either taking something out of the freezer into the microwave or ordering food in. It's part of a lifestyle view. You leave the office, you go maybe for a Happy Hour, you grab a quick dinner, or you have dinner at the office. A lot of tech firms provide meals either free or at low cost. The company I work at has breakfast, lunch and dinner." He explained his family cooking background, saying, "I was kept away from the kitchen as a kid, more from a safety perspective as my mom was nervous. Although she did bring me in to do manual labour. Obviously, I did cooking because I had to eat, but it's not something over the last number of years that I've made a priority, or just done because life is fast, days are quick. If it's just for myself, I don't see the reason to make a huge production. I'm a lot like any other tech worker in Silicon Valley. I can't think of anyone who actually cooks that I know. But I remember my mom back in the day. She'd come home from work and have to slave over the stove to cook food and stuff. We've gotten rid of that. We live in this generation of convenience: everything has an app; everything is fast."

Not only did I feel about a thousand years old, but his description of life begged the question as to why he'd paid so much money for a cooking trip. His answer: "I was fascinated because I understood the concept of what you were doing beyond the cooking. And, truth be told, part of it at the auction was that I'm super-competitive. When I saw that someone else was interested in the same thing, I upped the ante and, luckily, I live and work in Silicon Valley, so here I am."

One of our first dishes was a simple curry for him to experience the ingredients, with the spices dialled back to better reflect his taste. "What's nice is that I smelled all the spices, the cloves etc," he said. "Then just to taste it in the rice and smell it. All the other senses were turned on."

The poached pineapple was a triumph for his dexterity and strength. Drilling the cutter down through the fruit is no mean feat for a beginner, and far more difficult with only touch as a guide. The vacuum-packed banana-stuffed pineapple, plus a little rum and brown sugar, was cooked in the sous vide which was probably the most interesting piece of equipment he discovered with me. In comparison, he was irritated with his induction hob back home, saying, "The stove top is not accessible. The controls are buttons, but there's a menu so you have to kind of count and hope that you've gotten to the right temperature."

Such technology barriers inspired his co-founder to start a worldwide movement, explaining, "Most web developers have never heard of a screen reader before, or know anything about what accessibility is." He proposed an Accessibility Awareness Day, where people will take some time to learn about it. Together with Jennison, they used their extensive tech networks to stimulate interest and, in the first year, succeeded with events in several different countries and a governmental conference in India. Every year since, the event has attracted more international involvement of governments, businesses, charities, schools and colleges, running public events and in-house training. "They find it exciting, and they just want to be part of this global movement, to cause a conversation on any aspect of digital access or inclusion. It can be anything from showing someone how to use a sip-and-puff device (for people who don't have use of their hands or arms so they use their mouth, sipping and puffing, to control rather than using a keyboard), or they could hold a conference, or an event, or they could be presenting a new product."

In the past, designers have created features but not realised their extra benefit for disabled people, such as smart phones, "Like the voice recognition software that was never envisioned to be for people without use of their hands or arms." Increasingly industry is realising that design that works for disabled people can have mass market appeal too – win, win for everyone.

Jennison was understandably passionate about the LinkedIn commitment and said, "Part of the investment is to have full-time people whose accountability is strictly on accessibility. It's going to take more, with leadership from the top." And he's thinking of the whole global disability market: "There are 1.3 billion people with disabilities out there. More than that. People who are totally blind, like you and I, make up one of the smaller sub-groups. I would be doing a disservice if I advocated for and exclusively focused on making sure that things worked for people who are blind. That said, the argument is that, if you solve the technological challenges of people who are blind, those are the most complex and will end up helping everyone else."

He was equally conscious of market forces: "The big question for anyone who works in technology to ask themselves is, if you're not caring about accessibility or inclusive thinking or inclusive design, are you comfortable knowing that you're putting out a product and you're excluding that 20%? It's not that accessibility or inclusive thinking is something brand new, it's been around for a long time." My more jaundiced perception gained over quarter of a century is that too many businesses, government bodies and other organisations simply accept the risk of losing customers or legal action because they think it's easier and cheaper. Most have never moved beyond ignorance and prejudice to the point that they can see the market benefits.

Jennison suggested basic training was also an issue: "One of the frustrations we have is that a lot of engineers and designers have never been exposed to accessibility or inclusive thinking until they get to the companies. The big thing for me is engineering and computer science, at the college and university level, and at the bootcamps. They need to start teaching basic concepts of accessibility and inclusive thinking." These aren't just issues limited to technology. In any field, if your professional training excluded legal compliance affecting 20% of your potential customers, you'd think that it was negligent at worse, unfit for purpose at best.

More disabled people doing the work would help too. "Let me tell you," Jennison said, "as someone who's blind working in tech, it's a little lonely. We need to get more people with disabilities, impairments or long-term health conditions into tech because we know we have perspectives that we would bring. If a product is being spun up, no one's going to think about how a person with a disability or impairment is going to use that product." His concern went beyond initial design to product testing: "There is always talk about the need to have people with disabilities. Sometimes it's hard for companies to find those, but if we had full-time roles for testers with disabilities in all the companies..."

Video: HAMP Jennison garden chat

But enough of changing the world and back to the cooking. Jennison enjoyed the Scotch eggs, but was less happy about making them, saying, "I can never see myself squeezing out sausage again or peeling an egg. I'll let someone else cook them." My taxi driver/cook pal Jon was a vital element of the mission to encourage Jennison to spend more time in the kitchen. Jon had set the scene during the drive from the airport, and later arrived with more equipment to demonstrate classic fish and chips. His air fryer was a great success, having proper tactile buttons and knobs that worked for all of us and produced fabulous, hot crisp chips.

Video: Air-fryer potato chips and IT

The fish used a more hand-draulic method: both the fish and our fingers were first floured and then dipped in batter. Jon's logic was that, if the coating would protect the fish while cooking, it would do the same for our hands during the moments we laid it into the pan for shallow frying. With his close supervision, our hands survived unscathed, although I'm not sure I'd try this by myself!

Video: Beer-battered cod loin

Jon threw in a very simple sauteed prawn and leek starter to get the digestive juices flowing.

Video: Prawn and leek starter

At the end of our few days together, I wasn't convinced that Jennison would be doing much more cooking in the future, but at least he'd had some different experiences and lived to tell the tale. He was returning to California after some great food and with no lasting damage.

Recipes with Jennison.

Curried chicken thighs.

Video: Curried chicken thighs

4 pieces cinnamon.
1 heaped teaspoon coriander seeds.
1 heaped teaspoon cumin seeds.
5 green cardamom pods.
6 cloves.
6 black peppercorns.
1 teaspoon mustard seeds.
2 tablespoons oil.
2 heaped teaspoons garam masala.
1 flat teaspoon ground chilli.
1 flat teaspoon ground paprika.
1 flat teaspoon ground black pepper.
1 heaped teaspoon ground cumin.
1 heaped teaspoon ground coriander.
1 teaspoon turmeric.
3 onions, peeled and diced.
3 portions GGG (description below).
2 courgettes, diced.
4 tomatoes, diced.
2 tins coconut milk, plus half tin of water from washing them out.
About 8-9 chicken thighs, bone in but skinned.

Method.

Dry roast the whole spices in a large pan until they smell.

Add the oil and roast the ground spices.

Add the onions and sauté until soft and transparent.

Add the courgette and tomato, continue sautéing.

Add the coconut milk and water, bring to a gentle simmer.

Add the chicken thighs and return to a gentle simmer.

Reduce the heat to a very gentle bubble for a couple of hours, covered until the thighs have reached 70C.

My tips.

GGG is fresh root ginger, garlic and green chilli in proportions 4:2:1. Place the peeled and roughly chopped ginger, peeled garlic and de-seeded chilli in a food processor and whizz to a rough paste. Use straightaway or freeze in portions of a heaped teaspoon. Worth keeping a store for many curries.

The flavours develop if the curry is chilled in the fridge and gently reheated the next day, and freezes well.

Scotch eggs.

2 eggs.
300g sausage meat.
2 handfuls of breadcrumbs.
Spray oil.

Method.

Soft boil the eggs by pricking the shells and placing into boiling water for 3 and a half minutes.

Place in cold water to cool and then remove the shells.

Dry the eggs and wrap in the sausage meat.

Roll in breadcrumbs, spray with oil and place on a baking sheet.

Cook for about 25 minutes at 180C, Gas 4, 350F, turning over halfway.

My tips.

Flavour the sausage meat: salt and pepper; garlic powder; finely chopped herbs; lemon zest; chilli powder; some or all or anything else that inspires you.

Banana-stuffed pineapple sous vide.

Video: Pineapple sous-vide

1 whole pineapple.
1 banana.
Handful of raisins.
1 tablespoon brown sugar.
Small glass rum or brandy.

Method.

Using a pineapple cutter, core and slice the pineapple.

Insert the banana into the hole left by the pineapple core, keeping the pineapple shape intact.

Place the pineapple and all other ingredients in a plastic bag and expel/ suck out all the air before knotting the bag closed.

Vacuum pack the filled bag.

Place in a sous vide water bath at 70C, 158F for three hours.

Chapter 27.

Lessons learned.

Looking back over the months and years, I've realised how casually I chose cooking as the theme for the Holman Prize. It was just too comfortable and convenient at the time; something I could do and something others might follow. I hadn't imagined the importance of simply preparing food in relation to the broad spectrum of human experience.

Baking Blind taught me better empathy and sensitivity. Fred's bush tucker in Australia was the most obvious example of how food is closely intertwined with culture, geography and climate, but there were more subtle pointers. What we eat today is a product of historic and economic change over centuries. The maize kernels of Cephus's Malawian nsima had transformed across generations and continents to become Tania's grits in California, with other slave trade echoes in Mario's Caribbean chicken in Costa Rica. International influence and economic change still continue: Cephus was transforming those same kernels into his version of Italian polenta for the new generations of visitors.

Dani's kefir in Melbourne was telling another tale of migration, voluntary or not, with people clinging to all that they retained of the traditions of their cultural identity. The same family histories surviving relocation were repeated in Maribel recreating her mother's Spanish dish in Melbourne, Wendy's tribute to her Irish heritage, and Eddie's fire pit that echoed his Persian background. The cooking of our past generations is part of our histories and shapes our lives: those handwritten, dog-eared family recipe books are a treasure trove.

In comparison, Jennison's culinary experience was a stark contrast. Is food becoming no more than convenient, cost-effective body refuelling for new generations? Even if high-end demand for such delights as Luis's beach-after-bonfire dessert, and Dré's complicated caramel éclair survives, will we maintain everyday links to our history, cultures and environment? I'd prefer to avoid food being reduced to pre-prepared, pre-packaged calories which may sustain us but without enriching our lives.

On the other hand (and stepping back from foodie tub-thumping), modern technology is invaluable in the kitchen. Pounding cassava leaves by hand in Malawi was a reminder of the sheer joy of reliable electricity and a good food processor; refrigeration might have reduced Cephus's need for potassium permanganate; reliable hot and cold water supplies would have made washing up so much easier in Costa Rica. There's a delicate balance between the "naturalness" of our food and hygiene, between exploiting the planet and living well.

My most precious memory is of the generosity of all those cooks, all over the world, that went way beyond just providing sustenance. They all gave their time, enthusiasm, creativity, hospitality and even their recipes. If you want to hang out with a great bunch of people, cooks are a good bet.

A shared passion was the perfect ice-breaker. In this tale, it has all been about cooking, but anything from archery to zoo-keeping would have done. My basic skills, curiosity and enthusiasm meant I could just about operate on their wavelength. Our shared kitchen vocabulary demolished potential barriers of culture, experience and capability. Even blindness didn't matter.

There was a subtle intimacy when stirring a pot together, comparing techniques or sharing a tasting. A little time while cakes baked, pans heated or pasta rested was the chance to glimpse personal stories. Without cooking together, I might not have learned about Charlene's childhood transformation, Jo overcoming bereavement, and the lives of Wan Lin and Lisa in Chongqing. Once again, I'd forgotten the kitchen as a safe place for precious, companionable insights.

I learned a mantra from Luis: showcase a few ingredients to reinforce their flavour, texture and smell. Cooking with every sense fully loaded was a constant theme. Jack's simple tactile measure for cooking steak wasn't unique to Chongqing. We used the fingertip test of temperature, texture and "cookedness" with Jo's bakes, Rich's barbecued fish and Yinyishu's jiaozi dumplings. All were perfect examples of getting your hands dirty.

Janine from Melbourne wrote to me on the same theme: "I was pleased to hear that I'm not the only one who gets up close and personal with food frying away in the fry pan. I also use my hand to scrape food off a board into wherever it's going instead of using a knife. I love getting into the kitchen and getting my hands into foods, such as making rissoles. I love it and have been told that all good professional chefs employ their hands to prepare their food. Probably not all the time, but certainly to mix things like Christmas cakes and puddings." For my part, keeping one hand out of the mix or pan avoids spreading mess everywhere, and constant hand-washing is the order of the day.

Touch featured constantly: the increasing silkiness of pasta for Charlene's ravioli; Charlie's crisp pork and soft beef. Likewise, the Cheeseboard Collective bread makers wanted to feel the stretch of the gluten and the temperature rise of their dough. Everyone uses touch to assess if an avocado is ripe or a courgette has got too soft.

Taste is the sense of choice in the kitchen, although it's all too easy to forget the seasoning at the last moment. But the power of smell and hearing may be less obvious. In my own kitchen, I'm probably more attuned to burning than the smoke alarm. I can smell when cakes and bread in the oven or fish or fruit in the pan reach the right temperature. Hearing is even more important: the different notes of jam bubbling from start to final stickiness; the change of tone as mayonnaise thickens; the crackle of oil ready for roasting potatoes. The great advantage is being able to work on one side of the kitchen and know what is happening elsewhere. A complete 360 degrees of sensory input.

Organisation is absolutely essential: everything in the right place, to the millimetre. Kitchen design student Erica thought that some ideas might work for others: pull-out metal baskets are much better than boring cupboard shelves, and even better filled with ice cream boxes to pack the contents higher. Forget all that tedious scrabbling around to find equipment when you can put a hand on anything.

Less-than-perfect kitchen gadgets have short lives. Other than talking scales and thermometer, I've tracked down standard off-the-shelf equipment with particular features: the one-press "kettle" for the perfect amount of boiling water into the mug; the straw-filled knife block for no more slot hunting; the chopping board with one side rim to catch spills; the clamp-down knife sharpener to leave both hands free. Charlene from Melbourne said cooking is all about senses and sensuality. If more kitchen equipment was designed with all five senses in mind, there might be fewer of them languishing at the back of cupboards, unloved and unrecommended.

Most used are masses of stackable Lakeland boxes, three different sizes that all take the same lid – no more searching for one to fit. Each ingredient can be weighed into a box and arranged in the right order for the professional chef's mise en place, which keeps everything neat and tidy. Once the cooking is done, more boxes store the results with lids colour-coding their contents.

Like most other people, life has been punctuated by a series of blows, disasters, knock-backs or whatever you want to call them. The words don't matter, but being able to stagger up again and find a new way of surviving does. Different directions that still satisfy life's ambitions.

My school hopes of architecture and the law were early fallers, my number skills too weak and financial demands on my mother too high. Since I was 15, engagement to Simon promised marriage, children and, ideally, work at the Brighton Museum, which had been my home-from-home. He was killed as a passenger in a road traffic accident at the start of my post-graduate year, and the world changed.

Amidst the misery and medication, I explored every job opportunity I could find, advertising and building society to publishing and retail. Eventually I stumbled upon the Women's Royal Naval Service. I liked them and they liked me. It was a fabulous career, varied, challenging and stimulating for over 20 years. I had the chance to get to the top, and had even become one of about eight women commanders by the time blindness resulted in the medical discharge.

Prejudice and discrimination were common and less discreet in those days. Getting a job seemed impossible, so self-employment and starting a business were my only hope. My new disability was my Unique Selling Point (USPs were all the craze). Over the next 15 years, that company grew with a team of sub-contractors. Alongside, work at high levels in government, business and the voluntary sector ticked all the boxes: varied, challenging and stimulating. Life was back on track again.

Austerity policies, insensitivity, maladministration and injustice put paid to all of that. The dispute with the government department brought my business to a halt. There was no room for the consequences of the uncertainty and financial instability they created in the Wild West of commercial contracting. Graceful retirement and a less demanding life seemed no fun at all, so Baking Blind emerged. All the familiar satisfactions were back and the future seemed unlimited.

While those ambitions came to a grinding halt with the accident, I didn't throw in the tea towel. Recovering the previous level of physical and mental fitness continues to be a long, hard road. There was more time back in France for breast cancer follow-ups (all seems fine), and surgery on the hernia. Fatigue reached crisis; a downward spiral of sleepless nights, daytime naps, confusion and depression, all fuelled by frustration at not being able to return to a fully-functioning life. Months of professional coaching helped me recognise that constant pain and distress were prime causes. Embarrassingly simple and obvious solutions had been beyond my muddled thinking: painkillers, daily exercise, light suppers and early bedtime routines. Another long course of physiotherapy is starting to reduce the causes of pain until, over-confident with new vitality, I was moving too fast to remember a wall and fractured my vital right hand. Progress continues and, even if I can't yet spot the light, I'm moving down that particular tunnel.

My mind still isn't the same. Memory is vital for anyone without sight. We have to remember that 360 perspective, where everything is, who everyone is, the shopping list and where did I put down my keys. The alternative is either doing very little or endlessly hunting. I've heard it described as having to do the Financial Times crossword without a pen; having to remember all the clues and all the answers until the puzzle is done. I still have reasonable 3D images of various locations but, after the accident, there are a lot of blank holes.

There's a glimmer around the distress too. A psychologist, counsellor and neuro-psychologist have all worked on reducing the terror from that yawning door tempting me to death. I'm slowly moving forward and, with less fatigue, still hope to fill the word-finding gaps and regain whatever logical decision-making I used to have. Leaving hospital, I had no idea that recovery would take years and might never be 100%.

Now I have to face the reality of additional disability and make it less grim.

On that more positive note, all the tour videos were edited and published, speaking engagements and demonstrations were gathering momentum, and new ideas were bubbling away. Not even a pandemic was going to stop me. Live online bake-ins and centenary celebrations with Open Sight Hampshire (www.opensight.org.uk), weekly Covid cookbook postings and a couple of hopeless home-videoed TV auditions have kept me motivated. The DWP battle that started so many years earlier continued and, although Baking Blind emerged from the debris, my business had crumbled. Closure was a painful end to 20 years' hard work. Writing this story, reliving many happy times, and recalling wonderful people has been a powerful therapy. I'm still determined and ambitious, waving not drowning. Looking for new challenges, imagining that fourth career with all the variety, challenge and stimulation that makes life worthwhile. What's next?

Video: Baking Blind: good, bad and ugly experiences

Index.

Main ingredient/ Product	Recipe	Page number
Almond	Galette des rois à la frangipane	24
Beef	Red-cooked beef	184
	Marinaded and steamed beef	188
	Doner kebabs	229
	Italian ragu	300
	Sri Lankan beef and tamarind curry	308
Biscuits	Croustillant to top eclairs	263
	Tuile	22
Bread	Sourdough	58
	Sourdough focaccia	60
	Sourdough zampanos	60
	Sourdough bialys	61
	Sourdough starter	107
	Soda, wheaten bread	111
	Soda, yoghurt bread	112
	Four-minute bread	257
Cake	Honey cake (Steven Edwards)	31
	Seagrass cake	38
	Victoria sponge, chilli and coriander	78
	Banana bread	124
	Pumpkin bread	127

Main ingredient/ Product	Recipe	Page number
	Chocolate cake	201
	Caramel mud cake	202
	Chocolate mud cake	203
	Victoria sponge, coffee	311
Cake, icing	Salted caramel buttercream	264
	Coffee buttercream	312
Chicken	Chicken Marbella	30
	Buttermilk fried chicken	48
	Pollo con patatas	85
	Caribbean chicken	85
	Chicken with lemon, rosemary and garlic	93
	Sichuan-style Kung Pao chicken	142
	Chicken, pancetta and leek pie	309
	"Roadkill"	313
	Curried chicken thighs	327
Chocolate	Chocolate mousse with cream	147
	Chocolate mousse with eggs	147
Crackers	Seagrass crackers	40
Dessert, crumble topping	Apple crumble	314
Dessert, filling	Lemon mandarino curd tartlets	75
	Caramel Bavarois	263
	Caramel Chantilly	265
Duck	Braised duck	189
Eggs	Overnight egg casserole	128
	Eggs a la flamenco	244
	Scotch eggs	328

Main ingredient/ Product	Recipe	Page number
Fish	Salmon, baked with goat's cheese	95
	Puppy drum, fish pie	105
	Yellow croaker, battered fish	161
	Seabass, steamed whole	191
	Snapper, barbecued	211
	White fish fillet, baked Asian-style (en papillote)	217
	Rockfish, apple smoked	109
Fruit	Peach galettes	20
	Blackberry coulis	22
	Passion fruit cream	39
	Peaches, warm with honey and rum	98
	Strawberries, macerated	149
	Lemon, preserved	222
	Melon, hygiene	235
	Banana-stuffed pineapple sous vide	329
Lamb	Rack of lamb, roasted	221
	Shoulder, fire pit	230
Pasta	Dough	258
	Smoked egg, pumpkin and goat's cheese ravioli	259
Pastry, choux	Lemon curd choux buns	96
	Eclairs	262
Pastry, shortcrust	Lemon mandarino curd tartlets	75
Pastry, sweet	Peach galettes	20
Pork	Cantonese braised belly pork	143
	Chinese breakfast dumplings jiaozi	159
	Chinese breakfast dumplings baozi	160

Main ingredient/ Product	Recipe	Page number
	Spareribs sweet and sour (Charlie)	182
	Spare ribs sweet and sour (Mei)	193
	Fatty pork	194
Prawns	Creole shrimp	47
	Wok cooked prawns	162
	Risotto with butter-fried prawns	275
Pumpkin seeds	Pepitas	245
Rice	Rice and beans	84
Salad	Cabbage	84
	Broccoli crunch	130
	Waldorf	146
	Wood ear mushroom	187
	Needle mushroom	190
	Cauliflower, roasted	231
	Rocket, avocado and mango	232
	Beetroot, chickpea and spinach	232
	Watermelon, mint and feta	233
	Lentil, Kale and potato	233
	Halloumi	273
Salad, dressing	Avocado dressing	61
	Yoghurt dressing	220
	Basic	234
	Passionfruit dressing	275
Sauce, savoury	Creole sauce	45
	Teriyaki sauce	75
Sauce, sweet	Apple cider syrup	52
Scones	Lemonade scones	200
Soup	Mushroom soup	113

Main ingredient/ Product	Recipe	Page number
Soup	Chicken and prawn soup stock	186
Spices	Creole spice mix	45
	Sri Lankan curry powder	309
	Ginger, garlic and green chilli (GGG)	328
Tofu	Lao Lan Ma or Sichuan-style braised spicy and hot tofu	145
Turkey	Oriental lettuce cups	122
Vegetable	Aubergine, fried	192
	Aubergine baba ganoush	219
Vegetables	Maize white cheddar grits	46
	Vegetable sauté	109
	Oriental green beans	123
Waffles	Cornmeal waffles	50

Printed in Great Britain
by Amazon

35130569R00190